Created and Directed by Hans Höfer

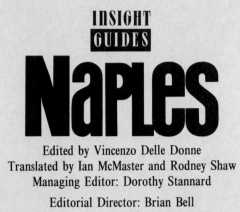

**INSIGHT
GUIDES**

Naples

Edited by Vincenzo Delle Donne
Translated by Ian McMaster and Rodney Shaw
Managing Editor: Dorothy Stannard

Editorial Director: Brian Bell

APA PUBLICATIONS

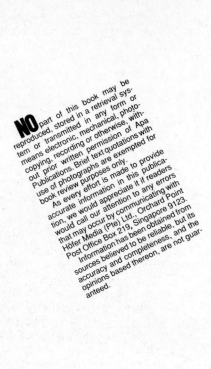

First Edition
© **1992 APA PUBLICATIONS (HK) LTD**
All Rights Reserved
Printed in Singapore by Höfer Press Pte. Ltd

ABOUT THIS BOOK

The approach of Insight Guides has always been to pay due tribute to a location's beauty spots while not neglecting to mention its warts. Such a philosophy is particularly appropriate to the Naples area, combining as it does the devil and the deep blue sea (with the city, needless to say, assuming the satanic role).

Writers especially have long been attracted to this alluring mix. Edward Gibbon, in 1796, found that its inhabitants "seem to dwell on the confines of paradise and hell-fire." And Percy Bysse Shelley, visiting in 1818, wrote home: "On entering Naples, the first circumstance that engaged my attention was an assassination."

Perhaps Shelley's experience was not entirely typical, because today's visitors speak highly of the warmth and character of Naples and the Neapolitans. But on the tail of every recommendation comes a string of caveats about the ills that beset the city, the headlines that tarnish the romantic image. Yet tantalisingly close are holiday haunts such as Capri, Ischia and the Amalfi Coast, retreats of Italy's wealthy and glamorous. If all human life is here, Apa Publications has captured it in *Insight Guide: The Bay of Naples*, portraying in words and pictures the good, the bad and the ugly.

The Writers

Only those intimately acquainted with Naples can fully extract the city's essence, and so many of the guide's contributors hail from Naples itself. Project Editor **Vincenzo Delle Donne** grew up near the city. He studied in Germany, embarked on a career in journalism with Italian newspapers and now works for the Cologne-based Westdeutscher Rundfunk TV and radio station and the *Suddeutsche Zeitung* newspaper in Munich. In his contributions to this book, which include "Centuries of Foreign Domination", he explains the ways in which modern Naples has been forged by its past, making the Neapolitans what they are today. He explains why they have their cliques and their Camorra, and why the lottery plays a crucial role in many Neapolitan lives.

Neapolitan **Franco Scandone** is especially interested in art and art history, a field of interest which he developed through his involvement on local guides such as *Napolicity* and *Napoliguide* and by producing art-historical features and documentary films. But he earns his living principally by working in the editorial department of Naples' most popular daily newspaper, *Il Mattino*. In addition to sharing his intimate knowledge about the city and surrounding region, he provides a step-by-step guide to Herculaneum, Pompeii and Vesuvius, helped by geologist **Mario Privileggi**, and escorts us round the National Museum, home of the stunning archaeological treasures recovered from these sites.

Sandro Castronuovo works for Naples' oldest daily, *Il Roma*. He shares the Neapolitans' favourite passions, in particular their enthusiasm for *canzoni*, love songs written in the Neapolitan dialect. The melody makes the music and listening to his amusing, melodious banter over a cup of coffee is an experience in itself. In "Melodramatic Love Songs", he takes a look at some of the most famous *canzoni*, including the immortal "O Sole Mio". He has also made a name for himself as an historian and here he describes

Delle Donne

Scandone

Privileggi

Castronuovo

Bloss

some of the more colourful events in the city's past – such as the legendary founding of the city by sailors from Rhodes and the story of Masaniello, the fishmonger turned revolutionary who toppled the Spanish viceroys. He also explores the origins of the pizza, the undisputed star of the region's long and varied menus.

Susanne Bloss has been commuting between her native Germany and Italy for years, and has acquired a deep appreciation of the muses which inspire Southern Italy. Together with Vincenzo Delle Donne, she looks at Naples' cultural development; its philosphers, writers, film directors and painters. She also discusses the Neapolitans' penchant for worshipping idols, as well as their obsession with death.

During a frenetic stint as a journalist for RAI TV in Rome, **Lisa Gerard-Sharp**, a regular contributor to the series and project editor of *Insight Guide: Sicily*, frequently took off for Capri and the Amalfi Coast for what she calls "sea views and serenity". In this book, as well as sharing her knowledge of these popular holiday destinations, she has written a revealing introduction to the Neapolitans. She also adds her own recommendations to the article on food, appraises the region's wines, and writes about the Neapolitans' talent for faking whatever they cannot make.

Another regular Insight Guides contributor, **Rowlinson Carter**, covers two of the most interesting chapters in the region's history: the rise and fall (under volcanic ash) of the Romans, and the aftermath of World War II, when, in a famine-stricken Naples, the Neapolitans' most prized quality, resourcefulness, reached new heights.

The Photographers

Most of the photographs are the work of **Bill Wassman,** a New York-based Insight Guides stalwart, and **Marc Aurel Rettenbacher**, with extra material from, among others, **Hansjög Künzel**, **Martin Thomas** and native Neapolitan **Luciano Pedicini**.

The book was translated into English, under the supervision of **Tony Halliday**, by **Ian McMaster** and **Rodney Shaw** (main text) and **Susan Sting** (Travel Tips). It was compiled in Insight Guides' London editorial office, under the direction of **Dorothy Stannard**, and proofread and indexed by **Carole Mansur**.

Gerard-Sharp

Carter

Wassman

Künzel

History

Features

Places

Maps

TRAVEL TIPS

**For detailed information
see page 273**

DANIELE
CORRADO
22-11-88.
23-3-90
FRANCESCO
LEONE
2/4/90
2/5/90
CARMINE
O'
BEL
Barbara
e
Massimo
ITC GALIANI

BAY OF NAPLES

The Bay of Naples and the Amalfi Coast, tucked into the other side of the Sorrentine peninsula, between them claim one of the most interesting and varied corners of Italy. Fynes Moryson, a 17th-century traveller to the region, said: "Here the beautie of all the World is gathered as it were into a bundle."

In a radius of only 50 miles (80 km) lies a hectic European city, incomparable archaeological sites – Pompeii and Herculaneum included – Vesuvius, which, along with its terrible twin, Sicily's Etna, forms Europe's biggest pressure cooker, and what many consider to be the Mediterranean's most picturesque bays and islands. It lies as close to Africa as it does to Milan, and not only in the geographical sense.

Here, in the temperament and lifestyle of the people, you will find the rich flavours of the Italian South, the *mezzogiorno*: warm, extrovert, anarchic, tragi-comic, and sometimes, in its less public moments and places, stricken.

Although often denigrated as outlaw territory by Rome and cities north, this part of Italy is not devoid of culture. Naples itself is an energetic city, with first-rate museums and strong theatrical and musical traditions. The playwright Eduardo de Filippo was born here, as was seminal post-war film director Vittorio de Sica, and both of them drew on the powerful influence of their native city. Perhaps the most telling expressions of the Bay of Naples and its people, however, are the *canzoni*, the haunting Neapolitan love songs full of yearning for loves and summers past, which singers such as Enrico Caruso transported all over the world.

Preceding pages: going to to the wall; bauble seller; life on the tiles; news vendor. Left, checking the books.

9th century BC: Anatolian and Acadian (Greek) colonists settle on the island of Megaride and the Pizzofalcone foothills. They name their city *Parthenope*. At first it consists of a small settlement at the port and a larger settlement on the mountain.

6th century BC: Settlers from nearby Cumae found a new city, Neapolis, a short distance from Parthenope, which is itself renamed Palaepolis.

474 BC: The Greeks from Syracuse defeat the Etruscans and thereby extend their area of power to the Bay of Naples.

328 BC: Naples declares war on Rome and is defeated. However, the municipal authorities are allowed to remain in office.

90–89 BC: Rome grants the right to Roman citizenship to the inhabitants of Campania.

62 BC: A devastating earthquake destroys parts of the settlements around Vesuvius.

AD 79: Pompeii, Herculaneum and Stabiae are destroyed by an eruption of Vesuvius.

AD 337: The Roman Emperor Constantine dies and Byzantium becomes the capital of the Roman Empire.

395: After Emperor Theodosius I dies, the Roman Empire disintegrates into two parts: a Western Empire and an Eastern Empire.

476: The West Roman Empire ends when Odoacer assumes power in Italy, having been proclaimed king, in place of the Roman Emperor Romulus Augustulus, by Germanic soldiers. Romulus Augustulus dies in Castel dell'Ovo in Naples.

536: East Roman General Belisarius captures Naples, entering via an aqueduct.

763: Naples becomes a duchy, largely independent from the East Roman Empire in Byzantium.

1139: Naples falls to the Normans, who rule over a large part of southern Italy.

1191: The Hohenstaufen Henry VI (Emperor of the German Holy Roman Empire) fails in an attempt to capture Naples.

1194: Henry VI succeeds in his aim and also conquers the Norman Kingdom of Sicily.

1220: Henry's son Frederick II succeeds in achieving absolute rule over the city.

1224: Frederick II, a patron of the arts, literature and science, founds the first university in Naples. Frederick's court hears the first literary experiments in "vulgar Italian".

1245: Pope Innocent IV dismisses Frederick II at the Council of Lyon, on the grounds of being an opponent of the church. To end the power of the Hohenstaufens in Italy, the Pope turns to Louis IX of France, promising him the Kingdom of Sicily in return for help.

1250: Frederick II dies and the rule of the Hohenstaufens draws to a close.

1266: The Kingdom of Naples is given to the French Royal House of Anjou after Charles of Anjou, the brother of King Louis IX, conquers it on behalf of the Pope.

1268: Charles of Anjou defeats the last of the Staufens, Conradin, in the battle of Tagliacozzo, ending both the threat of the Hohenstaufens in the Kingdom of Naples-Sicily and German imperial rule in Italy. Charles I chooses Naples for his royal residence.

1282: A bloody rebellion takes place in Sicily under the pro-Hohenstaufen Ghibelline party. French soldiers in Palermo are killed (an event known as the "Sicilian Vespers"). Charles I loses Sicily to King Peter III of Aragon.

1309: Robert of Anjou becomes king of Naples.

1442: King Alfonso V of Aragon conquers the Kingdom of Naples and reunites it with the Kingdom of Sicily. His court becomes the centre of southern Italian Humanism.

1495: Charles VIII of France conquers Naples and reigns for a short time.

1501: Ferdinand of Aragon and Louis XII of France conquer the Kingdom of Naples.

1503: The Spanish defeat the French at Cerignola and regain the Kingdom of Naples.

1504: From now on the Kingdom of Naples and Sicily is ruled by the Spanish viceroy.

1529: Plague rages in the city. Over 60,000 people perish.

1532: Don Pedro of Toledo becomes the Spanish viceroy. Under his rule, extensive urban development is carried out.

1647: A Neapolitan fisherman known as

Masaniello leads a revolt against the Spanish after an attempt by the Duke of Arcos to collect an extra million ducats by means of a special tax on fruit. Masaniello is appointed as *capitano del popolo*, and deposes the Spanish viceroy for nine days, after which the revolt is quashed with bloody force.

1656: Plague returns, claiming 240,000–270,000 of Naples' 450,000 inhabitants.

1688: Another devastating earthquake destroys large parts of the city.

1707: As a result of the struggle between Spain and Austria (the War of the Spanish Succession), the Austrian Archduke Charles becomes viceroy in Naples.

1713–14: Naples and Sicily fall to the Habsburgs and Sardinia falls to Piedmont.

1738: Austria loses the Kingdom of Naples and Sicily to the Spanish Bourbons, receiving Parma and Piacenza in return. Under Charles of Bourbon the Kingdom achieves independence.

Preceding pages: fresco in the House of the Vettii, Pompeii. Above, mosaic, Pompeii.

1759: Charles III becomes king of Spain and his son Ferdinand succeeds him to the throne of Naples.

1799: The succession is briefly interrupted when General Championnet, head of a Napoleonic army, proclaims a Parthenopean Republic. Ferdinand returns to the throne.

1806: Joseph Bonaparte is proclaimed king of Naples and is succeeded in 1808 by Joachim Murat.

1815: Murat is shot in Calabria, and Ferdinand of Bourbon becomes king of Naples.

1820: After the so-called July Uprising the king agrees to a constitution.

1859: The Italian War of Liberation begins, led by Giuseppe Garibaldi on behalf of the Piedmont Royal House of Savoy.

1860: Giuseppe Garibaldi lands at the West Sicilian port of Marsala on 11 May. Initially he has a force of just 1,000 freedom fighters. They find popular favour and sweep through the Apennine peninsula from the south. On 26 October the troops of King Victor Emmanuel II and Garibaldi meet at Teano in Calabria, thus sealing both the defeat of the Bourbons and, to a large extent, the unification of Italy. The resistance of the Bourbon King Francis II is broken a few months later.

1884: A severe cholera epidemic breaks out.

1885: The Italian Parliament passes a law providing for the first relief action for Naples. The aim is to improve social and sanitary conditions. Many of the *quartieri bassi* (slum areas) are demolished.

1943: The city is bombed during World War II. After a four-day uprising by the people, occupying German forces decide to withdraw their troops from the city.

1973: Severe cholera epidemic.

1987: With the help of Diego Armando Maradona, SSC Naples become champions of the Italian football league.

1989: The Christian Democrat Prime Minister Ciriaco de Mita opens the Centro Direzionale di Napoli, the new administrative HQ.

1990: Pope John Paul II visits Naples and calls upon the Neapolitan people to revolt against the "degeneration of public life".

Eight centuries before the birth of Christ Greek colonists sailing from the island of Rhodes drifted into a bay off southwest Italy. Impressed by what they saw, they decided to settle on a hill rising off the coast at the bay's northern point.

The hill, later to be called Pizzofalcone, was chosen in part for its beautiful location and agreeable climate, but also, and more crucially, because it met all the important strategic requirements of the time. In addition, the tuff caves carved deep in its base offered the settlers protection while they set about building their new city. The glowering presence of Vesuvius across the bay appears not to have deterred the new inhabitants in the slightest.

The cult of the Sirens: The new settlement was named after the Siren Parthenope. According to myth, it was here that Parthenope was washed up after crashing to her death when she and her sisters' spell was broken by Odysseus.

The cult of the Sirens originated in Asia Minor and came to play a central role in the Hellenic world, particularly among the inhabitants of Crete and Rhodes. Sirens, who lured sailors to their island with their seductive songs, were both feared and adored in ancient mythology. It was precisely because Odysseus was aware of the dangers a singing Siren could pose that he ordered his crew to lash him to the mast and stop his ears with bees-wax when his ship passed the Sirens' island.

As is so often the case with legends, there are numerous versions of the Siren stories. But some measure of agreement has been reached regarding the Greeks' idea of what they looked like, even if there is still uncertainty about details. Basically, they were described as a cross between a woman and a bird. Often they were portrayed as birds with a woman's head, but sometimes as women

Left, Hercules, Greek symbol of strength and courage, from the Farnese Collection. Right, a luring Siren beckons.

with wings and claws. It was only in the Middle Ages that the definitive picture of the Sirens emerged, presenting them as half-woman and half-bird.

The colonists from Rhodes built their new city between the Pizzofalcone hills and the small Megaride peninsula, near the caves made from volcanic tuff where they had originally found shelter. Today this area lies between Via Chiatamone and Via Domenico Morelli. In the course of time, the Megaride

peninsula became the island on which the first fortress of Naples, the Castel dell'Ovo, was later built. Although Parthenope was a relatively small settlement, it was soon able to hold its own against larger cities in the Mediterranean area, and increased its trade considerably in the ensuing period.

The original city centre: In recent times there has been much argument over the exact location of the original city centre of Naples and only the very latest archaeological findings have shed much light on the matter. In particular, the excavations on the foothills of the Pizzofalcone and on the Vomero hills in

Via Nicotera near the Chiaia bridge appear to confirm that Parthenope evolved here.

This theory is supported by the geological composition of the coast, most of which must have been virtually uninhabitable at the time – something which was to change over the centuries. The hill which the Greeks chose for their settlement was surrounded by water on three sides and could be reached only via a deep and difficult ravine, through which the rainwater flowed into the valley. The hill fulfilled every possible strategic requirement: any attack, whether from the open sea or from the mainland, could easily be repelled.

control of the hinterland. The Etruscans' continual expansion of their area of control in their attempts to become the sole rulers over Campania eventually led to a decisive battle, in 524 BC, in which the Greeks of Cumae were defeated. During this battle Cumae was destroyed and many of its inhabitants fled to the old city of Parthenope.

Even though the heart of Etruria was actually in Tuscany and Lazio, archaeologists have found evidence of advanced Etruscan civilisation in Campania. Many interesting discoveries – mainly in the form of graves and necropolises – have been made near Salerno. One of Italy's leading archaeolo-

In the course of a century, Parthenope developed into a model Greek city and achieved enough importance to be mentioned in records of the ancient world.

In the middle of the 7th century BC, descendants of the Greeks who had founded Cumae, the oldest Greek city in Italy (1050 BC), in the nearby Phlegraean Fields, came thundering on the city's door. Their arrival heralded the decline of the original city of Parthenope.

The city fell victim to wranglings between the Greeks of Cumae, who ruled the whole coastal area, and the Etruscans, who were in

gists, Sabatino Moscati, believes that the scattered Etruscan settlements in Campania were bridging stations – for both trade and cultural exchange with ancient Greece and the Orient.

New city of Neapolis: The Etruscans wielded power over the Bay of Naples for only a short period of time. In 474 BC the Greeks defeated the Etruscan fleet in the seas off Cumae (the Battle of Cumae) and regained complete control of the region. They then founded *Neapolis*, the new city, close to Parthenope, leaving Cumae to decline into a quiet country town.

From then on Parthenope was effectively on the outskirts of town. The new city quickly surpassed the old in terms of importance, especially following the influx of refugees from Ischia following a volcanic eruption. But there remained a close connection between the two settlements, and in the end they merged to form a single city.

By 400 BC this was the recognised commercial and intellectual capital of Campania. Neapolis coins were imitated and its weights and measures set the standard for other Greek cities.

One of the things binding the two centres was the cult of the Sirens, whose monument

point where the Greek colonists came ashore. Even though there is substantial evidence that the river existed – in the oldest documents it is known as the Clanio, the Greeks are believed to have called it Sebet, and both Virgil and Papinius Statius sang its praises – it has since disappeared without trace. How that happened is a matter of conjecture. Some experts suspect that its waters just evaporated as a result of dramatic geological changes.

Whatever the truth of the matter, the river is immortalised on many of the ancient coins of Neapolis and also appears in numerous representations of the landscape, sometimes

became the spiritual focus of the city. No-one knows exactly where the monument might have been situated, but one thing seems certain: it must have been clearly visible from the harbour, which would have served both Neapolis and Parthenope.

Long-lost river: Anyone investigating the origins of Naples inevitably comes up against the question of the river which is thought to have flowed into the sea at the

Left, Funeral Dance, fresco dating from the 5th century BC, National Museum, Naples. Above, Greek fresco from Paestum.

just hinted at, in other cases portrayed realistically. On some coins the river is personified as a beardless youth, wearing a laurel wreath on his head and with a forehead decorated with a small horn bearing the word Sebeitos. On the fountain in Santa Lucia (a gift to the Spanish viceroy), on the other hand, the river is represented by an old man with a long beard, lying on his side and contemplating his surroundings with obvious pleasure. This mysterious river is a symbol of the way the city has achieved a masterly balance between fantasy and reality for nearly 3,000 years.

Roman army officers on active service against Rome's early imperial enemies, like Hannibal and his infernal elephants, must have regarded the Gulf of Naples, and priapic Pompeii in particular, in much the same way as caused GIs in Vietnam to rub their hands at the prospect of a spot of R&R in Bangkok. There was also the food to look forward to. While the Greeks were wretched cooks at home (notoriously "one kind of porridge followed by another kind of porridge"), they did wonders in the kitchens of their southern Italian colonies.

Naples was convenient to the main military theatre of the age. The world as the Romans then knew it – the one they set out to conquer – revolved around the kidney-shaped Mediterranean. The paramount goal was to control the narrow straits between Sicily and North Africa, the bottleneck that divided East from West. To gain control of these straits, Rome had to acquire a navy and go on to defeat both Greek and Carthaginian opposition, especially the latter, whose city lay almost directly opposite at what is now Tunis. Two Punic Wars were inconclusive. Rome threw everything into the third.

Samnite resistance: In order to enjoy the Neapolitan flesh-pots between or even during these wars, Rome first had to conquer Campania, the name given to the whole area between the foot of the Samnite mountains and the sea. The Samnites, who had descended from the mountains first to overwhelm and then to co-exist with Greek colonists, were not going to give it up without a struggle. They had been lucky to catch the Greeks when Greece itself was locked in the Peloponnesian civil war. The hapless expatriates could expect no help from that quarter, although they had gone on to do what Greeks were always very good at: Hellenising their conquerors. Setting a precedent for Goths, Visigoths and even the Vandals, the tough Samnites demonstrated that a taste of Greek good life in a seductive

Left, fresco of Spring, National Museum, Naples.

Italian setting meant they were no longer, in the course of time and in a military sense, the men they had once been.

The first intimation that Naples would one day shed its Greek character and become Italian was given in 302 BC when Romans and Samnites were engaged in their second war for supremacy in the south. A Roman admiral, a certain Publius Cornelius, led a sort of commando raid through what served as Pompeii's harbour and up the Sarno River. They managed to get as far as Nuceria (Salerno) which, against what should have been better judgement, they plundered in a terrific uproar. By the time their boats were stacked high with booty, the inhabitants of neighbouring towns and cities had been alerted to what was going on and were waiting for them downstream.

Very few Romans regained the sea, and of course the captured booty added to the feeling among the Samnites that Rome had been taught a salutary lesson. In the event, the Romans had learned only too well, and within a decade or so the Samnites were utterly crushed – or so the Romans thought.

The occupation of the south meant that Rome was in a position to address the question of Carthage. In the meantime, the consolidation of the conquered lands took the form that was to become standard practice in the future empire. The sight of what the Greeks had achieved gave the Romans a sense of cultural inferiority, no doubt justified but sensibly accommodated not by destroying everything, as the Goths were later inclined to do, but by adopting Hellenic civilisation and adding Roman touches as they developed confidence in their own abilities in this field.

Flourishing Naples seemed to need not much more than bigger public buildings, baths, and refinements like underfloor heating, a source of great pride to Roman engineers and apt to be installed even where not strictly necessary. As long as the population behaved themselves, Rome was content to let them administer their own affairs.

The major distraction of the Punic Wars – with Hannibal famously crossing the Alps in order to attack Rome from the north – led to an early example of Italian irredentism, in this instance of Samnites who thought they saw an opportunity to regain their lands. They welcomed Hannibal as a potential liberator and applauded his impressive victories. In Naples and throughout the south, Roman garrisons were taunted with the catch-phrase of the day: "Hannibal is at the gates!" As things turned out, Hannibal roamed around northern Italy for years before having to return to Carthage without attacking Rome, let alone capturing it.

whole of Lower Italy was at Rome's feet.

The terms of the peace were magnanimous. Naples and its companion cities were allowed to maintain a high degree of self-government but they were forced to abandon rules which made it virtually impossible for outsiders to take up residence. Cities had traditionally regarded themselves as completely self-contained states, not part of some larger political entity. The thought of being part of an empire took some getting used to. Rome understood these sentiments and decided that the wholesale infusion of loyal army veterans in the cities would be a safeguard against any dangerous nostalgia

The Confederates' War: Rome's ultimate victory over the Carthaginians did not extinguish the flames of Samnite irredentism, which the Greeks were happy to fuel. Civil unrest in Rome in 91 BC was the cue for them to launch what became known as the Confederates' War. The Roman commander, Lucius Cornelius Sulla, put down the insurrection with unscrupulous brutality. Stabiae, just two miles from Pompeii, was completely wiped out, whereupon Herculaneum prudently surrendered. Pompeii fought on valiantly for a further two years, but the cause was hopeless and before long the

about lost independence. The policy of accelerated Romanisation included a new name for Pompeii: Colonia Veneria Cornelia Pompeianorum. It did not catch on.

The merchants of Naples were quick to see that an integrated place in the empire was not without compensation. Naples and the surrounding towns were put on a map which brought in Roman visitors with bulging purses. They came on holiday, liked what they saw, and were struck by the idea of buying or building a place of their own. Not a little place, a big one, the bigger the better.

It was an age that did not sneer at conspicuous consumption. Umbricius Scaurus, a Pompeiian who made a fortune out of a popular fish-sauce, made provision in his will for an extravagant tombstone depicting the monumentally extravagant gladiatorial games which he had laid on for his own funeral. His fish-sauce recipe is lost, which of course only encourages conjecture as to which of the present-day sauces it may be. Caius Quinctius Balbus and Maurus Porcius tried to make amends for their notoriety as the worst kind of property developer, the kind who got the owners of desirable property banished, on trumped-up charges if necessary, and simply took the keys. They were

ing it in his mouth. The pear went down his throat and he was dead, alas, before a doctor could be found.

Nero in Naples: While a genuine wave of sympathy probably went out to Claudius, the locals found it hard to love Nero. He was not a passionate violinist, as the legend about the fire of Rome suggests, but a truly awful singer. His preposterous ambition was to win the singing contest at the Olympic Games, and it was towards that end that in AD 64 he made his public debut at the annual music festival in Naples. He was in full voice when an earthquake shook the building for several seconds. The emperor carried on as if

forgiven for the price of Pompeii's 13,000-seat amphitheatre, complete with detachable canvas roof.

Members of the imperial family were naturally part of the throng who took their holidays in and around Naples, and of course there were accidents. In AD 21, Drusus, the 13-year-old son of the future emperor Claudius, was playing a game which involved throwing a pear into the air and catch-

Left, mosaic from Pompeii. Above, Roman sculpture embraced and emulated Greek ideas and forms.

nothing were happening. The city had been badly damaged in an earthquake only the year before, and it was said that the applause at the end of the performance had far less to do with his singing than with relief at still being alive. As the audience filed out, the theatre collapsed. It had obviously been more shaken by the earthquake than anyone realised. On the other hand, no other building in Naples was as badly affected. The catastrophic eruption of Vesuvius followed 14 years later. In the meantime, Nero won his Olympic medal, but only by inventing an imperial prerogative which kept him on stage throughout and prevented other entrants from getting a note in edgeways.

While Rome rebuilt Carthage, having previously sworn that no city would ever stand on the site again, it seems never to have occurred to any of the emperors to do anything about Pompeii and Herculaneum after the eruption of 79. Emperor Marcus Aurelius simply mentions the fate of the towns as an example of the transitory nature of earthly things. In any case, they sank into oblivion for 1,600 years, and in the 4th century it looked as if Rome might be going the same way. The Emperor Constantine transferred the imperial capital to Byzantium in 330, the

empire was divided in 395, and almost at once the Germanic tribes poured into Italy. Alaric sacked Rome in 410 and, marching on Sicily, ravaged all Campania, Naples included. There was more of the same under Genseric's Vandals in 455. Romulus Augustulus, the somewhat ephemeral Western Emperor, ran for his life. He locked himself in the Villa of Lucullus in Naples, where Tiberius had died, and there, in 476, he died too. There was no successor.

Naples has a legendary propensity to shrug off adversity, but even so it is surprising to find the historian Flavius Cassiodorus

saying that after 30 years under the Ostrogoth Theodoric the city "rejoiced in every kind of pleasure and delight by land and sea". Theodoric died in 526 and the good times came to an end soon afterwards in the person of General Belisarius banging on the gates of the city and demanding surrender in the name of Byzantium. The Byzantine Emperor Justinian had launched a personal crusade to drive the Goths out of Italy and restore the old imperial glory.

The Neapolitans would probably have let Belisarius in but they were prevented from doing so by the Goth garrison who, only numbering 800 themselves, were expecting reinforcements from King Theodahad, their ruler. A man of cautious disposition, Theodahad would not move until he had performed a peculiar mode of divination which involved live pigs representing Goths, Romans and Byzantines. He was still mulling over the implications of some pigs which died and others which merely lost bristles when Belisarius found a way into the city through a broken aqueduct (the Ponti Rossi, below Capodimonte). A battalion crawled through the hole and they let in their comrades. The customary killing and looting commenced, but Belisarius put a stop to it.

The Goths, under the more decisive King Totila, recaptured Naples in 543 and reached the curious decision to dismantle the walls. As things turned out, however, it probably did not matter because the Goths were defeated under Vesuvius so comprehensively that they never recovered. Naples thus became part of the Byzantine Empire and in due course was allowed to elect its own Dux.

The city managed not only to avoid the depredations of the later Lombards all around but also to become extremely rich. Saracen pirates plagued Naples' neighbours, but hardly ever Naples. In fact, Neapolitans found Oriental pirates easy and possibly even nice people with whom to do business. They were so little inclined to conform to orthodox attitudes towards these Moslem heathen that, in the end, Pope John VIII excommunicated the lot of them.

Left, Pozzuoli, once a testament to Roman wealth. **Right**, petrified Roman, Pompeii

"Nobody ever came here except as a conqueror, an enemy or an unappreciative visitor," wrote Carlo Levi of southern Italy in his autobiographical novel *Christ Stopped at Eboli*, published in 1945. Levi, an anti-Fascist from Turin, was banished to the *Mezzogiorno* by Mussolini, along with other opponents of the Fascist regime. He found in this southern wasteland, as he described it, a people completely different from their northern counterparts, in behaviour, speech

Aversa, a few miles north of Naples. Thirteen years later, in 1043, the battle-hardened knights seized Apulia from the Arabs and went on to conquer Calabria and Sicily. In 1130, the Norman King Roger II was crowned King of the Two Sicilies by the antipope Anaklet II, an appointment reluctantly confirmed by the real Pope, Innocent II, when he was captured by Roger in 1139.

Naples became the capital of Roger's Norman Empire. As later conquerors were also

and mentality, a people conditioned by the need to survive centuries of foreign rule.

Norman knights: Southern Italy and Sicily were the centre of the known world until long after the dark Middle Ages had passed. Whoever controlled this area effectively had the key to world power. As well as being of great strategic importance, the area was a stopping point for travellers to and from the Orient, particularly for Norman knights en route for the Holy Land.

In 1027 crusading knights returning from Palestine put down more permanent roots in southern Italy and founded the city of

to do, Roger made his triumphant entrance through the Porta Capuana. Crowds of cheering citizens greeted him. To secure his welcome he granted five *moggie* of land and five serfs to each man of noble birth for as long as they remained faithful to him.

Later dukes found it harder to win such allegiance. William I (1154–66), reputed to live like an Eastern potentate with an extensive harem guarded by eunuchs (hence, perhaps, his nickname "the bad") spent most of his reign fighting the rebellious barons, whose cause was backed by the Pope.

Although the city was constantly shaken

by war during this period, it had a superb defensive location – a sheltered harbour to the sea, and high mountains to the rear – and could repel most attacks easily. Henry VI of Hohenstaufen was forced to recognise its strength in 1191, when his first attempt to capture Naples ended in failure.

It wasn't until Henry conquered the Sicilian Kingdom (whose heir, Constance, he had married in 1186) that he also gained Naples. The Neapolitan people showed little

Breaking with the convention that poetry could be written only in classical Latin, Frederick encouraged writing in the vulgar Italian style, the *dolce stil nuovo* (the "sweet" new style). In fact, Sicilian Italian almost became the standard Italian language instead of that from Tuscany.

Frederick also did great things for Naples. He completed the Castel Capuano and Castel dell'Ovo and, most importantly, in 1224, he provided Naples with the *Studio*, Italy's

liking for their new monarch, but their hostility changed to enthusiasm under the rule of his son Frederick II. Born and bred at the crossroads of the Byzantine, Arab and Norman cultures, Frederick was tolerant in his politics. His artistic nature found expression in a love of Italy, and he chose to rule the German Holy Roman Empire from Palermo on Sicily and his Appian castles.

Frederick's court in Palermo became a centre for writers, artists and scientists.

Left, Roger II. **Above**, *Tavola Strozzi*, **1465, our earliest pictorial record of Naples.**

third university after Bologna and Padua, thus breaking the clergy's monopoly on the dissemination of knowledge.

Struggles against the popes: Success in ruling southern Italy was dependant on maintaining good relations with the popes – who saw themselves as superior to all worldly authorities – and a power struggle with the papal authority could spell the end for any dynasty, including the Hohenstaufens, as Frederick was to learn to his cost. Pope Innocent IV had Frederick dismissed at a Council in Lyon, on the grounds of being an opponent of the church – amongst other things because he had conquered those cities in Lombardy which had opposed the expansion of Hohenstaufen power to northern Italy. In fact, the Pope was worried about inroads on his own territorial power.

Pope Innocent IV turned for help to the French King of the time, Louis IX, and promised him the Kingdom of Sicily in return for ending the rule of the Hohenstaufens in Italy. The request was eventually fulfilled by the King's brother, Charles of Anjou.

Demise of the Hohenstaufens: Frederick II died at Castel Firentino, near Lucera, thus fulfilling a prophecy that he would die at Florence, a city he had studiously avoided

jewels to help her husband (her own motivation being to equal her three sisters who were already queens). Manfred was finally defeated at the Battle of Benevento, in 1266. An excommunicate, he was denied a Christian burial, and the Bishop of Cosenza, in accordance with the Pope's decree, had the body dug up and cast out of the kingdom.

The last of the Hohenstaufens, Conradin, tried in vain to win back his ancestors' land. As soon as the young man was old enough, the Ghibellines urged him to claim his kingdom. Against the wishes of his mother, Elizabeth of Bavaria, the 17-year-old accepted the challenge and advanced on Italy

until then. After Frederick's death Hohenstaufen rule disintegrated. He was succeeded by his son Conrad, whose reign was short (1250–54) and then by Manfred, an illegitimate half-brother of Conrad's, who acted as guardian for Conradin, Conrad's son. Manfred, abetted by his Saracen troops, tried his best to re-establish Hohenstaufen power over Naples, but in 1268 Charles of Anjou was offered the Kingdom of Naples-Sicily by the Pope, by then Urban IV (a Frenchman), and chose Naples as his seat of power. His ambitions were spurred on by his wife, Beatrice of Provence, who even pawned her

with an army of 3,500 horsemen. Disaffected subjects of Charles flocked to join Conradin's army, but in spite of initial success Conradin was beaten by superior tactics. He was captured and publicly executed, along with his nobles, in Naples' marketplace on 26 October 1268. Elizabeth, Conradin's mother, who on hearing of Conradin's capture had hastened to Naples with a large ransom sum, arrived to find her son dead. The popular Hohenstaufen dynasty was finally at an end.

Angevin rule: What followed, the rule of the Angevins, was one of the most brutal chapters of foreign rule in Neapolitan history. The only benefit to Naples was the wealth of churches and monuments built during this period, including the Castel Nuovo, under Charles of Anjou, and the monastery of San Martino, the cathedral and Santa Chiara church, all built under the most powerful of the Angevins, Robert the Wise. Under the Angevins, Naples was raised to the dignity of a capital.

Under Robert, French influence gained its first real hold on Naples. The Castel Nuovo rose to its greatest brilliance.The Piazza delle Corregge became the scene of dazzling jousting tournaments. Boccaccio described

ruler, Alfonso I of Aragon from Spain, laid siege to the city. For a long time it looked as though his troops wouldn't overcome the bitter resistance. But, at the dead of night, his troops finally penetrated the city, entering via an aqueduct shown to them by two workmen which emerged in the well of a tailor's shop.

As in the wake of every new occupation, there was a series of executions, the nobility was driven out, property was confiscated, and special taxes were imposed to rebuild the parts of the city which had been destroyed. But at this point Naples was still an independent state, and Alfonso was not alto-

how the young men, "with their fair hair flowing over their snow-white shoulders, clasped round the head by a thin circlet of gold or a crown of fresh leaves", ran in the tournaments. But such gaiety was to change with the untimely death of Robert's only son, Charles. Then the sobered king preferred to surround himself with theologians, scientists, astrologers and monks.

Angevin rule lasted until the middle of the 15th century – indeed, until the next foreign

Twin threats: left, the plague; above, Vesuvius, both depicted by Domenico Gargiulo.

gether unwelcomed by the Neapolitans who, after all, had never known a dynasty of their own. Alfonso liked Naples, preferring it to Sicily and Aragon, and demonstrated this fact by walking about the city unattended. When his courtiers remonstrated against this, he was in the habit of saying, "What has a father to fear among his children?"

Alfonso's successor, Ferdinand, generally known as Ferrante (1458–94), combined all the worst vices of a sovereign and was described as "naturally cruel". He was also extremely cunning, and hit upon a highly effective way of raising revenue, by buying up all available goods and then refusing to let his subjects compete with him in the open market. He nearly lost his kingdom twice, first when disaffected barons called in René d'Anjou to help them oust him, and again in 1485 when the barons conspired once more. Ferdinand eventually dealt with the problem with characteristic brutality. Feigning conciliation, he prepared a splendid banquet in the Castel Nuovo to celebrate the marriage of his niece to the son of the chief conspirator, the Conte di Sarno. When all the guests, which included the barons, were firmly ensconced at the banqueting table, he sealed all the gates and draw-

liance between Louis XII of France and Ferdinand the Catholic of Spain.

The Spanish viceroys: From the beginning of the 16th century until the beginning of the 18th, Naples was a province of Spain and under the domination of the Spanish viceroys – a period generally considered to be the nadir of Naples' history.

The portly Don Pedro of Toledo was the first and most memorable of the regents; among other things, he is credited with commissioning the first real urban development plan (the Via Toledo was named after him). That is not to say, however, that Don Pedro was a popular ruler. One of his priori-

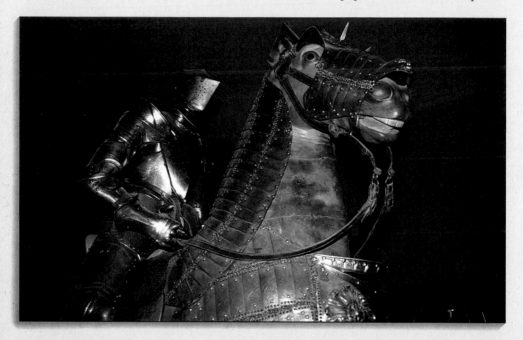

bridges, incarcerating even the women and children. The barons' wealth was seized, making a handsome contribution to the king's coffers.

Ferdinand's successor, Alfonso II, reigned barely a year, for in 1494 Charles VIII of France invaded and Alfonso abdicated, fleeing to Sicily with his treasure and a great quantity of wine. His son, Ferrantino, regained the kingdom (Charles turned out to be no less cruel than the Angevins) but, dying prematurely of a fever in 1496, was soon succeeded by his uncle Federigo, who was quickly driven from the kingdom by an al-

ties on coming to power was to fortify the Castel Nuovo against the uprisings of the Neapolitan people, who were being taxed into grinding poverty. The costly wars and dissolute lifestyle of the Spanish king forced tax collectors to search with increasing desperation for new ways of raising money. It was this which led to rebellion under Masaniello (*see page 45*).

In 1707, after the War of the Spanish Succession, Naples fell into the open hands of the Habsburgs. They reigned over the Kingdom of the Two Sicilies for three decades (1707–38). To begin with, like so many newcomers before them, they were warmly welcomed by the Neapolitans for, as the historian Giannone said, "There is no people more eager for liberty or less capable of using it than the Neapolitan. It hates the present and, in its ill-regulated passions, either dreads the future immoderately or counts upon it ridiculously."

The taxation policies of the Habsburgs were virtually identical to those of the Spanish viceroys, but their downfall was the pursuit of anti-papist policies. Eventually they were forced to hand over the Kingdom to the Bourbons, receiving the north Italian duchies of Parma and Piacenza in return.

amounted to a few prestigious buildings and grandiose facades.

Most of Charles's time was occupied by his two great passions – fishing and hunting. The Capodimonte castle, along with the one at Portici were both designed with sporting interests in mind. In Caserta, around 12 miles (20 km) north of Naples, the Bourbon monarch built a castle that was to become known as the Versailles of the south, boasting 1,200 rooms and an enormous park. Charles intended to move his seat of government to this castle, and would have done so had he not been called to succeed to the Spanish throne (in accordance with European treaties, the

The Bourbons: To begin with, the Bourbons were welcomed by the people of Naples, if only because their Austrian predecessors had been so disliked. Charles of Bourbon (Charles VII, known as Charles III) even gave the impression of being genuinely interested in addressing the problems of his subjects, for example in his attempt, albeit timid, to deal with Naples' immense urban problems. The final verdict on his rule, however, is not very favourable: the sum of his achievements in urban improvements

Left and **above**, relics of foreign rule.

two monarchies had to remain separate and independent). The building cost 9 million ducats, an extortionate sum for that time.

When Charles left for Spain – a departure witnessed by the whole of Naples – his third son, Ferdinand (the first son was certified an imbecile and the second son was in line for the Spanish throne) stepped on to the throne in Naples, albeit with the help of a council of regency until he should attain his majority.

The Parthenopean Republic: The Bourbon succession was interrupted in 1799, when effects of the French Revolution spread to Naples. Like Europe's other monarchs,

Ferdinand IV had feared the mounting threat in France for some years, not least because he was related to the French Bourbons and the two queens were sisters.

He sought to increase the size of his defence forces, but the Neapolitans were not disposed towards war, neither by nature nor habit, and the decision to join forces with other European powers against Napoleon culminated, in 1799, in a disastrous war with France. As one military historian put it: "The conscripts, remembering the injustice to which they had been subjected, considered themselves the victims of superior force, and not feeling bound to the army by duty, by their oaths, or by law, only continued to serve from the fear of punishment."

In 1799 General Championnet led a Napoleonic army into Naples and proclaimed the Second Parthenopean Republic (the first had been under Masaniello), promising peace, abundance and a better government. Many Neapolitans welcomed him. Unfortunately, what ensued was famine and punitive taxes, and as soon as the French army withdrew the Parthenopean Republic foundered.

The city was again captured by French troops in 1806, but the ensuing period of French rule, under Napoleon's brother Joseph Bonaparte and Joachim Murat, lasted only until Napoleon's final defeat at Waterloo and banishment to St Helena.

After Napoleon's defeat the rightful Bourbon rulers returned to the throne. Although they were in power only for a short period, they brought about important changes in Naples. A decree was issued bringing the city's administration into some sort of order, and a number of new streets were laid out. The Bourbons turned the monasteries in the old city centre into schools, hospitals, and public offices; but their most significant act was the reorganisation of the school system along the line of the French model. French influence didn't stop there. It is said, for example, that on returning to power Ferdinand was delighted with the way the French had renovated his palaces. He called Murat an excellent upholsterer.

Risorgimento: After the Congress of Vienna in 1815, King Ferdinand II (known as King Bomba, after his bombardment of Messina in 1848) was given the right to return to the throne of Naples. Nonetheless, he must have suspected that his days in power were numbered. The signs were unmistakable: all over the country the patriotic rebellion of the *Risorgimento* – the Italian unification movement – blazed into life. The Neapolitan people began to follow suit. Ferdinand's response was ruthless oppression. To make matters worse, another severe cholera epidemic broke out at this time, hitting the harbour area particularly badly.

Not even the passing of a constitution in 1820 was able to help the Bourbons. By this time, the concept of belonging to a unified Italian nation was firmly implanted. The attempt by King Ferdinand II to save his Kingdom from disintegrating inevitably ended in failure. On 13 February 1861 his weak and cowardly son Francis "Bombino" II capitulated to the troops of the Piedmont Royal House of Savoy, led by Garibaldi. He was forced to watch as the Kingdom of Naples was incorporated into the new Italian nation. His final words to his subjects were: "As a descendant of a dynasty which has reigned over this country for 126 years, my affections are centred here. I am a Neapolitan, and cannot without feelings of bitter grief, speak words of farewell to my dearly beloved people. Whatever may be my destiny, prosperous or contrary, I shall always preserve for them a lasting and affectionate remembrance. I recommend to them concord and peace, and the observance of their civic duties. Do not let an immoderate zeal for my fate be made a pretext for disorder." In fact, the Neapolitans were delighted. When Garibaldi entered the city 48 hours before the vanguard of his troops he was greeted by a vast cheering crowd.

This ended the long epoch of foreign rule over Naples. "We have created a nation," Garibaldi said. "Now our task is to shape the people." This remark remains pertinent even today: many Italians still regard the country as being divided into two halves. The border between north and south runs almost exactly along the line where the Bourbons clashed with the House of Savoy.

Right, Francis II, Naples' last foreign regent.

MASANIELLO, THE REVOLUTIONARY

In 1647 Tommaso Aniello, better known as Masaniello, led a successful uprising of the common people against the despotic Spanish monarchs. It began on Sunday, 7 July 1647, and lasted for nine days.

It was prompted by the introduction of a new tax on fruit, in summer the staple diet of the poorest Neapolitans. The viceroy's decision to press ahead with collection, in spite of potests, proved a fatal miscalculation. It was the proverbial straw which broke the camel's back. The range of taxable goods had become so large that there was hardly anything left.

The discontented Neapolitans rallied under the leadership of 27-year-old Masaniello, a humble fishmonger. His leadership was skilful and his knowledge of strategy instinctive. Taking advantage of the fact that nearly all the Spanish and Austrian troops had been sent north to oppose the invading French, he gathered together some 300 young men. His slogan was: "Long live the King of Spain, and down with this maladministration", which expediently swore loyalty to the Spanish throne while encouraging the people to rebel against the nobility. He transformed a brawl into a well-organised and successful revolution of the common people. The followers of the people's leader – *capitano del popolo* – obeyed his every word and were prepared to march on the viceroy's palace.

The spark which ignited the uprising flared up in front of the Santa Maria church on the Piazza del Carmine. In a flash, a mass rebellion developed. Market stalls were demolished, the houses of the tax collectors plundered, and the viceroy's soldiers put to flight. Looting and destruction spread.

The whole administration, from the highest nobility to the lowliest tax collectors, took flight – if they had time. Those who were unable to escape ended up on the scaffold. Their heads were mounted on spikes and displayed on the piazza, where the

Left, the fishmonger who became a hero.

capitano had set up his headquarters on a mountebank's stage.

The viceroy, meanwhile, barricaded himself in his palace on Via Toledo. He appeared on a balcony, promising the abolition of the duties on wine and fruit and throwing down written pledges, but he was unable to appease the mob. In the end, he fled. How he made his escape to Castel dell'Ovo is unclear. Some accounts say he was rescued by a group of nobles with drawn swords; others claim he made good his escape by scattering handfuls of gold coins in his wake.

What nobody could have predicted came about: Masaniello, succeeded within a matter of days in becoming so powerful that he was received as an equal by the viceroy. Donning a suit of silver brocade, he made his way to the palace.

Unfortunately, however, the fight was not won. The viceroy used this meeting as an opportunity to spread dissension among the rebels' ranks and generated rumours that Masaniello was showing signs of recklessness and tyranny. The policy worked, and Masaniello became isolated, even among his own ranks.

The uprising ended as quickly as it had started. On the ninth day of the revolt Masaniello was executed by a firing squad of eight and thrown into the Piazza del Mercato where his body was dragged about by youths. At the time of his arrest he was on his way from the Chiesa del Carmine to the adjoining monastery, after delivering an angry speech accusing the people of betrayal. His manner was desperate, his countenance deranged. When it came to his execution, the mob greeted his death with cheers.

The only popular revolt in Naples' history thus came to an end. A few days later the people saw the consequences of Masaniello's death and repented. They dug up the body, sewed back the head and gave him a military funeral. The viceroy, meanwhile, returned to the Neapolitan throne. Despite the promises made *in extremis*, his tax policies remained virtually unchanged.

A scholar who had written about Naples at the beginning of the 20th century returned in the 1950s to see how the place had been getting along. He looked forward to seeing the old sights, but in the event it was his sense of hearing that worked overtime: "Here more than in any other city in the world [the noise] overwhelms everything in its confusion and meanness, the howling of children, the cries of the women, the shouting of the men vainly competing with the hooting of horns, the explosion of the open exhausts of motor vehicles... the mind indeed being half-paralysed by the flood of indistinguishable things, not one of which was characteristic, but rather all together."

The Naples on which he reflected had just emerged from the most traumatic quarter-century in its entire history. In 1922 it was Benito Mussolini's springboard. "Either the Government will be given to us," he told 40,000 cheering Fascists at a rally in Naples, "or we shall seize it by marching on Rome." He marched on Rome and in due course on Abyssinia, Albania and Greece. "That great man south of the Alps," Hitler called him. "That absurd man," according to Lord Curzon in England. "I believe that there can be counted among my qualities one of being able to act in good season and to strike at the right moment without false sentimentality where the shadow of a weakness or of a trap is hidden," said Mussolini of himself.

World War II rolled on, and Mussolini professed to be gratified when Naples was bombed. A good dose of air raids, he said, would turn Neapolitans into a Nordic race, and he gave orders that sirens were to be sounded and anti-aircraft batteries were to blaze away whenever possible, even when not strictly necessary, to make the illusion of danger more exciting. With military disasters mounting, however, Mussolini eventually concluded that his countrymen were "not mature or consistent enough for so grave and decisive a test".

Left, **Il Duce, Benito Mussolini.**

The Italian Armistice, Hitler's seizure of the North, and the subsequent Allied invasions via Sicily and Salerno in the South meant that Italy was divided by a front-line, the so-called Gustav Line, which cut across the peninsula about 50 miles (80 km) north of Naples, from which the Germans had withdrawn in 1943. A strong point on that line, the gate to the Liri valley, was Cassino, a battleground remembered for the ferocity of the fighting and the controversial Allied destruction of the monastery.

Symbol of resistance: There is still no universal agreement on whether German troops were actually occupying the monastery; in the opinion of one of the Allied commanders, it was sufficient that they might. Fred Majdalany, a British soldier who wrote a brilliant chronicle of the battle, explained how he and his comrades on the ground viewed the monastery: "Because of the extraordinary extent to which the summit of Monte Cassino dominated the valleys: because of the painful constancy with which men were picked off by accurately observed gunfire whenever they were forced to move in daylight within its seemingly inescapable view: because of the obsessive theatrical manner in which it towered over the scene, searching every inch of it, the building set upon that summit had become the embodiment of resistance and its tangible symbol."

"To the ordinary German soldier," wrote Major-General John Strawson, who was also there on the British side, "the bombardment seemed like hell on earth. When a thousand aircraft bombed their positions and artillery concentrations simply went on all day the ground would shake like an earthquake, nothing but dust and smoke was to be seen, there was not a moment's peace, just the dreadful thunder of guns and mortars, enemy aeroplanes always overhead discharging their deadly and terrifying cargo; nothing like it had happened before, not even in Russia... Yet they held on."

The battle lasted four months. It ended with Majdalany's adjutant picking up a telephone in late May, 1944, with three words for headquarters: "Take-over completed."

Future generations wanting to know what Naples was like during all of this can consider themselves extremely fortunate in that Norman Lewis, a giant among contemporary travel writers, was on the spot as a member of the British Field Security Service, a branch of military intelligence. *Naples '44*, his anecdotal account, which Luigi Barzini described as "reading page after page as if eating cherries", is probably most easily found in the paperback version published by Eland Books of London in 1983.

"The city of Naples," reads Lewis's entry at Posillipo I stopped to watch the methodical dismemberment of a stranded German half-track by a number of youths who were streaming away from it like leaf-cutter ants, carrying pieces of metal of all shapes and sizes. Fifty yards away a well-dressed lady with a feather in her hat squatted to milk a goat… Hunchbacks are considered lucky, so they were everywhere, scuttling underfoot, and a buyer of the lottery tickets they offered for sale touched or stroked their humps as he made his purchase."

The desperation of the food shortage was evident in Neapolitans leaving the city every day in their thousands to scour the country-

on his arrival, "smells of charred wood, with ruins everywhere, sometimes completely blocking the streets, bomb craters and abandoned trams. The main problem is water. Two tremendous air raids on 4 August (1943) and 6 September smashed up all the services, and there has been no proper water supply since the first of these. To complete the Allies' work of destruction, German demolition squads have gone round blowing up anything of value to the city that still worked."

His impressions mounted as he moved around the city in the weeks ahead. "Today side for edible plants. As winkles and sea-snails had long been removed from the rocks piled up along the sea wall, children prised off limpets which, if boiled long enough, added a fishy flavour to broth produced from absolutely anything remotely edible. Resourceful butchers made the most of what they could find, making a showpiece of, for example, chicken heads from which the beaks had been neatly trimmed.

Lewis went along to try one of the first restaurants to re-open. The place was full of middle-class patrons who wore overcoats made of stolen army blankets, hot items on the burgeoning black market. The ritual in the restaurant, he learned, was for a waiter to pass through the tables bearing what was called "the show-fish" for the patrons to admire. "This had a good-looking head… but the body didn't match the head, and from its triangular backbone evidently belonged to the dogfish family." The Milanese-style veal, which looked a bit too dry, turned out to be horse. Lewis ordered macaroni. General Mark Clark, the American commander, had been feted with a banquet little knowing that the boiled fish with a garlic sauce put before him was a raw specimen fished out of Naples' famous aquarium.

Love among the ruins: In Naples, Lewis decided, food came before love, and the latter was no easy matter. One of his colleagues, a Captain Frazer, had taken up with a widow named Lola whose rear was covered in hundreds of tiny scars, the result of *iniezione reconstituenti*, injections that were available in many of the pharmacies of Naples to keep women at the peak of their sexual powers.

For the most part, however, sex in wartime Naples was prostitution born of utter desperation. A prince, the head of the second or third noble family in southern Italy, brought his 24-year-old sister into the Field Security Service offices and asked whether she could be given a position in an army brothel. On being told that the British Army didn't have official brothels, he replied in faultless English: "Ah well, I suppose if it can't be, it can't be."

Lewis calculated that the shattered economy meant that the average family with five children and perhaps a couple of grandparents to look after was expected to get by on about two dollars per month when shortages and inflation were soaring. The black market was the only recourse, and it was estimated that the cargo of one Allied ship in three unloading in the port of Naples was stolen. The black-marketeers even contrived to sound air-raid sirens in order to clear their way to particularly desirable cargoes.

The intelligentsia, who depended on

black-market supplies like everyone else but refrained from stealing themselves, managed as best they could. A venerable, non-practising lawyer wrote occasional newspaper articles on folklore and astronomy which enabled him to subsist on cups of coffee substitute and pumpkin seeds. Another of Lewis's acquaintances, also a non-practising lawyer, earned his keep by posing as the "uncle from Rome" which Neapolitan families would hire to make an appearance at weddings and funerals. An agency handled his bookings and provided a car with Rome number plates, in which he was conspicuously delivered to the event, and appropriate

clothing. All he had to do was affect a Roman accent and talk about life in the capital.

"Last week," wrote Lewis, "a nobleman in our street was lifted by his servants from his deathbed, dressed in his evening clothes, then carried to be propped up at the head of the staircase over the courtyard of his *palazzo*. Here with a bouquet of roses thrust into his arms he stood for a moment to take leave of his friends and neighbours gathered in the courtyard below, before being carried back to receive the last rites. Where else but in Naples could a sense of occasion be carried to such lengths?"

Left, Blackshirts swarm into Naples in October 1922. **Above**, liberation.

Annalisa III-D

Anne Buckland, an Edwardian visitor, was scathing about the un-British Neapolitans. "They form the element of national discord, the Irish of Italy: quick, gay, careless, noisy and impulsive; but vindictive, cruel, discontented, indolent; a people always ready to give trouble to their rulers but never likely to improve their own condition." The Irish snub aside, there is some truth behind this jaundiced assertion.

Certainly, the Neapolitans are troublesome. They welcome new rulers, if only out of eagerness to see the comeuppance of the previous regime. When Garibaldi's forces arrived from Sicily in 1860, a stranger could have been forgiven for not noticing the change of regime. George Gissing observed that the only sign of revolution was the disappearance of the Bourbon *fleur de lys* from the tops of lampposts. In Naples, today's jubilant crowds are tomorrow's jaded *Camorristi*: subversion not confrontation is the city style.

Maradona, the footballer, was an adopted Neapolitan but, curiously, its most archetypal. In looks, he was the stereotypical *Napolitano*: small, dark, swarthy, with a trace of Greek blood. In character, he was the incarnation of Neapolitan manhood: lawless and subversive, sociable and spirited. Maradona was the street urchin who always landed on his feet. He acted the part of good husband and devoted Catholic. He was also a notorious womaniser who wore out prostitutes in pairs, like football boots. As a player, he was a magician who deceived on and off the pitch. As a Neapolitan, he was God.

The old slogan of "see Naples and die" has been supplanted by *"vedi Napoli e scappa"* (see Naples and run away). A city of two million anarchists is not a recipe for a quiet life. The local outlook is as suicidal as the city traffic. The Neapolitan writer, Luciano

Preceding pages: marriage without the carriage; a master of display; peace in the cloisters of Santa Chiara; ship aloft. **Left**, member of the *scugnizzi*, street kids. **Above**, southern bloom.

de Crescenzo, offers an insight into the warped Neapolitan mind. "And what about the orange light?" the author asked an old man who spent his days at traffic lights waiting for accidents. "The orange? That doesn't mean anything. We keep it to brighten the place up."

Naples is in perpetual motion, matched by the wit and operatic intensity of the people. Naples is essentially street theatre reenacted every day. An entrepreneurial Nea-

politan sees opportunities everywhere. In crumbling tenements, business can be conducted by means of a basket suspended from the end of a rope. If the price of the tomatoes below sounds right, the elderly woman responds to cries of *"Signo! Acalate'o panaro!"* (Signora, lower your basket.)

But even on the street, there is order behind the chaos. The Neapolitans are anarchists only in that they don't follow other people's rules. In the manner of Eastern souks, similar trades cluster in the same alleyway. Whether a wedding dress or a Christmas crib, goods have their niche.

Bridal shops are clustered on Via del Duomo; Via dell' Annunziata is naturally for baby clothes; designer boutiques and antique shops occupy Piazza dei Martiri; second-hand bookshops line Via Port'Alba, near Piazza Dante.

Old-school spivs: The entrepreneurial spirit is rampant even amongst the *scugnizzi* (street kids) in the Forcella market. They dabble in anything from handbag snatching to heroin trading. Haggling is infectious in the ramshackle capital of Campania but importuning, touting and extortion are also market mechanisms. Still, as writer Ian Thomson says, the Forcella traders are not

our), the boy is then expected to prove his worth by serving the cause.

Even the humblest individuals are threatened unless they pay *dovuti* (dues) to the Camorra. The celebrated Neapolitan film director Franco Rosi condemned corruption in *Hands over the City*, dealing with the Camorra's control of the 1950s building boom in Naples. Their greed still causes the disfigurement of the city and the degradation of local culture.

Afragola, Fratta and Acerra form the so-called Triangle of Death, a Camorra-run homeland of half a million people. This *triangolo della morte* is a battlefield for rival

controlled by the Nuova Camorra Organizzata, the local mafia, "but by the old-school spivs who have probably learnt their dubious trade through selling nylon stockings at the end of the last war".

Nevertheless, Naples' nefarious reputation is justified: it is a hotbed of intrigue, crime and Camorra activities. The criminal culture is deeply ingrained in the Neapolitan character. As a Camorra stronghold, Naples presents citizens with daily choices between grey and black. It is a small step from sharp street kid to unpaid apprentice to the Camorra. As *piccioto di onore* (lad of hon-

gangs and a desperate place for the unemployed locals. A group of vigilantes, headed by a bishop, briefly fought the Camorra in the 1980s but the struggle came to nothing. Yet even here are small triumphs for the Neapolitan spirit. Elderly traders share an old van to the town centre. There they concoct new trades, from selling tripe to babies' rattles. At the end of the day, it is home to the Triangle of Death.

Poverty has pushed the Neapolitans into improvised jobs. An Edwardian visitor, Frances Power Cobbe, was unpleasantly reminded of her birthplace: "In Naples, they resemble more closely in ignorance, squalor and degradation the most wretched Irish who dwell in mud cabins amid the bogs."

Although the glow-worm vendors and tortoise trainers have disappeared, many bizarre or dispiriting trades have taken their place. The poverty is palpable: nothing is wasted in Naples.

The Neapolitan street economy depends on the rag trade. Clothes are produced in the overcrowded tenements on the outskirts. Leather is worked in dingy sweatshops in historic Naples. In the *bassi*, airless one-room hovels, families gather to sew shoes, gloves and bags. Over 100,000 people still

to an obscene dance. The entertainers are rewarded with bread or money. Outside Naples, they would barely be tolerated while, in countries with better social services, few would be allowed out.

Natural disasters are part of life in Naples and one of the causes of *miseria*. The 1980 earthquake killed 5,000 people in Campania. Since then, many citizens have been housed in makeshift places, including museums. Known as *terremotati*, these earthquake victims live in such refuges as Castello di Baia, a tumbledown 16th-century Spanish castle in Baia, outside Naples. By contrast, the 1983 earthquake in Pozzuoli had only one

live and work in such slums. This insalubrious quarter is the heart of the most densely populated city in Europe.

Surreal entertainers: Even so, overcrowding has only reinforced the respect for genuine poverty. Without romanticising it, Neapolitans are responsive to real need and give generously. Surreal entertainers, known as *pazarielli*, are appreciated. Each performance is individual but could feature anything from an impersonation of an African trader

Left, dressed in Sunday best. **Above**, making headroom.

fatality, who died of fright. Perhaps, on this occasion, Sophia Loren was watching over her birthplace.

In Naples, natural disasters are soon compounded by social catastrophes. Money destined for the earthquake relief fund was swallowed up by the Camorra. The housing crisis has been exacerbated by the need to provide refuges for the homeless.

Neapolitan social services are among the worst in Europe. Hospitals are so woefully overcrowded and inadequate that it is hardly surprising that there was a cholera outbreak in Naples in the 1970s. In city hospitals, patients jokingly complain of eating *grasso di rinoceronte* (rhino fat).

The Naples' Policlinico regularly makes the headlines for its *degradazione inumana* (inhumane conditions). In addition, Naples has the poorest refuse collection service in Italy. To make matters worse, funeral parlours are often closed down if they are suspected of having links to the Camorra. In 1992 the authorities faced the threat of unburied bodies piling up and relented on an order to close down 12 funeral parlours. The undertakers promptly went on strike. The Neapolitan reaction to such disasters is stoical suffering or fatalism.

The Neapolitans have long been pawns in a political power game. Grandiose projects, known poetically as "cathedrals in the desert", litter the industrial scene. Such white elephants are irrelevant or of limited advantage to the region. These car plants and refineries tend to employ few people and run on northern-produced equipment and imported expertise. Instead of revenue, they produce pollution and an increased cost of living. As writer Luigi Barzini commented: "The South is known as the cemetery of public works. But it may now be the cemetery of industrial plants as well."

Cemeteries, real and metaphorical, provide good cover for the Camorra and gangsters often negotiate there or hide arms in the family vault. On the wider stage, the links between Camorra gangsters and politicians are rarely touched upon. The Christian Democrats rely upon the Camorra to ensure that locals vote for the right, even to the extent of ballot-rigging. In 1992 Italian Budget and Planning Minister, Paolo Pomicino, was involved in a local corruption scandal. The Neapolitan-born protégé of the Prime Minister was accused of swindling the state of earthquake relief funds.

As a result of such corruption and mismanagement, the Neapolitans are torn between fatalism and extremist political measures. The locals have always been right-wing, drawn to the Christian Democrats or the MSI, the ultra-right Neo-fascist party. Unemployment is currently 30 percent and emigration to the North or abroad is no longer viable.

Heir to Mussolini: Cashing in on her Neapolitan inheritance, the glamorous Alessandra Mussolini stood as an MSI candidate in Naples during the 1992 parliamentary elections. Known as La Mussolina, she has generated almost as much controversy as her legendary grandfather. Amusingly, the PSDI socialist party opposed her with Prince Amadeo d'Aosta, the popular heir to the throne of ex-King Umberto. Such theatre could only happen in Naples. As a former actress and the neice of Sophia Loren, she is also a mistress of disguises and therefore a true Neapolitan.

The Neapolitans' inner life is as devious as their outer life. If Italians are masters of *l'arte di arrangiarsi*, manipulating the system, the Neapolitans are the supreme fixers. Given the city's history of absolutist regimes, cunning was a better tool than rebellion. The Neapolitan is renowned for being *furbo* (cunning), considered a virtue not a vice. A handbook to *scopa*, a traditional card game invented in Naples, begins: "Rule Number One: always try to see your opponent's cards."

Deception comes naturally to a Neapolitan. In this, homeopath Antonio Manzi sees Maradona, the city's fallen hero, as the true

Neapolitan: "His hand goal, the famous hand of God, reminds one of Ulysses for its deception and cunning."

In academic circles, cunning is often promoted to hypocrisy. The professors of English at Naples University were recently embroiled in scandal. The staff conducting the oral exams were sent to luxury hotels on Capri, paid for by the students' parents. The University examining board claimed that this had no bearing on the pass rate.

Visual tricks: The Neapolitans' love of the baroque is also an expression of their talent for deception: *trompe l'oeil* and tricks of perspective are fundamental to the style. As

higher than their compatriots. The Neapolitan imagination ran riot, from the baroque *duomo* to Domenico Vaccaro's rococo *palazzi*. One Neapolitan touch is the *guglia*, a freestanding ornamental spire. However, the dramatic curves and contrast of light and shade indicate virtuosity bordering the vapid, another Neapolitan trait.

The Neapolitans nurture a taste for the picturesque and painterly that verges on the kitsch. Lurid neon shrines in niches are only too common. Yet the cribs (*presepi*) on Via San Gregorio Armeno belong to a touching tradition. Father Rocco, a Dominican preacher to the poor, used the figures to bring

the English art historian Anthony Blunt said: "The architecture of Naples is like its inhabitants: lively, colourful, with a tendency not to keep the rules." Naples had long slumbered under the Spanish viceroys but Roman artists like Caravaggio brought a style which struck a chord with local sensibility. Pragmatism also played a part.

From the 16th century onwards, space constraints led the Neapolitans to build

Left, pause for thought. **Above**, in Naples' *bassi*, the pavement provides a spacious extra living-room for extended families.

the Christmas message home to his flock in the 1750s. These lavishly decorated Nativity scenes adorn churches over the Christmas period. Likewise, every family flaunts its prized collection of terracotta figures. While echoing displays in German and Scandinavian Christmas markets, these scenes outdo their rivals in sentimentality and showmanship.

Father Rocco also established shrines all over the city and, until 1806, these were the only sources of light. In memory of this, Neapolitans still cross themselves as the evening lights come on. Despite the sentimentality, the citizens are fiercely Catholic. In the Montecalvario quarter of Naples, each alley has its own shrine to a local saint. San Gennaro, the city's patron saint, competes with Santa Lucia and the Madonna. The shrines are tended by wizened old ladies who change the oil, light candles and collect pitiful offerings. The English travel writer Eric Newby slyly notes that in the hot grottoes beneath, the terracotta figures, including a priest, "fry in purgatory".

Beware the evil eye: Yet Naples is the most superstitious city in Europe. The citizens use amulets to ward off the evil eye and also dabble in numerology and black magic.

sion winds through the heart of the city to the Madonna's shrine. The sanctuary was founded in 1500, after a miraculous outpouring of blood from a statue of the Virgin. A kitsch effigy of the Madonna, draped in pink tulle and palm leaves, is borne aloft by a tumultuous crowd. Ian Thomson, a visiting journalist, found the celebration as superstitious and voodooistic as any in the South: "Girls and boys prostrate themselves in humble supplication. Old women, tearful with emotion, hobble shrinewards on their knees, seemingly oblivious of pain."

Other festivals have clearer pagan origins. The Whit Monday Return of the Pilgrims

Even Catholic ceremonies are imbued with superstition. The liquefaction of San Gennaro's blood is the greatest display of collective paranoia. Yet when it failed to liquefy in 1941, Vesuvius erupted; when the miracle faltered in May 1988, it was before a football match in which Naples was defeated by archrivals Milan. If the miracle succeeds, crowds prostrate themselves before the reliquary and the kissing of the phial lasts a week. On the first Saturday in May, the phials of blood are paraded through the old city as a ritualised blessing of all Neapolitans.

The Madonna dell'Arco Easter proces-

from Montevergine is a Christian version of an ancient Bacchanalian rite. The procession is accompanied by beribboned donkeys and costumed revellers bearing staves decorated with fruit and flowers. Animals also feature in the Festival of Sant'Antonio on 17 January. The horses are blessed at Sant'Antonio church, much as in the more famous Sienese Palio. The festival harks back to Bourbon times when Neapolitan horsemanship was unequalled. The locals miss no opportunity to congratulate themselves.

Fancy dress: Some see the love of elaborate ceremonial as the Spanish inheritance, a legacy of the Bourbons. But theatricality and buffoonery are innate to the Neapolitan character. Even so, the *Struscio* is an extravaganza dating back to the Spanish court. It is even named after the rustling noise of silk dresses worn on the occasion. On the Thursday and Friday before Easter, the Neapolitans play at being grandees for a day. Dressed in all their finery, the crowds sweep along Via Roma to view the gorgeous Easter displays in the shops.

Extravagance and mystique merge in a traditional funeral. As fatalists, the Neapolitans have perfected a cult of death which feels closer to ancient Egypt than present-

phans if the deceased's estate can carry the cost. At Camorra funerals, the bereaved wear diamond-studded shirts so expense is rarely an issue. However, when the firm dared put in a bill for one Camorra funeral, they received a bomb by return of post.

A taste for the ghoulish: The weird Prince Raimondo, an 18th-century alchemist, built the Cappella Sansevero as a human laboratory. His avowed goal was to extract phosphorus from urine. Two mysteriously preserved corpses are still visible in the crypt below. Shortly before Raimondo died in a botched experiment, the Pope had the sense to excommunicate him.

day Europe. The *Bellomunno* funeral processions are a direct inheritance of Bourbon times. Even the name is a sick joke referring, in dialect, to *bello mondo*, beautiful world. A gold and black rococo hearse is pulled by eight, 10 or 12 jet black horses and driven by a single coachman.

Most such lugubrious affairs are reserved for the Camorra chiefs who can afford such a send-off. In theory, *Bellomunno* can assemble a cast of hundreds of professional mourners, nuns and real or simulated or-

The San Gennaro catacombs depict the ghoulishness of the Neapolitan imagination. Amongst the mosaics and frescoes are funeral niches and the remains of the saint. Yet even in death, the Neapolitans exhibit a passion for life: a priapic goat dances above the early Christian throne.

An 18th-century traveller was astonished by the lavish lifestyle of the Benedictine nuns at San Gregorio Armeno. At the banquet were "so many victims to the pride of family, to avarice and superstition. Many of these victims were in the full bloom of health and youth, and some were remarkably hand-

Left, street musicians. **Above**, street vendor.

some." No aristocratic community believed in abstinence.

By the end of the 19th century, Naples was condemned for its "contaminated atmosphere and filth" by Dr Henry Bennet, a criticism still heard today. "Where the sun does not enter, the doctor does," runs a Neapolitan saying. Yet it was also considered the foremost city of fun, a warm and wicked place and a cure for British ennui. As historian John Pemble remarked, "Naples had too much native vitality to submit to anglicisation."

The vitality, theatricality and instinctual humanity still survive. The Neapolitans re-

Spagnolesco, the Spanish nobility who despised work. Their *dolce far niente* approach to life colours the Neapolitans' vision. The *passeggiata*, or evening stroll, is a charming custom inherited from the Bourbon rulers. It is an opportunity for finery, flirtation and flattery. As Barzini says: "Naples is the capital of hyperbolic and meaningless flattery."

The Spanish quarter is the place for theatrical street life and female gossip. The crisscrossing balconies allow no privacy, a word alien to the natives. The intimacy of the city allows little space for smothered sensibilities. Luciano de Crescenzo mused on the effects of transporting a Neapolitan house to

main the most demonstrative of Italians, and the quickest to anger. An early 19th-century book, *The Mimicry of Ancient People Interpreted Through the Gestures of the Neapolitans*, lists 10 typical gestures for expressing rage. Curiously, these include "biting one's fingers individually" and "pretending to bite one's elbow".

The harsh, Arabic-sounding Neapolitan dialect is spoken at incredible speed but masks another Oriental trait, a fatalism in the face of adversity.

Spanish legacy: Yet one side of Neapolitan character yearns for the ease of the so-called

Heaven. "Imagine… the vast line of bunting, houses and washing lines and washing and all the singing."

The gentler side of Naples opens up in the breezy gardens of the Villa Comunale. Along the seaside promenade, strollers are tempted by coconuts, cold drinks and water melons. *Venditori di volanti* (pedlars of "flying objects") attract children to their floating balloons and kites. Picnickers and ice-cream sellers snooze under the blue and white parasols that echo the colours of Naples beloved football team.

The arts remain a mainstay of Neapolitan

life, a chance to indulge in release. While the city has been celebrated in films and literature, music is the Neapolitans' natural forte. The locals are refreshingly unsnobbish and unacademic about music. Naples may be the capital of melancholy yet joyous *bel canto* but a rock band is as common as a maudlin mandolin. San Carlo opera house, the largest in Italy, staged premieres of works by Rossini and Bellini. Samuel Sharp visited in 1763 and was astonished by the noisiness of the audience during the music but their rapt attention for the dancing. He was informed: "The Neapolitans go to *see,* not to *hear,* an opera." This remains true today.

Naples is second only to Milan as a centre for modern music. In fact, Neapolitans complain that they create the music but the Milanese only produce it. Neapolitans have a talent for improvisation and inspired borrowing. American jazz infused local folk music with new vigour in the 1950s. In the 1970s, the urban Blues scene sprung up around Pino Daniele and the Alfa Romeo factory in Pomigliano. However, popular music has not drowned out the Neapolitans' passion for baroque music. In summer

Left, throw-away gesture **Above**, tactile tactics.

classical concerts are held in the San Francesco cloisters.

A sense of belonging, the *cultura dell' appartenenza*, is the glue that binds Naples together. The September Festival di Piedigrotta commemorates the Battle of Velletri in 1744 with rousing popular songs at the Grotta Nuova. A fierce pride unites the lively yet secretive Spaccanapoli quarter of old Naples. Summer festivals held in the *rioni*, all the historic quarters, celebrate the city with firework displays and pageantry. Local sports clubs join in processions of the *rioni* but only football not folklore aspires to religious status.

Machismo versus mammismo: A common Neapolitan saying runs: "*E meglio cumanna che fottere*" (domination is sweeter than fornication). Naples has never had an empire and never dominated – until Maradona brought the illusion of conquest. Yet pride, prestige and the trappings of power are as important as the power itself. As Luigi Barzini writes in *The Italians*, a southern male "wants to be obeyed, admired, respected, feared and envied".

Honorific titles are important as a sign of prestige. Any prospective male client is automatically promoted to *Dottore*. He may even rise to *Commendatore* (knight) if he is middle-aged and slightly distinguished. Neapolitans have an ingrained sense of status. Bootblacks used to have seats as glittering and gaudy as thrones. The idea was, quite simply, to make the client feel like a king. But power and money are not of equal worth. As Barzini says: "Southerners tend to make money in order to rule, Northerners to rule in order to make money." In a city where status is all, no one has a more mythical role than a Neapolitan *mamma*: a rogue might sell his grandmother but never his mother.

The sulky Neapolitan male traditionally suffers from *mammismo*, an infantile dependence on his mother, and *gallismo*, machismo in its lady-killing guise. One joke is that Christ must have been a southern Italian since he lived at home until he was 30, thought his mother was a virgin and that he was God. Certainly *braggadocio* is not unknown to Neapolitan men. It is accompanied by an ambivalent attitude to sex. As Oscar

Wilde wrote from Naples in 1897: "It is not for pleasure that I come here; though pleasure, I am glad to say, walks all around."

John Evelyn, a 17th-century visitor, was equally impressed by the women who were "well-featured but excessively libidinous" compared with his prim compatriots. Neapolitan women are a visible presence, unlike their counterparts in the rural South. Their contribution to the black economy is vital, whether as traders or home-workers. Retirement barely exists: elderly women are unofficial museum custodians or sit outside churches collecting alms. Their survival skills are sharply honed; in the poorest sub-

urbs, this can mean reconditioning rags or living off restaurant scraps.

Subversiveness, a city characteristic, applies to both sexes. Recently, a number of women have risen to high rank in the Camorra, with one section run by the formidable Pupetta Maresca. In 1981, Carmela Provenzano delivered the death sentence on "Angel Face" Turatello, a Camorra boss then serving a jail sentence. The next day he was stabbed 60 times by male and female *sicari* (cut-throats).

On a more legal level, women have a high profile in the city's cultural life, partly thanks to the liberalising influence of the university. But, at home, Naples is still semi-medieval southern Italy. When a Neapolitan maid goes to work for an unmarried man, her possessive husband generally waits outside. Bourgeois Neapolitan girls fare no better; they are over-protected, often escorted to English classes on chic Via Chaia by sullen brothers. Still, Neapolitan women are less sheltered and less subservient than most southern women. A curious custom is to wish a woman *"figli maschi"* (boy children) whenever she sneezes, whether she wants them or not.

The way to celebrate: Neapolitan theatricality is best appreciated at a fireworks display. This custom of appeasing the *popolo*, the common herd, is yet another custom with roots in the city's Bourbon rule. According to Don Ciccio, the major fireworks chauvinist in Naples, the Chinese may have discovered fireworks but they've invented nothing since. "Believe me, Naples is the world's fireworks capital." The whole community pays for a display, held to celebrate anything from Easter to New Year. Such extravaganzas are suitable for a volatile, spectacular people. A Neapolitan display begins with a dramatic *colpo scuro*, a detonation in the dark and ends with the finale, when all hell breaks loose. Don Ciccio raises his glass: "To Vesuvius. Sooner or later, he'll get us all".

Being a Neapolitan is about salvaging success from the jaws of defeat. The battle is between self-respect and fatalism. After Naples won the Italian football championship in 1987 for the first time, fans waved the flags of the American Confederacy and chanted: "We're better than the North." Even now, gratitude outweighs regret: "We give thanks to Diego who for once made the South win without distorting it or alienating it," is how one intellectual put it. The fans' reaction is blunter: "*Grazie Napoli*" graffiti is still daubed on the city walls.

The king is dead, but *Evviva Napoli* – long live Naples.

Cesare de Seta's history of Naples, published in 1981, is generally regarded as the most comprehensive work on Naples ever produced. "The history of the city," the author writes in his introduction, "can be gleaned from her streets and squares, from the cathedral and the Palazzo Municipale, from the monasteries and churches, from the city gates and the markets, from the people and the slum areas and from the topology and transformation, or rather destruction, of the natural environment."

To help reconstruct the history of urban development in Naples, de Seta analysed many paintings, not because they record particularly accurate views of the city but because their intention was to satisfy the personal vanity of those who commissioned them, a *raison d'être* which he finds reflected in the city's architecture.

As de Seta points out, the various ruling dynasties who wielded power in Naples left very different marks on the city's urban development. The confusion of styles and concepts of city planning is therefore considerable. In de Seta's view the problems caused by the inappropriate development policies pursued blindly by the various rulers have never been brought any closer to being solved. Many of the problems of present-day Naples, such as the precarious sanitary conditions of several districts, are not just ills of our time, but have roots reaching deep into the sub-soil of history.

City views: The earliest picture we have of Naples, an important document of the city's urban development, is a panel painting by a man whose purpose was to pay homage to the Spanish ruler from Aragon. The *Tavola Strozzi* by the painter Strozzi (it can be admired in the Museo di Capodimonte) shows Naples from the sea at the time of Ferdinand of Aragon's triumphant return from the bat-

tle for Ischia in 1465. This view of Naples was later to represent the popular image of the city abroad.

At first sight, the Naples depicted in the *Tavola Strozzi* looks like a medieval city. In reality, however, when Strozzi carried out his commission in 1474 the city was in a vigorous state of flux, something which can be recognised from minute but important details on the painting. Under the express instructions of the Spaniards, urban develop-

ment was effectively turned on its head. Their architects took as their inspiration Naples' ancient past.

Nevertheless, it was under their rule that a successful symbiosis was achieved between aesthetic considerations and the need for sound defence. The Spaniards' greatest concern was to reinforce the city fortifications as soon as possible – after all, these bulwarks were the key to power over the city. They also summoned a number of renowned Renaissance architects to Naples to lay out gates, churches, chapels and squares. One particularly impressive feature in this respect is

Preceding pages: view from Vomero; the Royal Palace; some of the worst slums in Europe. **Left**, closely packed and steeply stacked. **Right**, Galleria Umberto I.

the triumphal arch which Alfonso of Aragon built between two of the towers of the Castel Nuovo. All in all, however, the Spanish made only cosmetic changes to the urban landscape; nothing came of their ambitious scheme to bring lasting order to the city by implementing a well-coordinated development plan. The city continued to grow uncontrollably and the living conditions of the people deteriorated.

Antonio Lafrery's painting of the city (1566) shows Naples approximately 100 years later, when it was the seat of the Viceroy Don Pedro of Toledo. Like the earlier picture, it is a good record of the radical changes the city underwent during this period. Don Pedro was another ruler who nursed grandiose plans for the city's urban development; unfortunately, he was thwarted in his aims by the explosive growth of the population.

The main reason for such growth was the increasing volume in migration from the countryside, the result of the short-sighted tax policies of the monarch. The extravagant court life of the Spanish viceroy and the consequent impoverishment of the rural population through the taxes levied to pay for it led to more and more people pouring into the city. Many of the migrants settled on the fringes of Naples. The Spanish viceroy, alarmed at the increasing urbanisation, could think of no way of dealing with the problem except by issuing bans. A decree of 1565, for example, forbade building in various districts of the city or on the San Martino hills.

After numerous decrees went unheeded Don Pedro's architects took drastic action, demolishing all the houses which had been built without permission. This policy ended in failure, creating the foundations of the miserable conditions which exist in some parts of the city today. In the middle of the 17th century the city had around 450,000 inhabitants, whilst comparably large European cities had less than half this number. Epidemics were therefore continually devastating large sections of the population: over 250,000 people died during the plague of 1656.

Capital city: Naples was chosen by the House of Aragon as the capital of the empire.

As a result, the city's developers found themselves torn between the desire to erect prestigious constructions and the need to plan administrative buildings, stimulate the economy, and design a decent network of thoroughfares.

The Bourbons, who followed the Spaniards, tried to resolve this dilemma in the 18th and 19th centuries by establishing two priorities: first, the extension of the most important streets; and second, the building and furnishing of new administrative centres, which they took care to locate at strategically important points in the city. The Teatro San Carlo, the Palazzo degli Studi,

the Serraglio, the Caserma al Ponte della Maddalena and the poor-house were all built during this time. However, in reality much of this building work was no more than a patch-up job, even though some of it was masterfully carried out.

Naples was already a metropolis under the Bourbons, but the kind of radical social and economic changes which took place in other large European cities failed to materialise. Not even the Bourbons were able to channel the unstoppable growth of the city properly: they, too, took decisions which made the city's dilemma worse rather than better.

When it was clear, for example, that new development areas were necessary, the city's planners decided to create them on the eastern outskirts of the city, even though other, more accessible sites were available. The utter foolishness of this decision is evident in the fact that the areas chosen consisted largely of marshland, which first had to be systematically drained. The main railway station was built on these eastern outskirts in the 19th century, and with it came the urbanisation of the green spaces on the hills of Posillipo, Vomero, and Capodimonte. The modern city landscape was thus shaped.

the wretched sanitary conditions, the Italian government ordered the demolition of many of the housing complexes in the heavily populated areas. Sadly, among the complexes earmarked for redevelopment were some important remnants of the city's medieval architecture, in particular many buildings from the time of the Anjous. Incidentally, the Galleria Umberto I (1876–83) by Emanuele Rocco, was built during this last period of urban development, based on a design similar to that produced by Giuseppe Mangoni in Milan.

Urban jungle: At present, the politicians are hopeful that the centuries-old problem of

The inhabitants of the new districts had to cope with severe traffic problems from the very beginning. The city centre could be reached only with difficulty – a problem which still hasn't been resolved.

The last attempt to bring some order to this jungle of houses and streets was just before the cholera epidemic of 1884, at a time when Naples was already part of the new Italian nation. To prevent further epidemics, the risk of which was increased considerably by

Left, facade in Spaccanapoli. **Above**, Porta Capuana, one of five extant gates.

urban development will be resolved by the Nuovo Centro Direzionale, which was officially opened in 1989. There are high hopes that this ultra-modern city, built behind the main railway station, will provide a solution to the city's transport problems. Not that the people of Naples have much faith in the new arrangement: an integrated transport plan to regulate the flow of the 700,000 cars which roll into the city each day still hasn't been passed. At this rate, the Neapolitans look like remaining dependent on their finely tuned wits to cope with the traffic conditions until well into the 21st century.

In most cities, the areas where the wealthier citizens live are clearly separated from those of the less well-off by invisible demarcation lines. However, in Naples – at least in the old part of the city – affluence and poverty live cheek by jowl. The town residences of the bourgeoisie stand next to run-down hovels, and luxury buildings share the same views as dilapidated tenements. Narrow streets criss-crossed by lines of drying washing, a sight so evocative that it has become a symbol of Naples' poor, run into thoroughfares of gracious mansions. The only exceptions to this rule are the areas on the hills between Via Petrarca and Via Manzoni which were built after World War II.

Forcella, however, situated in the centre around the main railway station, is the most famous slum district in Naples. The locals call it the *kasbah forcella*, a name which dates from the period after the liberation of Naples in World War II. This is where the Neapolitans established a flourishing black market. There was nothing which was not available for those who could pay the price; butter and coffee, meat and bread, cigarettes and chocolate, and even medicines and condoms. The products were obtained from the Allied troops, either by stealing or bartering.

Now the area is one huge open-air market, which still does a roaring trade in contraband goods. Unfortunately this also extends to hard drugs, and drug peddling has become the main source of income.

In other ports the seedier areas are usually grouped around the harbour, the reason being that sailors with a raging sexual appetite and legs used to a rolling deck wouldn't want to go too far to spend the pay in their pockets. In Naples, however, they are a little further away, beyond the Maschio Angioino, the famous opera house of San Carlo and the Galleria Umberto, in the *quartieri spagnoli,* the Spanish quarter, which, in the 17th century housed the soldiers of the Spanish viceroy. This is the area of the notorious

Left, bringing home the bread

bassi, one-room, windowless basement dwellings.

The *quartieri spagnoli*, also called *pallonetto*, stretch from Via Santa Lucia to the hills of Pizzofalcone, and are often rightly described as labyrinths. It is an area of steep steps, winding alleys and innumerable washing lines fixed to crumbling facades. It shows better than any other part of Naples how the city must have looked in the 18th and 19th centuries, as comparisons with old prints and engravings of the city prove. But, lamentably, though much of the district may look the same, most of its inhabitants have moved with the times, and former fishermen have become cigarette smugglers or hench-men of the Camorra.

Nowadays nothing much can be seen or heard of the bustling everyday lives of the inhabitants of these neighbourhoods. At one time it was possible to peer into the rooms and perhaps catch a glimpse of unmade beds or an old woman preparing *ragú*, the tradi-tional spaghetti sauce made of tomatoes and meat. Closed Venetian blinds and tinted glass now shield against the inquisitive eyes of voyeuristic tourists.

Less infamous than Forcella is Sanità, the old and dilapidated area between Via Foria and the hill of Capodimonte. This area, built over 200 years ago, was named after the Church of Santa Maria della Sanità. Its most notable feature is the Cimitero delle Fonta-nelle, a cave cemetery containing the bones of plague victims, where the superstitious come to consult the spirit world.

The most revered skull among the col-lection of bones is that of the so-called *capitano*. Not only is the skull credited with being able to predict the lucky numbers in the lottery but it is also said to cure rare diseases. The strangest anecdotes are told about the *capitano* – comical and tragic, to-tally improbable, they are essentially a re-flection of the Neapolitan soul. Scenes here are more reminiscent of the developing world than a major centre of one of the leading countries in Europe.

The *Cassa del Mezzogiorno* aroused great hopes of a better life in Naples, a life made richer through industrialisation. And yet it turned out to be a complete fiasco. This government compensation fund for the Mezzogiorno, the economically underdeveloped south, was set up in the post-war period in an attempt to stimulate the industries of the region and create desperately needed new jobs. Billions of lire of public money were pumped into it.

In reality, however, it was an opportunity for a lot of people to make a financial killing at the state's expense in the shortest possible time – and all perfectly legally. The trick was very simple: all you had to do was set up a firm with the aim, say, of producing and exporting wine.

It had to be an area of production that didn't already exist in a particular region, but for which sufficient raw materials were available. Providing these conditions were met, the state was prepared to provide investment. Local authorities made land available, the state subsidies flowed both plentifully and legally, and production began.

In theory, this was all well and good. But, because of corruption and government inefficiency, the desired economic miracle failed to materialise. In the case of the wine industry, because wine was already in excess supply and the sales potential in the export markets virtually negligible, most of these new firms declared themselves bankrupt within a few months. Only a handful survived for more than a few years. The end result: large amounts of money were raked off by sharp individuals, the majority of the people employed by such industries were jobless once again, and the landscape was scarred by yet more ugly industrial ruins. Experiences such as these typified the sad history of industrialisation in the Mezzogiorno.

Preceding pages: the sun sets on the industrial Phlegraean Fields. Left, industry in the Spaccanapoli. Above, worker in Santa Lucia,.

Bagnoli steelworks: Bagnoli, once Italy's third largest steel plant, suffered from Economic Community steel quotas and the drop in demand for cars and white goods. The steel trade union accepted closure in return for 1,500 new jobs in tin production on the outskirts of Naples. However, Bagnoli was ultimately the sacrificial lamb that enabled the Taranto steelworks to survive. Unlike most Neapolitan industry, Bagnoli was not Camorra-controlled so its downfall can

partly be seen as a victory for the Camorra.

At the end of October 1990 the steelworks was closed down altogether. Only a handful of newspaper photographers were there to record the moment when the last drops of molten iron flowed from the last operating blast furnace.

The dream of prosperity through industrialisation quickly faded. Industrial failure wasn't limited to the steel sector: it hit even those branches of industry which had once been booming. In Bagnoli the firms of Eternit and Agip, along with several tobacco manufacturers, were forced to close virtually simultaneously. Although a new venture is is planned for the site, namely a seaside leisure park, hardly anybody believes that it will compensate for the thousands of jobs which have been lost in the old industries.

A deep recession: In the meantime the mass exodus of businesses out of Campania has reached alarming proportions. The managing director of the finance company Sofin, expressing himself carefully in a document addressed to Franco Nobili, the president of the state-holding company IRI, had this to say on the matter: "The progressive complexity of economic life and the increase in organised crime are forcing the best part of their own by the skin of their teeth. A new factor in the current situation is that the medium-sized businesses, which once formed the economic backbone of the city, are also being hit hard by the crisis.

According to the regional employers' association, some 1,300 businesses were forced to close over an eight-year period; on average, each of them employed 10 people. To set against that, only 857 new firms were founded during the same period. All in all, over 35,000 jobs have been lost over the past decade. According to Giuseppe di Vagno, the president of the financial holding company Isveimer, the shortage of private in-

the population, and the entrepreneurs in particular, to withdraw from certain activities and areas." The result, he believes, is that only the very largest companies, such as Fiat and Olivetti, can survive in such conditions.

Naturally there are welcome exceptions to this bleak picture. For example, the Alfa-Lancia plant in Pomigliano d'Arco almost doubled its car production in 1990. And the aeronautic company Aeritalia managed to boost profits to around £35 million on a total turnover of £1.1 billion. These are excellent figures but they still can't hide the fact that most of the other industrial concerns hold vestment, as well as the absence of the infrastructure necessary for a well-balanced economic development, are the reasons why more and more industrialists have left the region.

Against this bleak background, public investment and subsidies have a vital role to play in ensuring the economic survival of the region. But private business people can only receive these payments when they have a *raccomandazione* – when they find favour with one or other of the politicians responsible for these funds, a situation that invites corruption.

A reluctant management: A further pressing problem is the difficulty of filling the leading positions in many companies. Around 80 percent of managers turn down management posts in Campania, something which the leaders of IRI know only too well, having recently tried in vain to fill three directors' posts. In part, this is because of common North/South racism and fear of finding suitable accommodation in Naples, but the biggest deterrent by far is the Camorra. According to official statistics, 70 percent of companies are threatened by the Camorra, and 58 percent end up paying protection money.

Those few managers who are willing to

skilled workers from the industrialised north of Italy. All that remains for the Neapolitan people themselves are unskilled and odd-job positions, which are badly paid and likely to be cut at the first whisper of recession.

Inevitably under these conditions, the motto for both firms and workers becomes the same: do whatever you can to survive. For many there is no alternative but to become involved in black market activities. Naples has become the "European capital of imitations". French bags and perfumes, Rolex watches and Scotch whisky, Lacoste T-shirts, fashion articles of all sorts, records, cassettes and even tickets for the most im-

move to the region demand such high salaries that you would think they were being asked to work in a Third World country. And their demands do not stop there: free private schooling for their children, private health insurance and a civil servant's limousine have become standard perks.

As well as a great shortage of top managers there is a dearth of skilled workers. Training has been a major problem for a long time now. As in the past, the area still has to recruit

Left, one of many industrial ruins. **Above**, workers take a break.

portant SSC Naples matches, as well as best-selling novels – there is nothing which cannot be forged in the backstreets of Naples, when there is sufficient sales potential. And who cares whether the woollen pullover with the Armani or Valentino emblem is really made in Naples if it is sufficiently realistic? The main thing is that its wearer can appear to belong to the circle of people who can afford the real McCoy.

And as many commentators have pointed out, if this black economy did not exist, the Mezzogiorno would probably have gone bust decades ago.

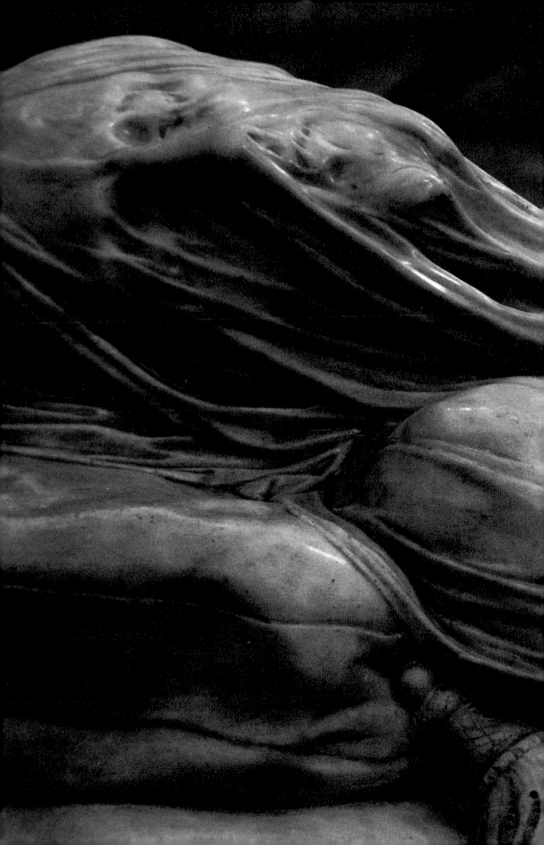

Every little street in Naples has a newspaper stand, a crucifix and a picture of a saint beneath which passers-by occasionally stop and pray. For nearly seven years the saint was invariably flanked by pictures of Diego Maradona, because the Argentine footballer – who attributed his prowess to a "direct line to God" – was worshipped with religious fervour by the Neapolitans.

Then, as the 1980s gave way to the 1990s, the god-like status given to the football star took a noticeable dive when he revealed the side of his nature which preferred cocaine and beautiful women to early nights in preparation for the next day's game. When Maradona played his first season for the club in 1984–85, some 63,000 Neapolitans bought expensive season tickets. By the 1990–91 season the number had plummeted to 43,000.

But football stars are not the only idols to rise and fall in Naples: take, for example, the undisputed patron saint of the city, San Gennaro (St Januarius).

Naples' patron saint: San Gennaro, the Bishop of Benevento, was beheaded in the amphitheatre in Pozzuoli on 19 September 305 during Diocletian's persecutions of the Christians. After the execution his followers collected his blood in two phials. These, it was said, would henceforth determine the life of the Neapolitans, for better or for worse.

The Neapolitans made San Gennaro into the most powerful saint in the Catholic church, and they hoped to be rewarded for their devotion. When they had exhausted all possibility of helping themselves, and in every hopeless situation whether financial or personal, great or small, they sought help from San Gennaro. The same holds true today. Whenever SSC Napoli, the local football team, faces a relegation battle supporters cry, *"San Gennaro, aiutaci tu!"* ("San

Gennaro, help us!") – not the usual chant to be heard on stadium terraces.

Good and bad omens: Belief in the saint's powers is directly associated with the two phials of his blood, kept in the cathedral. On three days a year the blood is said to liquefy. If it fails to do so it is considered a bad omen for the coming year. The three days when the miracle can occur are 19 September (the day of the saint's execution), the Saturday before the first Sunday in May (his birthday), and 16 December.

Proceedings are conducted according to a well-known ritual. When everything is ready, the cardinal fetches the relic with the holy phials from a safe behind the altar. At this stage of the miracle, the dark substance half-filling the phials is in a solid state. The cardinal then raises the relic repeatedly in the air, in front of the congregation, at which point there is a storm of camera flashes and a collective gasp of anticipation.

Anyone who wants to be sure of capturing the moment of liquefaction has to keep the man standing next to the cardinal in view. He is specially chosen from the San Gennaro Committee (consisting of 10 nobles and two representatives of the people). From his gestures and calling, but above all from the cloth in his hand, it is possible for the people to see how the miracle is progressing. Waving the cloth from one side to another, the notary of the miracle cries out to the people: *"Il miracolo, il miracolo!"* – the miracle has taken place. With luck, the substance in the phials is now blood-red and liquid.

At the same time, on a stone in a church in Pozzuoi, said to be the one on which Saint Gennaro was beheaded, a spot of blood takes on a brighter hue. With this, all the conditions are fulfilled to ensure that the next year is one to look forward to with hope.

Perhaps the most dramatic of these liquefactions occurred during the French occupation of Naples in Napoleonic times when a French army general with the distinctly un-French name of Macdonald went along to witness it. When nothing happened

Preceding pages: the Veiled Christ, Chapel of Sansevero. **Left,** San Genarro, guardian of the Neapolitans.

he threatened to shoot the Archbishop and his staff if the blood did not liquefy within 10 minutes. It liquefied there and then. "The benign saint hearing the brutal menace had saved his devoted adherents just in time," reported a staunch believer. "Can one expect a better proof of the validity of the miracle?"

In 1980, when the region was hit by a severe earthquake, the miracle of the blood failed to occur.

Theories of the cynics: Disbelieving eyes regard the whole ceremony as nothing more than a clever conjuring trick and have proposed all kinds of explanations, including the theory that it is caused by the heat gener-

makes them heavier and lighter in a ratio roughly but not exactly proportioned to their apparent bulk."

Even so, the importance attached to the miracle appears to be waning. Monsignor Pignatiello fears the decline may be irrevocable. Reflecting on one recent ceremony, he said: "The procession was short and only reached from the cathedral to Santa Chiara. The only ones who went were those who had to; the top representatives of the church, and the politicians. Hardly any of the ordinary people joined in." Even in the cathedral, he claims, the faithful were restrained, with no shouting or cries for help.

ated by the exceptionally large congregation. The phials have not been opened to allow chemical examination of the contents, but in 1902 a Professor Sperindeo shone a ray of light through it and said it gave the spectrum of blood. In 1926 a Father Thurston, a Jesuit who was said to have no time for bogus miracles, declared that "the supposition of any trick or deliberate imposture is out of the question as candid opponents are now willing to admit... We are forced to accept the fact that contrary to all known laws a change goes on in the contents of the hermetically sealed vessel which

"In the past," says the monsignor, "this religious festival was a cause of unadulterated joy, helping to promote a feeling of togetherness in the community."

The monsignor attributes declining interest to detrimental changes in modern society and thinks the original spirit of the occasion is irretrievably lost. That it was the church authorities themselves who wanted to curb this extremely unorthodox miracle, as some people claim, he flatly denies. In the words of Cardinal Michele Giordano, attempts are now being made "to rescue the spirit of the festival with theological reflection".

By this, the cardinal is referring to theologians who are trying to put the San-Gennaro cult on to a purely religious footing, something unlikely to find favour with the people.

The church expresses the same misgivings about the modern lack of a spiritual element in other religious festivals in the city, such as the one honouring the Madonna del Carmine, the holy virgin from Mount Carmel. This festival begins in the market area of the city, and reaches its climax in a spectacular firework display over the church tower.

There are many other religious festivals in the year. A festival to celebrate the virgin birth takes place on 8 September in the area

technology: a helicopter brought him to the near sell-out San Paolo stadium, and the *tifosi* (fans) came just to see him. He was a present from heaven, and treated as such by the people of Naples. He received the unconditional loyalty of the city's footballing public not only when he was in action for Naples, but also when using his unique ball skills for the benefit of Argentina, his national side.

"He's one of us, so similar to us that he could have been born in Forcella or in the Sanità," was a claim heard again and again. The fact that he was capricious, and didn't seem to care for discipline, was regarded as natural for a man after their own heart.

around the Piedigrotta church, thought to have been the site of a heathen temple. The mystical power of the various madonnas is regarded by the Neapolitan faithful as being only slightly less effective than that of San Gennaro. When they are in need of some spiritual help, they cover themselves by turning to both.

Maradona's magic: Diego Maradona arrived from the heavens like a figure from classical mythology, albeit using modern

Before going out on to the turf Maradona would go through an elaborate ritual to conjure up supernatural sources of help, from praying to the Virgin Mary to performing various rites. The Neapolitans could indeed believe he was one of them: in no other city in Europe are belief and superstition so closely allied and nowhere else is the magic potential which some atribute to numbers and letters (*cabbala*) taken so seriously.

Maradona's sense of the theatrical was equally well-suited to Naples. In the city where every street is a theatre and everything seems to oscillate between extremes, it

seemed perfectly natural when Maradona sank dramatically to the ground after a foul, as if fatally wounded.

Intrigue also goes down well with the Neapolitans. What does it matter, they said, if the idolised superstar used his hand to help him achieve what was beyond the reach of his considerable skills? Cheating and trickery are an integral part of life in Naples, without which the local people would never have been able to survive their chaotic history. No wonder, then, that the city's people identified so totally with their "adopted son" – particularly in the slum areas where the poverty and misery is pronounced and survival tactics are inborn.

If the Neapolitan fans ever wavered in their adulation Maradona was ready to jog their memories. In the semi-final of the 1990 World Cup, for example, the Argentine superstar displayed his essentially Neapolitan character. He also showed amazing skills as he went about weakening the front of the Italian fans. According to Maradona, for 364 days in the year SSC Napoli and its fans were contemptuously abused in the stadiums of northern Italy as being *terroni*. And then, when he was playing in Naples against the Italian national side, Italian fans from the North demanded that his truest supporters should desert him and support the Italian team. Italy lost to Argentina in this vital match. Afterwards both the Italian players and the team's trainer, Azeglio Vicini, complained that the side had not received sufficient support from the people of Naples.

Unceremonious downfall: There was a still less attractive side to Maradona, however, which even truest fans could not fail to see: his womanising and his liking for cocaine. When the judiciary stumbled on Maradona's misdemeanours in 1991, his days in Naples were numbered. The stories about his womanising could be overlooked by the *tifosi* (fans); after all, in the hot, sensual city of Naples, sexual misbehaviour is regarded more as a virtue than a vice. But drugs were different. In the end, Maradona, the gift from God, was forced to exit to Argentina, under the cloak of darkness in the dead of night.

<u>Left</u>, the maestro in action.

In Naples gambling is an integral part of life. An expression of hope, it has a long tradition. Charles Dickens remarked on the Neapolitans' passion for the lottery – "which is very comfortable to the coffers of the state, and very ruinous to the poor"– but was more amazed by the Neapolitan belief that it was possible to foretell the winning lottery numbers by examining mystical messages hidden in events in daily life, particularly accidents:

"Every accident or event is supposed, by the ignorant populace, to be a revelation to the beholder, or party concerned, in connection with the lottery. Certain people, who have a talent for dreaming fortunately, are much sought after, and there are some priests who are constantly favoured with visions of the lucky numbers." Citing a typical example of this, Dickens wrote: "I heard of a horse running away with a man, and dashing him down dead at the corner of a street. Pursuing the horse with incredible speed was another man, who ran so fast, that he came up immediately after the accident. He threw himself upon his knees beside the unfortunate rider, and clasped his hand with an expression of the wildest grief. 'If you have one gasp of breath left, mention your age for Heaven's sake, that I may play that number in the lottery'." *(Pictures from Italy*, first published in 1846.)

Conjuring up numbers: *Cabala* (cabbala) is the name given to the medieval practice of numerology. A system of Jewish origins, it was originally used to explain the creation of the world. The Neapolitans still employ the *cabala*, using numbers, letters and figures to predict the future. As far as the lottery is concerned, the arithmetical laws of *cabala* are used to predict the winning numbers.

Yet the roots of the lottery do not lie in Naples. The game was discovered in Genoa in 1576, when the Republic of Genoa decided to select its three governors and two administrators by drawing lots from an urn

containing the names of the heads of the 90 leading families in the city. The aim was to give everyone an equal chance and avoid any dispute. Those Genovese whose names were not in the urn gambled on the results.

The numbers 1 to 90 were substituted for the names of the families and a new game was invented. It was taken to Naples, where it became famous. According to the history books, "In the year 1682 of our Lord, a group of traders from Genoa came to Naples, rented a house near the Pignasessa and began the fascinating game of lottery, calling it *bonafficiata*." The speed at which the game became popular reflected the depressed economic conditions at the time.

Still dreaming: Reality is generally regarded as being something objective, beyond doubt. In Naples, however, it is a malleable concept, which can be interpreted at will. The *smorfia*, a mystical book of dreams published at about the same time as the lottery was invented, a time when intellectual notions of what is and what is not reality were preoccupying all of Italian society, catered to a need. Following this philosophy, destitute Neapolitans could think that virtually everything they saw was imaginary: people who had enough to eat, fine clothes to wear, a bed to sleep on and a roof over their heads, for example.

The church added to the pervading climate of mysticism. Monks, nuns, vergers, priests and bishops greedily exploited the hundreds of crypts and churches reputed to work miracles. The number of relics and statues reputed to bleed spontaneously proliferated yearly and, as those who sought a saint's grace first had to give a suitably high donation to the priest, the church was profiting handsomely. The "administrators of the estates" preached incessantly that nothing in life was a question of chance, and that the sun and the moon, sunset and sunrise, snow and rain, were all acts of divine providence. From here it was only a small step to the mystification of human life by means of numerical symbols.

Spiritual help: Today, if you get three correct numbers in the lottery, it is known in the jargon as *terno secco*, hitting the jackpot. In Naples the people are convinced that this is impossible to bring off without help from the dead, a conviction that has spawned a whole industry of people with different roles to play. Those who are able to commune with the after-life are popularly known as *assistiti;* they are said to be told the winning numbers in dreams. But, popular wisdom goes, not all dead souls are cooperative: some lead people astray (for example, by revealing the numbers in the reverse order), so dreams have to be interpreted by special

people, known as *santoni.*

A "number interpreter" is then required to translate the meaning into numbers. In some cases, this is relatively simple: for example, a dream of dead relatives indicates 48, representing death; if there is an accident in the dream, the number is 17; and if the victim suffers head injuries, the number is 34. It becomes more complicated, however, when the numbers have to be added or subtracted. For these cases the "number interpreter" is deemed essential.

In recent times the lottery has had a rival – the football pools. Although the pools in-

volves filling in only 13 correct numbers on the coupon – i.e. the results of 13 football matches – the system for interpreting the numbers has remained the same. Occasional coincidences fuel faith in the system. When SSC Napoli signed Maradona in 1984, the number which came up most often was 10, the number on the back of his shirt.

Much of the gambling is organised by the Italian state – on the principle, presumably, that if gambling cannot be eradicated it may as well earn money. However, just as the Camorra has taken over many functions of the government in Naples, it also organises much of the gambling activity. Its turnover is estimated by experts to be well in excess of that made by state betting offices, not least because it offers certain advantages over state-controlled gambling: it pays out more quickly, pays higher prizes and allows people to play on credit.

Claims of rigging: But the definitive game – at least as far as lottery is concerned – remains the state draw, mainly because it is trusted. With the football pools it's a different story. Suspicions have often been voiced – and with good reason – that the results of certain matches have been manipulated by the Camorra. Shortly before the end of the 1987–88 season, for example, SSC Napoli was sitting at the top of the table with a four-point lead, and yet managed to bring off the remarkable feat of coming only second. The rumour at the time was that the Camorra had bet an enormous sum of money against SSC Napoli being champions for a second time and had succeeded in bribing the club's players.

In Naples gambling is not the prerogative of men. Women also indulge, though usually only in the ancient game of *tombolella*. This game of "small tombola" is a favourite pastime of many older women and children, particularly at Christmas, and only very small sums of money are gambled. In the slum areas especially it is an impressive spectacle, in which the magical numbers 1 to 90 once again appear.

Left, lottery stand in the Via Toledo. **Right**, *tombolella*, the preferred game of female gamblers.

The elderly courtesan knew of only one solution when the man whom she had served for so many years decided to leave her with three illegitimate children to go off and marry a younger, prettier woman: she pretended to be critically ill, and demanded that he fulfil one last wish – marry her on her death bed. There was no escape for her former lover; his deeply rooted respect for death and his new-found code of morality in its presence demanded that he comply.

This is the plot of Eduardo De Filippo's comedy *Filumena Marturanto,* and it strikes a chord in all Neapolitans. The wishes of the dying are considered sacrosanct in Naples, one reason being that they might be able to put in a good word for you in the hereafter, and the other, more urgent, being that without the active support of the spirit world it is considered impossible to win the jackpot in the state lottery.

Open to conmen: Inevitably, this extreme reverence for death is exploited. One Neapolitan, who later went off to seek his fortune abroad, described how, in a desperate attempt to get money, he exploited bereaved families: "First of all I discovered the names and addresses of all those who had died on a particular day," he explained. "Then I would buy a new off-the-peg suit and would go without delay to the place where one of them was being laid out. While feigning shock and deep sympathy for the relatives, I would claim that shortly before death the deceased man had given me an order for a made-to-measure suit. I would then say, as though merely in passing: 'But now it doesn't matter any more…' at which point the relatives would normally buy the suit from me, and for a much higher price than I had paid for it. Seldom was I chased away, and then only because the family had already fallen for a similar trick."

Like births and marriages, funerals are important social events in which the whole

neighbourhood participates. All Saints' Day, the day on which the church bids us to pay homage to the dead, is practically a festival in Naples. On this day the cemeteries of Naples are thronged with people. In the Fontanelle cemetery in the Rione della Sanità, where the dignitaries of the city are laid to rest, it is hard to find standing room.

Death ceremonies: In the *quartieri popolari* things have hardly changed for centuries in respect to death. Here, funerals and their rituals are still celebrated in unadulterated style. When someone dies, the female relatives and friends of the deceased immediately assemble to witness the laying out of the body. Dressed in black, they mourn according to an age-old ritual reminiscent of a scene in a Greek tragedy. "Why have you left us?" one will cry, and the others will repeat the question in chorus. Their wailing, which has the quality of a litany, reaches an ecstatic climax as the coffin is closed.

Although the deceased may have been one of the many thousands living on Naples' breadline, the route to his or her final resting place – maybe even to paradise – is always accompanied by pomp and ceremony. Even the poorest citizens scrimp and save for a decent funeral. The three or four undertakers in Naples who can provide a mourning coach, complete with six or eight horses and a brass band to provide a musical accompaniment to the funeral march, still do excellent business, in spite of the fact that the cost of the coach and horses alone is around £1,700.

Yet although the Neapolitans regard their mortality with stoicism, they like to keep an iron grip on the reins of life. *La salute –* health matters – are held to be of utmost importance and are a constant topic of conversation. And whenever they speak about the dead they always take the precaution of saying *"Salute a noi,"* either in advance or as a way of rounding off their thoughts about the deceased. Although this amounts to "God rest his soul", it literally means "health to ourselves" – in other words, give us a long and healthy life.

Left, gruesome reminder of mortality in Via Tribunali.

"No, the Neapolitans won't help us," says Sandro Federico, head of the Neapolitan *Squadra Mobile*, the special police unit responsible for fighting organised crime, "they are too afraid of being killed." These words of resignation are from a police chief who earned such praise in the North that the Florentines protested when he was transferred to Naples.

When the *commissario* came south he was confident of success. He knew that the Camorra, the Neapolitan equivalent of the Sicilian Mafia, reigned supreme. But he thought he could dislodge it with skill and public support. Such misplaced confidence stemmed from an ignorance of the Neapolitan nature. The locals' ingrained distrust of authority, whether the police or the government, makes a cosy nest for the criminal confraternity. In no time, the dynamic inspector was forced to admit defeat.

A new twist: The Neapolitans have long regarded the state as an enemy institution which collects taxes without delivering anything in return. The Camorra came into being in the 18th century as the incarnation of local alienation and anger. Created by illiterate convicts, the Camorra was never tinged with Robin Hood romanticism. The word itself derives from the Spanish for extortion, a reflection of Neapolitan plans.

This secret brotherhood used its new-found power to punish, blackmail and terrorise Naples. A Camorra henchman, known as a *guappo*, acquired his authority by assuming functions that had hitherto belonged to the state. The philosophy is simple: "Where state authority is lacking, I take the law into my hands and bend it to my own advantage."

Nowadays when the people of Forcella, the notorious slum quarter, are victims of crime, they turn not to the police but to the Giuliano family. Don Giuliano, a Camorra clan chief, is the arbiter in local disputes or

tussles with the law. It is he who fixes a *raccomandazione*, an entrée to a job in the public sector, his personal fiefdom. This amounts to a meal ticket for life in a criminal playground. While Don is an honorary title, some say that it is granted only to someone who has killed for the Camorra. In local eyes, the Don is the only real authority.

A similar situation applies in San Giovanni, Teduccio, Barra and Ponticelli, where the Camorra can mobilise over 400 armed men at any time of day or night. The criminal network consists of about 60 families who control Campania and Naples. Yet, unlike their counterparts in the Sicilian Mafia, the Camorra families have no umbrella organisation. As a result, fights between rival gangs are potentially even more obscure, blood-thirsty and long-lasting than a Mafia feud.

Raffaele Cutolo, born in Ottaviano in Naples' hinterland, revived the sleepy Camorra whilst in jail in the 1950s. By the end of the 1970s, he was regarded as the *capo di tutti capi* ("boss among bosses"). In the underworld he was simply *il professore*, the professor, because of his love of poetry. He turned the Camorra into a tightly-knit organisation. His main sources of income were drug trafficking, smuggling, extortion and the manipulation of public sector contracts for the service and building industries.

Despite receiving multiple life sentences, Cutolo continued to direct the organisation from his plushly furnished prison cell. With the help of his sister Mariuccia, he successfully ran the organisation from his cell for 30 years. The parties he held in prison, awash with champagne, attracted the attention of the world's press.

When Campania was struck by a devastating earthquake on 23 November 1980, billions of lire were pumped into the region. The Camorra's greed for a share of the aid led to a series of shaky alliances followed by internecine warfare. The Camorra families which Cutolo controlled joined forces to form the *Nuova Famiglia*. This "New Family" was soon confronted by a rival clan, the

**Preceding pages: outside the Banco di Napoli.
Left, an actor plays the part of a Camorra boss.**

Nuova Famiglia Organizzata. The furious gang warfare which followed led to more than 200 deaths and is not clearly resolved. At stake was the cigarette smuggling business and a lucrative drugs empire.

Over £4 billion in earthquake relief funds were earmarked for the region, with a large proportion allocated to industrial projects. Yet in 1990, when the parliamentary select committee examined the accounts of the organisations running these projects, it received a number of nasty shocks, particularly in the case of the Castelruggiano winery, set up in 1983 near Salerno. The committee was flabbergasted to hear the

rant, Camorra bosses carve up their drugs empires over mounds of mussels and *spaghetti marinara*. In the background drift deferential ghosts who have perfected the part of dumb waiter. Elsewhere, Camorra bosses bribe the prison authorities to release them for a " thermal cure in Tuscany" – and then travel back to Camorra country and the aptly named Triangle of Death north of Naples.

The rise of Mad Mike: In recent times, the most bizzare Camorra personality must be Don Michele Zaza. Known as *u pazzu* ("the madman"), he grew rich on smuggling cigarettes and drugs. In response to an Italian magistrate's question about his wealth, Mad

main shareholder, who had received around £6 million in state subsidies, openly admit that he had not paid tax since 1969, indeed had not so much as filled in a tax return. How was it possible that such a man could have been regarded as worthy of subsidies by the authorities? Outraged, the committee gave its incriminating evidence to the courts.

The Camorra stirs the shockable to new heights of outrage. "We all pay protection money," testify service industry employers and owners of small and medium-sized businesses before the parliamentary anti-Mafia commission. In Naples' U Cafone restau-

Mike claimed, "I worked and I saved," but could not account for the £100 million worth of Philip Morris cigarettes in his possession. Investigative journalist Claire Sterling describes him as "sly and falsely humble, illiterate, shifty, garrulous to the point of sounding as crazy as he hoped he looked".

In 1974 Mad Mike became the first member of the Camorra to be sworn in as a member of the Sicilian Mafia. The ceremony took place on the country estate of the nefarious Nuvoletta brothers outside Naples. During the honeymoon period, the Camorra and the Mafia co-operated over smuggling. The port of Naples was so choked with contraband that both sides took it in turns to unload their ships. But by 1976, cigarette smuggling was *passé*. Both organisations had moved on to morphine routes. After careful planning with the Turkish Mafia, a multinational heroin conglomerate was established, with factories all over Italy and the Middle East.

This peasant from the Santa Lucia district of old Naples is currently at liberty to enjoy his Beverly Hills mansion or his stretch of the Côte d'Azur. After a decade of "guarded" hospital beds and "daring" escapes, Mike was released from jail in 1991. He particularly annoyed the French for buying their Riviera casinos and using them as money-laundering facilities. On a memorable St Valentine's Day in 1989, Mad Mike carved up the European drugs trade with the Mafia. As a result, the Camorra is now responsible for South American, French and East European markets – a Valentine's Day Massacre indeed. As the chief of the *Nuova Famiglia*, the ascendant Camorra clan, Mad Mike is naturally planning a movie.

Public contracts form the economic backbone of the Camorra. Few government employees dare challenge these ancient privileges. Recently, the city privatised its refuse collection service, giving the contract, worth £90 million (US$150 million) a year, to a consortium rather than to the Camorra. Following attacks from the neighbourhood criminals, the refuse collectors have to be protected by special riot police.

Socialist civil servant Antonio Cigliano is in charge of allocating the contracts, and for him the situation is critical. "In recent months," he confides, "I've had to change my telephone number eight times, and have often had to stay in hotels." He is driven to such desperate measures by the need to protect his family from intimidation and a possible assassination attempt.

The Camorra is constantly seeking to consolidate its political power. It commonly bribes parliamentarians in return for extracting favours from Rome. But recently its tactics have become much more aggressive.

Left, the stretch limo, an essential accessory. **Right**, Raffaele Cutolo, "boss among bosses".

String-pulling has been overshadowed by a bid for direct power. The *Camorristi* now attempt to place their own people in key local posts. At stake is their control over the allocation of public service contracts. This cutthroat approach was evident in the 1990 local elections (dubbed the "bloody elections"). *Camorristi* stood as candidates across the political spectrum while honourable politicians who refused to be involved in corruption and ballot-rigging were gunned down.

In an attempt to prevent Camorra members from being elected, the editorial office of *La Repubblica* started its Fair Election Campaign. Readers were invited to provide

anonymous tip-offs about dubious candidates standing for local office. After checking the information, the newspaper handed it over to the courts. Hundreds of calls were received, and yet the campaign failed. Nearly all the suspect candidates were elected. Considering that their predecessors had been dismissed by President Cossiga on the grounds of their Camorra connections, this was particularly ironic.

Were the Camorra to be purged, the public services might disintegrate. A purge would need to be linked to fundamental reform of the public sector. In 1992 Domenico Sica, the top criminal prosecutor, announced that 15 percent of the administrative workforce was under investigation for criminal connections. According to Cencis, Italy's main political research agency, local extortion nets over £1 billion a year. In short, the Camorra has a turnover similar to that of Fiat. In the Naples area, 70 percent of businesses are regularly threatened with Camorra violence, and 58 per cent pay protection money. Yet if organised crime were curtailed, this would threaten an estimated 17 percent of Italy's GNP. In 1989 the President of the Anti-Mafia Commission wrote to the State President, "Dear Cossiga, the Mafia has won" –

As a last resort, a paid killer is employed.

School of life: One of the worst aspects of the Camorra is its policy of using children to carry out crimes. This is a cruel irony in a country which prides itself on its love of children. Originally these lads were simply street kids, known by the rather romantic name of *scugnizzi*. They played truant and worked in bars, garages or small businesses to make a meagre contribution to the family income. Then in the early 1970s, when Naples experienced a baby boom, and even menial jobs were hard to find, the *scugnizzi* turned to new dodges. The boys survived by selling paper bags, cigarette lighters or con-

an indictment of state paralysis.

Where it is unable to infiltrate the authorities, the Camorra resorts to the ancient methods of intimidation. This is particularly drastic for illegal immigrants in Campania. The Camorra annually imports several thousand Africans to work as virtual slaves in the fields near Caserta. The notorious Nuvoletta brothers run the city as a Camorra stronghold. The clandestine workers are forced into crime, drugs and prostitution. When they attempt to protest, death threats are issued. Initially, the henchman shoots targets in the leg or bombs personal property.

traband cigarettes. Others joined the *scippatori*, the motorcycle menaces. These artful dodgers snatched gold chains or handbags from well-heeled tourists and made a fast getaway on Vespas.

Trafficking has become big business for these youngsters. Typically, a criminal career begins with petty thieving, and soon moves on to drug dealing. Recently, minors have been involved in gangland murders. The latest trend is the emergence of the so-called baby-faced killers. These 10 to 15-year-olds are used to carry out serious crimes because they are too young to be sentenced.

They are trained to blow the kneecaps off the chosen victim (*gambizzare*).

"The street has effectively become the only school these children know," states a report by the Anti-Mafia Commission. Their on-the-spot investigations have helped establish a clearer picture of juvenile crime. "The number of children under 14 who are involved in crime is increasing all the time," says the report. But under the Italian criminal code, juvenile offenders can be charged only in cases carrying a minimum sentence of 12 years' imprisonment.

The complex causes for crime lurk in the Neapolitan street culture. Naples is a city of ing their backs on primary education is on the increase. Carulli believes that 5,000 youngsters have opted out of school in Naples. Yet despite the high truancy rates, statistics suggest that juvenile crime is decreasing. However, sociologists argue that these figures are misleading since they are only based on actual arrests. A better indicator is the number of reported offences in which young people are involved. Here, the official figures virtually doubled in the first six months of 1990.

Don Giuliano, the Godfather of the Forcella, recently lost his teenage grandson to a heroin overdose. To indicate the breaking of

dangers: the young face a double risk, as victims and perpetrators of crime. Ombretta Fumagalli Carulli, a crusading lawyer and member of the Anti-Mafia Commission, believes that the educational system is also to blame. By not striving to create a compelling alternative world, the schools fail to socialise the pupils. Equally well, the classroom cannot compete with the street.

The number of children deliberately turn-

Left, the chief of the anti-gambling brigade assesses the results of a raid. **Above**, apprehended minors.

a taboo, a relative's death through drug addiction, he forbade the traditional funeral cortège in his neighbourhood. Even so, the glossy limousines of fellow hoods still swept past in token mourning. The dead boy's father later denounced the heroin trade. Whether this was done out of conviction or showmanship, only the Camorra can tell. Still, if criminals survive childhood, the future is not too bleak. Professor Francesco Aragona has performed autopsies on Mafia and Camorra members since 1958. His cheery conclusion is: "More criminals die of stress than by the bullet."

Luciano de Crescenzo is without doubt the most famous of Naples' contemporary writers. Though for a long time he has preferred to live in Rome, he still likes to stress his Neapolitan heritage. When he says, with a touch of poignancy, that he is "the child of ancient parents", this has two meanings. First, he is mourning a world that no longer exists: he believes that a certain way of living, of thinking, of speaking the language and enjoying good food has died. Secondly, he is alluding to the fact that Naples has been a melting-pot for various cultures since its foundation by the Greeks.

An open city: Naples has been exposed to a constant stream of new ideas and influences over the centuries, and yet its culture has been characterised by as many troughs as peaks. Its most enduring cultural manifestation is probably Pulcinella, the famous Neapolitan comedy figure who came to Naples in the 17th century from northern Italy's *commedia dell'arte*. His crooked nose resembles a beak, his body is unshapely like a bird's; he has a hunchback, wears a white shirt and baggy trousers, and is clearly used to carrying heavy loads. He sports a white sugar-hat and a black half-mask. Although in love with a woman, he must contend with rivals and his love is unrequited. He tries to earn a living but his *signore* (master) always finds reason to beat him. On top of everything, his stomach never stops rumbling.

The only thing that saves Pulcinella is his cunning. In short, he is a quick-change artist who in spite of his buffoonery manages to escape the worst consequences of his actions at the very last minute. He represented, and still represents today, the very essence of the Neapolitan people: Pulcinella the actor, landlord, spy, waiter, lackey, leader, gardener, bandit, baggage handler, fisherman,

and cuckold. In Naples he is everywhere. And "*Siamo il paese del Pulcinella*," ("We are the country of Pulcinella"), a common saying in Italy, means that total chaos reigns.

The Neapolitan people have no difficulty identifying with this figure and his milieu. His adventures reflect the theatre of the street, of the *bassi*, the windowless houses with doors that are left wide open to let in the light. Such streets double as communal living-rooms, stages where the tragi-comedy of everyday life is played out. The ability and range of the acting are considerable.

A golden age: Naples' cultural life reached its zenith in the 18th century, when the city was the undisputed centre of Italy and was in constant touch with the other cultures of the Mediterranean area. This was the time of the idealistic philosophers Giambattista Vico and Pietro Giannone. Vico, the more famous of the two, was really a specialist in rhetoric, though he was always attempting to play down this area of his work; indeed, he tried on numerous occasions from 1723 onwards to exchange his Chair of Rhetoric for the

Preceding pages: inside the San Carlo Theatre. *The Story of Pulcinella*, by Pier Leone Ghezzi. **Left**, a lute-playing Pulcinella performs. **Right**, Eduardo de Filippo, the city's most distinguished playwright.

more prestigious one in Civil Law (which was also better paid). The fact that he remained a simple Professor of Rhetoric is now regarded by philosophers of history as a blessing in disguise, for through Vico the subject of rhetoric acquired considerably more status. His observations on the philosophy of history, which culminated in his principal work *Scienza Nuova* (the New Science), are regarded by today's philosophers as being a long way ahead of their time, indeed pointing the way to Romanticism. Vico's philosophical legacy was later taken up both by the German representatives of idealism and Benedetto Croce, the great 20th-century liberal.

Pietro Giannone, in contrast, was forced to flee Naples for heresy. He was excommunicated by the Pope because of his critical reflections on the role of the Papal States in his historical tract *Istoria civile del Regno di Napoli* and his call for "a free church in a free state". After seeking refuge at the court of the Habsburg Emperor Charles VI, Giannone was kidnapped by secret agents and imprisoned in Turin until his death.

After the founding of Naples University by the Hohenstaufen Frederick II, the city became a focus for inellectual life in the whole Mezzogiorno. The Neapolitan school of Jurisprudence and Medicine had no equal in the 19th century. This was also a golden period for philosophy in the city, when the leading positivists taught at the university. According to Giuseppe Galasso, the Neapolitan Professor of Medieval and Modern History and Secretary of State for the Mezzogiorno, all this changed at the beginning of the 20th century, but Naples' role as the driving force behind Italian culture from the Italian unification in 1860 to the early 1900s left an indelible mark on the cityscape. During this period Naples received a complete new face.

Strangled by Fascists: The various languages, customs and religions which have lived side by side in Naples for centuries, and the attendant climate of tolerance, quickly became thorns in the side of Mussolini's Fascists; the Neapolitans weren't remotely interested in the "putative revolution" of his blackshirts. The stocky dictator, with his exaggerated narcissistic behaviour, was regarded by the inhabitants of Naples as nothing more than one of the many outsiders that had tried to impose their will on the city over the years. As a consequence of this indifferent attitude, the Fascist regime attempted to strangle the cultural life in Naples, and met with some success. Nonetheless, after World War II, the city's cultural life blossomed afresh. Films and the theatre especially thrived.

Theatrical renaissance: The outstanding example of this was the *Compagnia del Teatro Umoristico*, the theatrical company set up by the actor and dramatist Eduardo de Filippo and his family. Eduardo de Filippo, the most famous of all the comedy writers in this century, learned his trade from the great Neapolitan comedian of the 1920s and 1930s, Scarpetta, and took his inspiration for his numerous tragi-comical Neapolitan dialect plays from the streets. His black comedies are sharply poignant. One of the most famous is *Natale in casa Cupiello* ("Christmas in the Cupiello Household"), in which an ageing, unsuccessful, *petit bourgeois* man channels all his energy and enthusiasm for life into the annual ritual of building the Christmas manger whilst his family life collapses around him, both financially and emotionally. De Filippo's pieces are written in both Italian and the Neapolitan dialect.

Another famous comedy is *Napoli milionaria* ("Naples the Millionaire"), a chronicle of a Neapolitan family during World War II and after liberation by the Allies, when the black market became the focal point of Naples' society.

His vision of Naples is never romanticised: "Nobody can deny it: the theatre must reflect life as it is, with its various customs and practices. It must be a picture which draws its life from reality, a reality which is at the same time prophetic," says one of de Filippo's characters, echoing de Filippo's own outlook on the theatre.

Honoured by the Italian president for his contribution to Italian culture, and thereby appointed as a senator for life, de Filippo committed himself shortly before his death

Right, painting the town.

to social issues in his home city. He took particular interest in young people who had fallen into the hands of the criminal underworld. He made many appeals to his fellow citizens in the *bassi*. "*Fuitevenn'*," ("Get out of here") he would tell them, using the native Neapolitan dialect.

De Filippo's comedies were originally performed in the Teatro San Ferdinando in Via Nuova, which has now been closed for long-promised renovation. As yet, nothing has come of this, and de Filippo's son, Luca, frustrated by the lack of progress, began eliciting the help of private sponsors. "I've had enough of the empty promises of the

local politicians," he says.

Talent spotter: Another Neapolitan actor and director to play a major part in the re-emergence of culture in the immediate post-war period was the neo-realistic film-maker Vittorio de Sica. His film *Ladri di Biciclette* ("Bicycle Thieves"), set in the working-class areas of Rome, was of seminal importance. Many of the actors and actresses in this film – slated by the critics because they thought it denigrated Italian life and its people before the eyes of the world – were "discovered" by de Sica on the streets of Naples. They included Sophia Loren. De Sica met her in one of Naples' alleyways when he was looking for an amateur actress.

How is it, then, that cultural life in Naples is in such a sorry state today? There is no question that the place which was once the driving force of Italian culture is noticeably less important nowadays. "The cultural future of Naples," says Professore Galasso, Professor of Medieval History at the city's university, "depends on the university. The rebuilding of this institution is therefore of critical importance." Professor Galasso believes that the university, which has over 100,000 students, could lead the non-academic culture of the city (from the theatre to the fine arts) out of its current lethargy.

Art galleries: It is typical that there is still no museum for contemporary art in Naples except the Palazzo Roccella, an unsatisfactory base for modern art for over 50 years.

"People always say to us that Naples has more important problems to solve than those of culture," laments Gianni Pisani, the Director of the Neapolitan Academy of Art. The Academy, better known as the *Scuola di Posillipo*, was founded by Charles III in the middle of the 18th century and is one of the oldest in Europe. Although hampered by lack of space and funds (the Academy receives the most meagre of subsidies from the state), Pisani has put together some first-rate exhibitions in recent years, including one on the key exponents of Expressionism and a retrospective on the German avant-gardist Joseph Beuys, an artist inspired by Naples.

According to Beuys, this beauty is based on an "extended concept of art, which is related to every kind of human activity, as well as on human creativity and dignity". His conception of art is thereby virtually identical to that of Johann Wolfgang von Goethe – at least as far as his appreciation of the Neapolitans is concerned. The latter ended the notes in his diary on 27 May 1787 with the following tribute to the Neapolitans: "I can't begin to describe the capabilities of the people, their customs and energy, and how many people they have conquered with their literature and artistic skills."

Left, Sophia Loren, discovered by Vittorio de Sica. Right, music while you shop.

Like Vesuvius and pizza, the *canzoni napoletane* – songs written in the Neapolitan dialect – belong to Naples' most celebrated products.

The melodies of these emotional and melodramatic love songs began enchanting the ears of the wider world at the end of the 19th century when emigrants from Naples exported them first to Europe and later to North and South America. By taking their distinct musical tradition with them, the Neapolitan emigrants maintained a strong cultural tie to their homeland; at the same time, the songs gained a new following among non-Italians. Nowadays songs such as *Funiculi-funiculà, O sole mio* or *Torna a Surriento* belong to the repertoires of orchestras and singers all over the world.

Neapolitan songs have been written for centuries, but until 1880 it was customary for the composers to remain anonymous. That all changed with the song *Funiculi-funiculà*, written by Peppino Turco and Luigi Danza, two Neapolitans who had moved away from the city. The former, the writer of the lyrics, earned his living as a journalist in Rome and the latter worked in London, where he lectured on the art of the *bel canto* at the Royal Academy of Music. They met up in the summer of 1880 in Castellamare di Stabia, halfway between Naples and Sorrento, in a new hotel belonging to the Danza family.

Here, just before the official opening of the hotel, they created *Funiculi-funiculà*, the tune which was later to become a standard number of the Red Army choir. The song, clearly influenced by Russian folk music, enchanted the Tsar and he had it performed at court by the Italian tenor Marconi, who happened to be on tour in St Petersburg at the time. It is said that the Tsar so enjoyed Marconi's performance that he sang along with the chorus.

Around the turn of the century, another song sprang to world fame – *O sole mio*, without question the most loved of all Neapolitan songs, written and composed by Giovanni Capurro and Eduardo di Capua.

Capurro eked out a meagre existence as a journalist with a leaning towards poetry, and di Capua was a conductor of a small group of musicians that supplied musical interludes in theatres. Both men were poor, so they tried to earn extra money by composing Neapolitan songs. *O sole mio* gained second place in a music competition organised by the Neapolitan music publisher Bideri.

Following this success, it was played everywhere, throughout Europe and beyond. Several sultanates chose *O sole mio* as their anthem, and it is supposed to have been played instead of the Italian national anthem on a number of official occasions.

The inspiration behind the song *Torna a Surriento* was rather less romantic. Although the song sounds like a simple love song, it is supposed to have been composed as a reminder to the Italian Prime Minister, Giuseppe Zanardelli, of a magical day he spent on the Sorrento peninsula. It was meant to encourage him to allocate government funds to that region with more generosity than usual. The song was composed in 1903 by the famous musician Ernesto de Curtis, at that time only 27 years old and on the threshold of his career (although his talent was evident from a number of songs already composed). The lyrics were written by his elder brother, Giovambattista.

The *canzoni* have helped numerous Italian tenors make the breakthrough to fame, both nationally and internationally. Included among them is the unforgettable Enrico Caruso, born into a poor family on 25 February 1873. Although he could hardly read or write properly, he was able to master countless opera scores. However, his debut, in front of his local audience in 1902, was lambasted by the critics, causing him to leave Naples for America and swear never to sing there again. This was a promise he was to keep, even after he had risen to be the number one tenor in the world. When Caruso did eventually return to Naples, it was to die.

Left, the unforgettable Enrico Caruso.

In the beginning there was the flat dough cake, a simple flour mixture that was baked in the oven. With this step forward in culinary evolution the problem of what to serve as the midday and evening meal was solved for thousands of years. Gradually the dough cake born out of necessity, also known as a *focaccia*, was refined to become the pizza, a triumph in terms of taste and colour.

This forerunner of today's pizza was invented in the backstreets of Naples where the problems of eking out an existence were greatest, and where survival was refined to an art. However, it has proved impossible to pin a more exact place for the origins of the pizza, even though academics have tried long and hard to do so. From time to time, an important document, letter or chronicle is discovered which prompts further research into the subject, but on balance the people of Naples are pleased that so little information is available, believing that uncertain origins serve the whole mythology better.

Enter the tomato: Experts agree that pizza as we know it first appeared in the 17th century. Despite the lack of scientific evidence, it can at least be established that pizza must have come out of the oven after the Neapolitans had become acquainted with the tomato. The tomato, brought to Europe by Christopher Columbus and originally known as the *pomme d'amour*, became the queen of the Vesuvian vegetable garden, for both the soil and the climatic conditions in the *campania felix* were uniquely favourable to the plant. From the tomato to the pizza is a small step, and today the success of this combination is recognised all over the world.

One of Italy's most vociferous champions of the pizza is the popular writer Domenico Rea. Sitting on the terrace of his house in Posillipo, Rea bubbles with enthusiasm, as if he had the *bassi* of Naples in his blood. Rea calls the pizza "a simple and therefore per-

fect discovery". With only the hint of irony he claims that the discovery of the modern pizza base should be ranked on the same level as the discovery of the law of gravity, electricity or the theory of relativity.

As Rea is the first to point out, pizza is also one of the world's most important fast foods. Pizza and pasta are big business. Experts reckon that in Italy alone they bring in a turnover of more than 20,000 billion lire, equal to that of the Turin car manufacturer

Fiat. These figures are confirmed by the Association of European Pizza Bakers (APES), which has its headquarters in Naples. This association recently organised the first conference of pizza bakers, and its membership now extends all over the world. Italy and the rest of Europe alone have over 100,000 members

The classics: Margherita and marinara are the two most famous types of Neapolitan pizzas; they are available in any pizzeria, from Tokyo to Cairo. But to what extent can pizzas bought outside Naples really be regarded as bearing any relation to those in

Preceding pages: street food includes fresh oysters. Left, "wine and oil" restaurant, Naples. Right, a pizza baker at work.

their hometown? "That's the problem," confirmed Neapolitan pizza bakers at their most recent conference. They proposed that the preparation of pizza should be protected in the same way as a trade-mark. The result was the formation of the "Cooperative of Genuine Pizza Bakers", which people can join only if they commit themselves to maintaining the traditional Neapolitan recipes and cooking methods.

Leaving aside confusing details, the following ingredients have been designated as necessary for a genuine Neapolitan pizza base: flour, sour dough or yeast, salt and water. As far as the preparation is concerned,

conflict with the basic ground-rules. As to which type of pizza is preferred in Naples, it is a close-run contest; but Pizza Margherita, which recently celebrated its 100th birthday, is said to be the first choice of born and bred Neapolitans.

Origin of the Margherita: This long-time favourite pizza is said to have been invented in homage to the spouse of the first Italian king, Umberto I. The Neapolitans referred to Umberto as the "good King of Savoy". According to the story, in June 1889 Raffaele Esposito, a famous pizza baker of the time whose premises were built on the slopes of Sant'Anna di Palazzo near the Via Chiaia,

the pastry should be made by hand, and must be rolled out without the use of any technical aids or a rolling-pin. In addition, the pizza must be baked on the floor of the oven, which should be bell-shaped and built from fireproof tiles. The guild of pizza bakers has also laid down rules about which pizzas can carry the seal *DOC*: they are the pizza marinara (oil, tomatoes, oregano, garlic and pepper), the pizza margherita (mozzarella, tomatoes and basil) and the pizza calzone, which is filled with curd cheese and salami. The guardians of pizza baking allow minor variations but only so long as they do not

was summoned to the royal residence at Capodimonte. The royal couple were staying there for a few days during their visit to Naples and had expressed a desire to eat pizza. It fell to Esposito – in Naples this name is as common as Smith in England – to represent the pizza bakers of the town in fulfilling the royal wish. Don Raffaele packed the necessary ingredients and, together with his wife, made his way to the royal kitchen.

He prepared three different pizzas, two from the classical repertoire of the time and one which he invented himself. The latter was described as being patriotic because its topping was based on the three colours of the national flag – red, white and green. Although the queen enjoyed all three versions, it was the new pizza which particularly took her fancy. Don Raffaele, pleased with the praise of the royals, christened the new pizza *Margherita*. The new pizza was confirmed with the royal seal and Raffaele's pizzeria thereby secured a place in the gastronomic history books. The pizzeria still exists today, albeit under the name Pizzeria Brandi.

A preference for pasta?: If the pizza is the queen of Neapolitan culinary art, spaghetti is the heir apparent, although it would be pos-

ghetti are worth a special mention: the *spaghetti vongole*, with Venus muscles (red or white depending on whether it is with or without tomatoes) and the *spaghetti aglio e olio*, with oil and garlic, rounded off with the obligatory parsley.

But there are literally hundreds of other pastas apart from spaghetti. Even an ordinary high street supermarket stocks several tens of different pasta shapes. According to connoisseurs, different varieties produce very different tastes, the exact flavour being determined by the surface area exposed to the sauce.

Likewise, great ingenuity has been de-

sible to argue long and hard about the correct order of standing. Be that as it may, in terms of the variety of different ways of preparing spaghetti, it is at least equal to the pizza. Although the Chinese are credited with inventing spaghetti, it is the Neapolitans who made it into what it is today. Until recently, this poor man's dish was prepared, cooked and eaten on the streets, as a large number of famous engravings testify.

Two particular methods of preparing spa-

Left, steaming *polpo*, a local speciality. **Above**, fish comes in many other guises.

voted to *antipasti*. As in all historically poor regions, cheaper produce such as vegetables, bread and cheese are combined, often with the judicious addition of herbs, to mouthwatering effect. Among the specialities are *panzanella alla napoletana*, a salad of crumbled bread, onions, tomatoes, anchovies and basil, and *gatto*, a delicious dumpling made from mozzarella, potatoes, egg and prosciutto.

Real mozzarella made from buffalo milk, a cheese produced near Naples and nowhere else, shouldn't be missed. It is white, round and soft, with a sweet milky taste and is

VOLCANIC WINE

Vineyards abound on the foothills of Vesuvius and on Ischia. Lacryma Christi, the region's most famous wine, has been grown there since classical times. Called "Christ's tears", it refers to Christ's sorrow on seeing that Lucifer had stolen this patch of paradise. Lacryma Christi shines as a medium dry white with an unforgettable aroma while the rich red Lacryma improves dramatically with age. The Vesuvian grapes give the wine a sulphurous or gunpowdery tang, a fitting preparation for the chaos of Naples.

Wine on Capri is delicious but scarce compared with the output of neighbouring Ischia. Capri is

a crystal clear, topaz-coloured wine with a fragrant bouquet. Red Capri is only slightly inferior and equally sought after – locals keep it to themselves. On ageing, it acquires the aroma and tawny glow of a vintage port. Ischia's wine is celebrated, whether as Biancolella, Bianco Superiore or Epomeo. Red Epomeo often accompanies a rabbit stew while Bianco Superiore is a crisp white, ideal with a seafood platter.

Denominazione di origine controllata (DOC) is the Italian equivalent to *appellation contrôlée* and embraces several Campanian wines. Taurasi, a renowned red wine, comes from Avellino, east of Naples. Produced from the Aglianico grape, Taurasi is recognisable for its blood-red colour and powerful taste. Taurasi is dubbed "the Barolo of the South" because of its impact and longevity but the high prices it commands are justified only by vintages at least 10 years old.

Fiano di Avellino and Greco di Rufo are also DOC wines from the hills of Avellino. Burton Anderson, the world expert on Italian wines, places them among Italy's most distinctive white wines. Greco di Rufo, a wine grown here since Greek times, has a pleasing peppery flavour but Fiano is an acquired taste. The wily growers claim that it needs to be sampled at least seven times before appreciation sets in.

Other thriving "archaeological" wines include the fabled Greco wines of Falerno. The straw-coloured wine is produced on the Phlegraean Fields near Pozzuoli and Cumae. Devotees say that Falerno matures well while its critics claim that it is best kept for 2,000 years. Falernum has also been revived as Falerno del Massico (DOC), a full-bodied red.

Wines not yet awarded DOC status can be surprisingly good, from tangy Ravello to the smooth but light reds on Capri. Fresh and fruity white wines and robust reds are produced all over Campania, from Posillipo to the Sorrento peninsula. White or red Solopaca is a basic table wine produced near Benevento but the only rosé of note is Rosa del Golfo. Aversa produces white Asprinio but there is no need for an aspirin afterwards. Red wines from Salerno have hitherto been used for blending bigger names in central and northern Italy but are now striving for an individual style.

According to Burton Anderson, Campanian wines from the plains are "hot-blooded blenders", while wines from the heights can be "as fresh, fragrant and stylish as northern vintages". Altitude and exposure are the key to the mountain wines while proximity to the water determines the success of the maritime wines. However, as southern wines turn from quantity to quality, standards are improving everywhere. Local wines are acquiring a reputation under their own labels. Still, Italian wines are noted for romantic individuality rather than classic consistency and, in this, Campanian wines are no exception.

Campania is also noted for its liqueurs. Capri produces Certosina, a slightly bitter concoction distilled from herbs. On the mainland, Benevento makes the sweet, yellowish Strega ("witch"), named for its magical powers. Perhaps it is mere coincidence that the Camorra places more confidence in the murky powers of whisky. ∎

easily digestible. It comes fresh every morning from Aversa and Battipaglia. *Mozzarella in carrozza* (mozzarella in a carriage), a thick slice of mozzarella fried between two slices of bread, is a Neapolitan sensation.

If you prefer meat then you shouldn't miss the grilled meats and the meatballs filled with eggs, cheese, sultanas, and pine nuts. *Braciola alla napoletana*, a large roll of beef or pork filled with provolone, prosciutto, raisins and eggs and cooked in a tomato sauce, is usually served on festive occasions. Alternatively, order loin of lamb *alla pizzaiola*, so-called because it is made with the same ingredients as a pizza, or serving it is *polpo all luciana* (octopus stewed with tomatoes, olive oil, peppers and garlic) which, as the name suggests, was invented by the women of Santa Lucia, where Naples' old shellfish market used to be situated. Also recommended in the fish line is authentic Neapolitan fish soup, made with dragon fish, and *anguilla in umido*, eels cooked in a tomato sauce and served on toast.

An excellent way to round off the meal, or indeed to start the day, is by trying a *sfogliatella*, an envelope of puff pastry filled with curd cheese, candied fruit and cinnamon. Naples' best *sfogliatelle* are to be had at Pintauro in the Via Toledo.

coniglio all'Ischitana, a rich rabbit, wine and tomato stew.

Another speciality – naturally for a city by the sea – is fish. Squid and *polpo* (octopus) are old Neapolitan favourites. It is said that at one time the favoured method of catching *polpo* was to lower mirrors into the deep waters it inhabits and wait until the curious fish fastened its cleaving suckers to its glassy image. The traditional though now seldom used method of killing *polpo* is by biting it firmly in the heart. The favoured way of

Left, vines. **Above**, some like it hot.

Campanian cuisine: The cookery writer Claudia Roden praises the eclecticism of Campania, its flair for blending culinary cultures: "The Greeks planted olive trees, vines and durum wheat; raisins and pine nuts, honey and almonds, orange blossom essence and the manner of stuffing vegetables came from the Arabs, who ruled Sicily, and from Byzantium; and there is a very strong influence from France and Spain."

But Campania has stolen, synthesised and shared its cuisine. No ethnic group has had as powerful an influence on American cuisine as the Neapolitans. Pizzas, pasta and ice-cream have travelled from the vine-hung courtyards of Campania to urban Chicago. The cuisine of Campania is imaginative, robust and addictive.

On the islands, food prices are high but even a simple picnic is a pleasure. In Ischia, locals make use of the scalding volcanic sands to cook lunch. Stuffed peppers and pastry pies are wrapped in foil and cooked on the beach of Maronti. Ischia's sulphurous Epomeo or Biancolella wines make a suitable accompaniment. The setting, near the lovely fishing village of Sant'Angelo, is mysterious: picnickers crouch over sizzling sands and listen to hissing fumaroles.

Fish, clams and lobster star in coastal cuisine. *Fritto misto* (mixed seafood) and *spaghetti con cozze o vongole* (with mussels or clams) are popular on the islands and the Amalfi Coast. *Gnocchetti al salmone* (gnocchi with salmon) is a variant on *spaghetti ai frutti di mare*, as is *risotto ai frutti di mare* (seafood risotto).

In fact, fishy rice dishes such as *risotto alla pescatore* appeal to most tastebuds. *Sardine alle scapece* (fried and marinated sardines) are a speciality of Praiano, a village near Positano. *Alici* (anchovies) are common enough for their presence to be assumed in any dish which calls itself *alla napoletana*.

Both Capri and Ischia concentrate on seafood specialities, including *pesce spada* (swordfish) and *aragosta* (lobster). Even so, a plentiful supply of wild rabbits on Ischia and Procida means that rabbit (*coniglio*) is synonymous with stew. Meat is more common on Capri than on Ischia; roast rabbit and chicken are traditional dishes, not concocted to appeal to cosmopolitan tastes. In the countryside, *zampone e cotechino*, trotter stuffed with pork and sausage, is a dish associated with winter pig-sticking. No part of the pig is wasted in the family production of bacon, blood sausage, salami, cured and smoked ham. Even the tail is good luck.

Vegetables, used as *antipasti* (hors d'oeuvres) or *contorni* (side dishes), are one of the culinary delights of Campania. The fertile, black volcanic soil yields four crops a year in Ischia and the plains north of Naples. Vegetables are often cooked in clay pots, reputed to give a richer taste. Called *tiella* or *pignatta*, these pots are a legacy of Spanish rule.

Antipasti include fried ravioli, *melanzane* (aubergines) and stuffed peppers (*peperoni ripieni*). Contrary to popular belief, *melanzane alla parmigiana*, that cheesy main course, was created in Campania not Parma. In Capri, mushrooms collected on Monte Solaro often find their way into *crepe al formaggio*, *fettuccine* or pizza fillings. The *formaggio* will usually be *mozzarella di bufalo*, a cheese produced on the marshy plains north of Naples since Roman times. Goat's cheese and broad beans sautéed with onion makes a tasty *antipasto*, a delicacy in Amalfi's Cappuccini Convento.

Dishes are often named after local celebrities. In Capri, La Pigna restaurant offers *fettucine alla Sophia Loren*, named after the fiery actress from Pozzuoli. *Spaghetti puttanesca* (whore's spaghetti) is a suitably spicy concoction of black olives, tomatoes, anchovies and capers. On the coast, *linguine Cosa Nostra* is a succulent pasta and seafood dish prepared with more than a nod and a wink to the Mafia.

Above, snacks for hearty appetites. **Right**, cave of culinary delights.

This region surely is not of the earth.
Was it not dropt from Heaven?
  – Samuel Rogers, writing on Naples in *Italy*
1822–34

In fact, the power which drew so many poets and artists to Naples had more to do with earthly charms than divine virtues, but by all accounts it was no ordinary city. A hidden principle of order was discovered in the chaos of Naples; the colourful hustle and bustle of the people in the narrow streets, and the variety of different cultures which lived side by side were regarded as expressions of an imaginative and lively city.

Percy Bysshe Shelley's famous *Ode to Naples* encapsulated its dual – divine and sensual – qualities: "Naples! thou heart of man whichever pantest/Naked beneath the lidless eye of heaven!" Everything in Naples was portrayed in such a fascinating light that from the end of the 18th century onward the city attracted artists and literary figures from all over Europe. The French writer Stendhal described Naples as the "most beautiful city in the world".

In the opinion of many visitors, Naples even knocked Rome, the so-called eternal city, into second place; those particularly enchanted were the English, German and French Romantics in search of its Greek and Roman heritage (for which just a century or so later a Naples-bound Henry James was to conceive "a tenfold deeper loathing").

One of these Romantics was Goethe, who alighted on Neapolitan soil for the first time on 25 February 1787, having travelled from Rome along the Appian Way. At first he was rather sceptical about the city's vaunted attractions and it took a number of experiences to fill him with the emotional raptures he is noted for in connection with the city. His entry in his diary for that day is rather nonchalant in tone: "Naples gives the impression of being happy, free and full of life, countless people run around all over the place, the King is away hunting, the Queen is expecting a baby, and things just couldn't be

better." He went on to complain about the level of comfort. But, step by step, he fell under the city's spell. Just a few days later he wrote: "I can't describe the location of the city and its beauty, which have so often been described and praised. *Vedi Napoli e poi muori* they say here: 'See Naples and die'."

Goethe was enthralled by Neapolitan life: "You only have to go for a wander in the streets and to keep your eyes open and you will see inimitable pictures," he said. "That

none of the Neapolitan people want to move away from the city, and that their writers sing with exaggerated hyperbole about the bliss of the life there, is something which couldn't be held against them, even if there were a few more Vesuviuses in the neighbourhood." He tried repeatedly to convey in writing the "indelible impression" which he took home with him but, as he admitted in retrospect, his efforts failed to capture the magic of the city.

But the Italian peninsula pulled visitors with less lofty motives than ruin-appreciation or the desire to study Vesuvius. Naples under Charles III and Ferdinand IV sported an exotic, liberated social life whereby foreign visitors could escape the restraints of home. Casanova was a regular visitor to the drawing-rooms, and bedrooms, of Procida, Chiaia and Posillipo. On one occasion he escorted the Duchess of Kingston and Sir William Hamilton, the English ambassador to the *palazzo* of the Principe di Francavilla in Chiaia where, Casanova reports, the prince amused the duchess by making his pages, "lads of fifteen to seventeen. sweet-

Lyon, from his nephew Charles Greville, with whom she had been living, in return for waiving some debts. She was installed in the Palazzo Sessa, Hamilton's magnificent villa overlooking the Bay of Naples and Capri, where according to Emma her lover did nothing all day but look at her and sigh. Naples was Emma's finishing school, where her dancing received instruction and her voice was tranformed into a beautiful soprano – Lancashire accent notwithstanding –

hearts of the Prince who preferred Ganymede to Hebe", strip naked and engage in a sort of synchronised swimming.

It was in Naples, too, that Hamilton conducted his *amour* with Emma Hart, the *femme fatale* whom he was later to marry and who, later still, captured Nelson's affections (also in Naples, in fact in Hamilton's villa). Hamilton had won Emma, born plain Amy

Preceding pages: the Bay of Naples, playground of Europe's élite. **Left,** Goethe strived to capture the magic of the city. **Above,** Virgil's tomb, draw to the Romantics.

which could make even the sentimental Neapolitans cry. The people of Naples adulated Emma, comparing her with the Virgin Mary herself.

A different view: All too often the praise and attention which the city reaped overlooked or underestimated the reality of life there. By the 18th century Naples was already a city of around 450,000 inhabitants and a victim of the ills of poverty and overpopulation. Goethe was one of the few visitors to see the city's other side, the slum areas or *bassi*, which are still inhabited today. He noticed the area on his way back from a trip to

Vesuvius and described them thus: "On our return to Naples I noticed some odd little houses with only one floor, strangely built without any windows, with rooms that were illuminated only through the doors leading out to the streets. From early morning until way into the night the occupiers sit in front of the house, before finally going back into their caves." Goethe's description is just as valid today, even with the addition of electric lights and the ubiquitous blaring radios.

But Goethe didn't probe far into this side of Neapolitan life. From Naples he went to Sicily. On his return, his admiration of Naples became a rhapsody. The city became to

pursued by a woman with a bludgeon, and a man armed with a knife. The man overtook him, and with one blow in the neck, laid him dead in the road. On my expressing the emotions of horror and indignation which I felt, a Calabrian priest, who travelled with me, laughed heartily, and attempted to quiz me, as what the English call a flat."

And when Shelley complains of what he called "the degraded, disgusting and odious" aspects of Naples, all he gives by way of illustration is the habit of young women of quality to eat garlic.

Sobering up: By the mid 19th century the stirrings of a more sober mood were felt in

him a land flowing with milk and honey, and the pervasive squalor shed its negative aspects entirely. "It is true you can hardly take a step without being confronted by a person in tattered clothes, but they are not layabouts or wastrels!" he wrote of the city's poor.

Other literary visitors likewise celebrated and glamorised the city's darker aspects rather than abhored them. Shelley muses on his first encounter with Naples in a letter to his friend Thomas Love Peacock in December 1818: "On entering Naples, the first circumstance that engaged my attention was an assassination. A youth ran out of a shop,

Naples, a change that had already affected much of the rest of Europe. Under Ferdinand II, the penultimate Bourbon ruler, a hypocritical concern for public morals evolved. There were fewer glittering balls and high society detached itself from Ferdinand's censorious court.

The criticism levelled at Naples also took a more serious tone. Until now the splendours of Naples had tended to eclipse the ills. Nineteenth-century social critics were keen to set the balance right. Charles Dickens, addressing those he called "lovers and hunters of the picturesque", cautioned: "Let us not keep too studiously out of view the miserable depravity, degradation, and wretchedness with which this gay Neapolitan life is inseparably associated. A pair of naked legs and a ragged red scarf do not make all the difference between what is interesting and what is coarse and odious."

But, in spite of caveats, Dickens too was smitten by Naples' "sun and bloom". He too endowed it with superlatives ("this most beautiful and lovely spot of earth") and in the end it took an altogether plainer man, the 19th-century social reformer William Ewart Gladstone, to turn the heavenly accolades awarded by earlier guests on their head: in a

plague and cholera swept through the city.

Later lovers of the Neapolitan region tended to focus on Sorrento, Ischia or Capri rather than Naples. One of the area's most devoted fans was Norman Douglas, who first took a villa on Posillipo in 1886 and died on Capri in 1953. He wrote several books there, including his acclaimed travel book *Siren Land*, about Capri and the Sorrentine peninsula, and held open house to artists, aristocrats and sundry sybarites.

Neapolitans frequently confused Douglas with another English resident, Lord Alfred Douglas, the infamous lover of Oscar Wilde who visited him there shortly after his re-

letter to the Earl of Aberdeen in 1851, Gladstone wrote: "This is the negation of God erected into a system of government."

With the arrival of Garibaldi the last vestiges of Naples' high society fled. In 1874 Ruskin called Naples "certainly the most disgusting place in Europe", an opinion which was reiterated a thousand-fold 10 years later when a devastating epidemic of

Far left, Lady Emma Hamilton enchanted the Neapolitans, but her greatest admirer there was the celebrated British admiral, Lord Nelson (**left**). **Above**, Capri, Norman Douglas's idyll.

lease from prison in 1897. When Douglas had to leave for Rome, Wilde – whose memorable quips on Naples include "The museum is full, as you know, of lovely Greek bronzes. The only bother is that they all walk about the town at night" – contemplated suicide in a Naples' garden noted for such acts. He was interrupted by the rustling noise of "the little souls of those who had killed themselves in that place." The thought that they were condemned to linger there ever after changed his mind."The cooking is really too bad," he later explained to his friend Vincent O'Sullivan.

There has never been a lack of words to describe Naples. Unlike many other European cities, it provokes reaction in the most laconic of visitors. What's more, any random selection of quotes about the city and its inhabitants is likely to include admiration and detraction in equal measure. Heaven on earth, then, or the very crucible of hell? The writer Peter Nichols sums up this polarised response: "Neapolitans still reproduce what must be the nearest equivalent to life in classical times. Naples is one of the great tests. Some people hate it and some people love it."

Nichols's following remark, "I think that people who do not like Naples are afraid of something", clearly showing which side of the divide he is on, invites the instant retort, "No wonder!" in those he is talking about, for the image of modern-day Naples is one of progressive deterioration and rising criminality. But, in reality, this unfavourable image, fuelled by the national and international media, is as misleading as the romantic image which preceded it. Above all, Naples is a unique feast for the senses; here, every aspect of life, including survival itself, has been elevated to an art form. There is no better place to encounter this phenomenon than in the famous Via Spaccanapoli.

Negotiating the city is not as fraught with danger as some people, including Neapolitans themselves, would have visitors believe. There are areas which are effectively no-go areas for tourists in the evenings (the slum areas of Forcella and Ponticelli, for example), but most of Naples is no more threatening than any other major city.

In the rush hour, when the traffic in the congested streets comes to its usual chaotic standstill, the best way to get around most of the city is to walk or, if need be, use public transport. The hills and the harbour and especially the castles and palaces, such as Castel dell'Ovo or Castel Sant' Elmo, provide reliable orientation in the maze of streets in the old part of the city.

Visitors should not be afraid to ask locals for help if they have lost their way. Neapolitans have a reputation for friendliness and hospitality, and encounters with most Neapolitans are rewarding. The constant advice and warnings to safeguard cameras and money, to remove any valuable jewellery and to keep a firm grip on handbags and camera cases is well-meaning, if unnerving. Time and time again, Neapolitans will offer to accompany you safely to your destination.

Preceding pages: forging a *ponte*; sea views, Sorrento; boating party; dining in Positano. **Left**, verging on paradise, Capri.

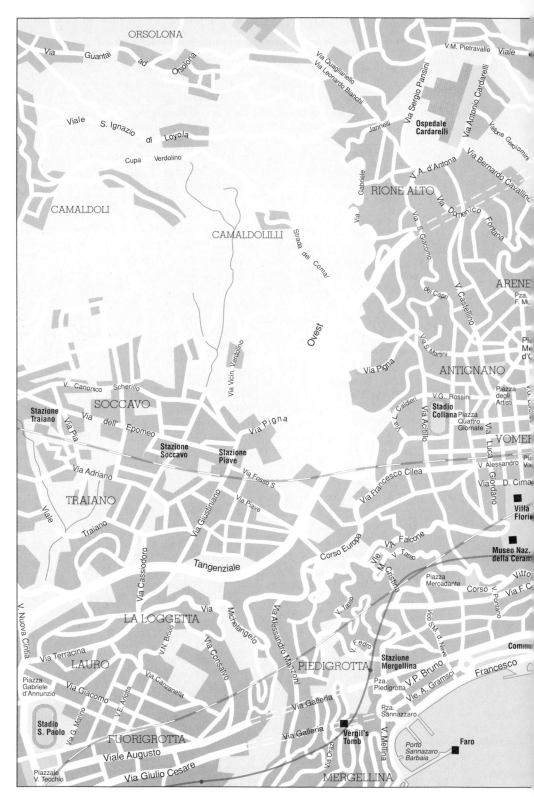

ORSOLONA

Via Guantai ad Orsolona

Viale S. Ignazio di Loyola

Cupa Verdolino

CAMALDOLI

CAMALDOLILLI

Strada dei Comal

Ovest

Via Vicin. Verdolino

V. Canonico Scherillo

SOCCAVO

Stazione Traiano

Via dell' Epomeo

Via Pla

Via Adriano

Stazione Soccavo

Stazione Piave

Via Pigna

Via Fosso S.

TRAIANO

Via Giustiniano

Via Piave

Viale

Traiano

Tangenziale

Corso Europa

LA LOGGETTA

V.N. Brixio

Michelangelo

Via

Via Consalvo

Via Alessandro Manzoni

V. Nuova Cinzia

Via Terracina

LAURO

Via Giacomo

Via Canzanella

Piazza Gabriele d'Annunzio

V.E. Aliotta

V.G. Marino

Stadio S. Paolo

FUORIGROTTA

Viale Augusto

Piazzale V. Teochio

Via Giulio Cesare

Via Quagliariello
Via Leonardo Bianchi

Jannelli

V.M. Pietravalle   Viale

Via Sergio Pansini

Ospedale Cardarelli

Via Antonio Cardarelli

Vallone Geolomin

Via Gabriele

RIONE ALTO

V. A. d'Antona

Via Bernardo Cavallino

Via Domenico

Fontana

Via S. Giacomo

Via Castellino

dei Capri

ARENE

Pza. F. Mu

Via S. Martini

Pi M d'C

ANTIGNANO

Via Pigna

V.G.. Rossini

Piazza degli Artisti

Via Caldieri

Via T.

Via Acitillo

Stadio Collana

Piazza Quattro Giornate

V.G.

VOMER

Via Luca Giordano

Via Alessandro

Pi Va

Via Francesco Cilea

Via D. Cima

Villa Flori

Museo Naz. della Ceram

Corso Europa

V.A. Falcone

V. Tasso

Vie M. Cristina

Piazza Mercadante

Corso

Vitto

Via F. C

V. Pontano

Via Tasso

Vico S.M. d. Neve

Commu

V. Pedro

Stazione Mergellina

PIEDIGROTTA

Pza. Piedigrotta

V.P. Bruno

Vle. A. Gramsci

Francesco

Via Galleria

Pza. Sannazaro

Via Galleria

Vergil's Tomb

V. Mellina

Via Orazi

MERGELLINA

Porto Sannazaro Barbaia

Faro

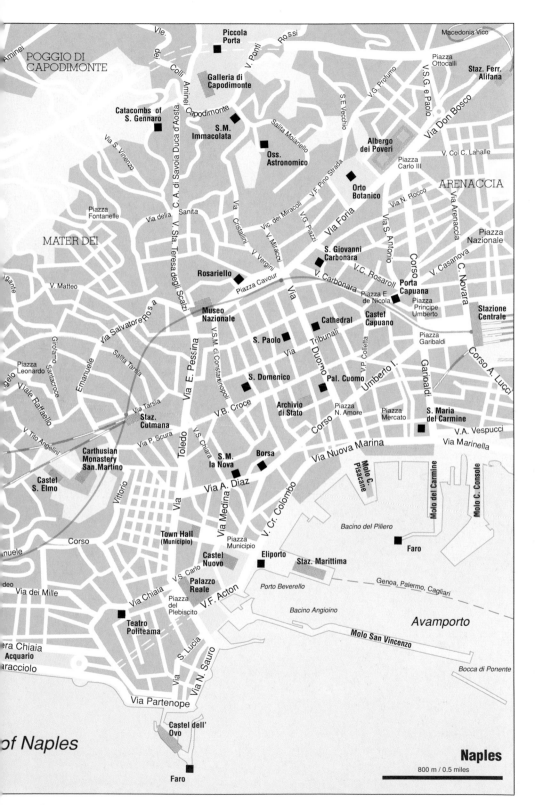

POGGIO DI
CAPODIMONTE

Piccola
Porta

Galleria di
Capodimonte

Catacombs of
S. Gennaro

S.M.
Immacolata

Oss.
Astronomico

Macedonia Vico

Piazza
Ottocalli

Staz. Ferr.
Alifana

Albergo
dei Poveri

Piazza
Carlo III

ARENACCIA

Orto
Botanico

Piazza
Fontanelle

Piazza
Nazionale

MATER DEI

V. Matteo

Rosariello

Piazza Cavour

S. Giovanni
Carbonara

Porta
Capuana

Piazza E.
de Nicola

Piazza
Principe
Umberto

Stazione
Centrale

Museo
Nazionale

Cathedral

Castel
Capuano

Piazza
Garibaldi

Piazza
Leonardo

S. Paolo

Tribunali

Piazza
N. Amore

S. Domenico

Pal. Cuomo

Piazza
Mercato

S. Maria
del Carmine

Archivio
di Stato

V.A. Vespucci

Staz.
Cutmana

Via Marinella

Carthusian
Monastery
San.Martino

S.M.
la Nova

Borsa

Via Nuova Marina

Castel
S. Elmo

Via A. Diaz

Bacino del Piliero

Faro

Town Hall
(Municipio)

Piazza
Municipio

Castel
Nuovo

Eliporto

Staz. Marittima

Via dei Mille

Palazzo
Reale

Porto Beverello

Genoa, Palermo, Cagliari

Piazza
del
Plebiscito

V.F. Acton

Bacino Angioino

Avamporto

Teatro
Politeama

Molo San Vincenzo

era Chiaia
Acquario
aracciolo

Bocca di Ponente

Via Partenope

Castel dell'
Ovo

of Naples

Faro

Naples

800 m / 0.5 miles

149

NAPLES' HISTORIC CENTRE

Naples' reputation goes before it. Since Victorian times, northern puritanism, prejudice and guidebooks have conspired to maintain that it is the Bay of Naples that is beautiful, not Naples. Even northerners closer to Naples, the Milanese, the Venetians, the Florentines, are wont to look down on Naples and its inhabitants as a nation apart, belonging to the impoverished Third World rather than Europe.

Undoubtedly, in many districts of the city there are few attractive qualities and this verdict is hard to dispute. But in the *centro storico*, the old town, the area fanning upwards from the harbour and bordered by the Via Toledo to the east and the Piazza Giuseppe Garibaldi to the east, the congestion, overcrowding and general dirtiness is redeemed, indeed transformed, by an insistent vitality. Site of ancient Neapolis, the *centro storico* is the cradle of Neapolitan life. In the shadowy alleys and handkerchief-size piazzas splashes of colour – the ubiquitous fruit and vegetable stalls, the drying washing, the occasional window-box – are all the more vibrant.

When one suddenly emerges into the sunlight-flooded larger piazza the beauty of the architecture also strikes. One glance can embrace a cluster of churches, palaces and convents spanning the gamut of architectural styles: Renaissance, Angevin, baroque, rococo, classical.

Walled city: Over 300 years ago, at the time of the Bourbon rule, the old centre of Naples was surrounded by a vast city wall with over 40 gates. Although many of these were *pertusi*, simple gaps in the wall, they were still controlled by the city guards. Only five of these gates have survived the centuries and nothing is left of the wall itself, for even in the early days the resourceful Neapolitans were knocking their own holes through the wall to escape the duty levied at the city gates. (Antonio Alvarez, the Spanish Viceroy and Duke of Alba, later legalised the *pertusi*, the holes in the wall, in honour of his dead father, Viceroy Don Pedro of Toledo.) Like a huge polyp, the city soon spread beyond its old borders, devouring the last crumbs of the old fortifications, apart from the five bereft gates.

Of these city gates, **Porta Alba**, built during the reign of the Antonio Alvarez, leads directly from Via Toledo and the Piazza Dante, at one time known as the Largo Mercatello, to the ancient heart of the town. Nothing remains of the original gate, but we know what it looked like from Mattia Preti's famous picture of the Mercatello at the time of the devastating plague in 1656. Porta Alba served as a quarantine ward during Naples' epidemics, and the gate can be clearly recognised in the painting.

A short distance inside the gate lies the area known as Costantinopoli, named after a 17th-century church dedicated to a Byzantine Madonna. The

remnants of ancient walls belong to a Greek fortress. Excavations recently begun here have uncovered remains of **Caponapoli**, confirming that a number of temples and villas were sited in this part of the Hellenistic *polis*.

The remains of the fortress lead to Via San Pietro a Maiella and the **convent of San Pietro a Maiella**, now the home of the conservatoire, a prodigious source of talented musicians, singers and composers. The conservatoire's graduates have included Domenico and Alessandro Scarlatti, Giovan Battista Pergolesi and Giovanni Paisello.

By turning right just before the monastery, down Via San Sebastiano, you reach **Via Benedetto Croce** (further west, Via San Biaglo ai Librai), otherwise known as Spaccanapoli ("split Naples") with its row of splendid old palaces. One of these is **Palazzo Filomarino**, where the philosopher and historian Benedetto Croce (1866–1953) held his literary and political salons, vital to the cultural life of Naples during the early decades of the 20th century. Croce was minister of education in the Italian government during 1920–21 but, as an opponent of Mussolini's Fascism, was thereafter forced to resign from his professorship at Naples University. After World War II he headed the Liberal party in Italy.

On the south side of this street, on Piazza Gesú Nuova, is the **convent of Santa Chiara**, whose cloister, elaborately decorated with majolica tiles and festooned with trailing greenery, is one of the most photographed corners of Naples. Although bomb damage in World War II destroyed much of the convent's baroque interior (dating from the mid-18th century), sensitive reconstruction has preserved its austere character. The original church was built by Gagliardo Primario for Sancia, queen of Robert the Wise, in 1310–28.

The restraint of Santa Chiara's interior is in marked contrast to the **Gesú Nuovo church** opposite, in which ornamentation is unbridled. This church

View over San Martino.

was built at the behest of Isabella della Rovere at the end of the 16th century. The frescoes include work by Corenzio, Stanzione and Ribera.

If we are to believe the city's guides, the most important piece of architecture in this district is the **church of San Domenico Maggiore**, "a jewel of Gothic architecture" as their spiel puts it, on Plaza San Domenico. The church was built in the 14th century and re-modelled in the 19th; its interior shows a distinct baroque influence. The scholastic theologian and philosopher Thomas Aquinas, canonised in 1323, spent almost two years in the neighbouring monastery. The small painting of the Crucifixion in the Cappellone del Crocifisso is reputed to be the one which spoke to Thomas.

Many of the works of art in this church were tragically destroyed in World War II, including Giotto's famous fresco, the remains of which are kept in the neighbouring Convent of the order of St Clare. Miraculously, the belfry remained unscathed by the war.

Just round the corner from here, up Via F. de Sanctis, is the **Cappella Sansevero,** built in honour of an oath made by Giovan Francesco di Sangro, the Duke of Torremaggiore. On recovering from a death-threatening illness, the duke vowed to show his gratitude for his cure by building a chapel for the **Madonna della Pietà**, a picture attributed with miraculous powers. The original chapel with its simple rectangular ground plan, the design of an unknown architect, was built in 1590. Later, the duke's son had the chapel extended to accommodate the streams of pilgrims who came to pray for miracles. At the same time the chapel was converted into a family mausoleum for the Dukes of Sansevero. Reminders of death are everywhere. In the middle of the 18th century important works of art, including sculptures and frescoes, which reflected the artistic style of their time, were added. The curious combination of the sacred and the sensual

Traffic rarely moves faster than trotting pace.

evident in their execution was characteristic of this era of art history.

One work which art historians immediately associate with the chapel is Giuseppe Sanmartino's statue **Cristo Velato** (Veiled Christ), sculpted in 1753. Sanmartino's remarkable artistic skill is exemplified by the thin veil appearing to cover the prostrate body of Christ. A closer look shows that this veil is fashioned out of extremely thin and thus transparent alabaster. For many years experts argued about the identity of the artist of this work; in the end, they agreed that it was most likely the work of the Neapolitan sculptor Giuseppe Sanmartino. It is said that before he decided on the statue's position in the chapel he experimented with the effects of light. It is the play of light and shadow which makes the innumerable folds of the cloth clinging to the body of Christ so effective. This technique became Sanmartino's trademark.

Further east, just after Via Benedetto Croce becomes Via San Biagio ai Librai, lies one of the richest ensembles of church architecture in Naples. The small area between Via dei Tribunali and Via San Biagio ai Librai presents a curious mixture of styles, ranging from the towering San Lorenzo Maggiore to the convent of San Gregorio Armeno, with its supporting arcade, and the splendid neoclassical building of San Paolo Maggiore.

The earth moves: It would fill volumes to record all the stories associated with **San Lorenzo Maggiore** and its adjacent monastery. The history of this church and the legends that have evolved have become irrevocably tangled. It was in this church, for example, on Easter Saturday 1336, that the master of early Italian story-telling, Boccaccio, is said to have met his Fiammetta (Maria, daughter of Robert of Anjou), the muse behind many of his greatest poems. On catching sight of Maria, the 23-year-old poet experienced a *coup de foudre*. "I had no sooner seen her than my heart began to flutter so strongly that it was as if I could feel it throbbing in the smallest pulses of my body."

Petrarch, the other great lyricist of Italian poetry and the earliest of the great humanists of the Renaissance, is also supposed to have passed an eventful time under San Lorenzo's vaulted roofs; during his sojourn in Naples – he was staying at the Franciscan monastery adjacent to the church – a massive earthquake occurred.

San Lorenzo Maggiore was commissioned by Charles I of Anjou, and work was carried out between 1270 and 1275 on the site of an early Christian church dating from the 6th century. Charles I had most of Naples' churches rebuilt and modernised. The main reason for his interest in religious architecture was his desire to find favour with the papal authorities. The Pope elicited Charles's help in driving the excommunicated Hohenstaufens out of the city.

The different architectural and artistic styles subsequently incorporated into San Lorenzo Maggiore provide a

Left, Chapel of Sansevero. Right, confession.

detailed guide to the development of art history in Naples. Nine chapels radiate from the apse, including the magnificent Cappellone di San Antonio in the left transept. Also of note is a 15th-century panel of **St Anthony surrounded by Angels** in the left-hand transept of San Lorenzo Maggiore.

A maze of streets: The exact position of of the original Paleopolis can no longer be determined. It was almost 3,000 years ago that the first city's inhabitants built their harbour on the island of Megaride where, centuries later, under the rule of the French House of Anjou, Castel dell'Ovo was erected. The neapolis, however – the "new city" – which was built according to the geometrical design of Hippodamus, is still reflected 2,000 years later in the precise chequerboard pattern of streets lying either side of Via San Biagio ai Librai. Little else remains of the Graeco-Roman Neapolis, and only a trained eye will find the remaining evidence of ancient roots; the one Graeco-Roman ur-

Left, San Lorenzo Maggiore. **Below**, votive chapel.

ban complex which has managed to resist the ravages of time is the catacombs of San Lorenzo Maggiore, on which the basilica of the law courts was built in the early Middle Ages. The ruins of the agora, with the remains of arches, taverns and the rooms of the cloth fullers, can be reached through the lovely cloister of San Lorenzo. Alas, the curia, where the archons, the annually appointed public officials, gathered to debate new laws, is irretrievably destroyed, as are the Greek gymnasium and the art gallery praised so effusively by the philosopher Philostratus. Little remains of the agora. All that is left are the ruins of the Diascori temple including the two Corinthian columns with the mutilated reliefs of the heavenly twins, Castor and Pollux, which nowadays support the neoclassical **church of San Paolo Maggiore.**

This church contains two notable baroque chapels: the handsome Cappella Firrao (1641) by Dionisio Lazzari and Valentini e Tacca, with its inlaid marble and mother of pearl, and the Cappella della Purità (1681) by Giovanni Domenico Vinaccia.

Get thee to a nunnery: The ancient city's temple of Ceres and the house of the vestal virgins have also disappeared without trace. They are assumed to have stood on the site of the **church of San Gregorio Armeno**, and its attendant convent, which boasts an interesting collection of oriental plants in its courtyard. Eucharistic bread has been prepared on these premises since 1897. It used to be made exclusively for the Pope, but these days the convent supplies only Neapolitan churches.

In the middle of the 19th century the convent shot to fame when torrid tales of sexual exploits within its walls were exposed by Enrichetta Caracciolo in her book *Mysteries of a Neapolitan Convent*, written as an act of vengeance against the mother who had banished her here in 1841. The nuns of this convent were not pious young women with a vocation, but the daughters of noble

MAKING IT AND FAKING IT

Naples mirrors Hong Kong. The city is both the meeting-place of clashing cultures and a master of counterfeit culture. But it is no pale Western copy. Here hawkers peddle and ragamuffins rob, but with flair and *fantasia*. A magician's touch transforms imitation into art – painted marzipan fruit looks finer than real peaches. Desperation coupled with imagination have led the city into deception: Neapolitans, from taxi-drivers to transvestites, sell fake services as readily as fake goods.

Via Chiaia is the chicest street, jokingly called the only place to buy genuine goods in Naples. Here Armani, Valentino and the other top designers reign supreme while just down the road traders flaunt counterfeit *couture* as superior to the real thing. Deception is a creative tool in Naples. Not for nothing are Neapolitan marketing managers prized in Milan or Neapolitan politicians powerful in Rome.

The Forcella market is the place for ersatz Scotch whisky, Fernet Branca liqueur and

French cognac. Fake leather goods include Louis Vuitton luggage and Gucci handbags. Recently, Gucci had to simplify its leather range in response to widespread copying. Fake Rolex watches, Ray-Ban sunglasses and pirated cassettes are readily available. At the top end of the market are well-made copies of Etruscan vases, ancient bronzes and classical figurines. However, the unsuspecting buyer might find a shoddy substitute in the well-wrapped package.

As for perfume, a few drops of fake Chanel Number 5 or Hermès Calèche may make you as desirable as a Neapolitan transvestite, a legendary breed. Lacoste T-shirts come with the crocodile logo sewn on upside-down. Disgruntled black-clad widows sell contraband Marlboro, Merit and Lucky Strike from makeshift stalls. Naturally, traditional Neapolitan coral necklaces are mostly made in Africa. Even the barefoot Senegalese street traders tend to be local students.

Neapolitans are never what they seem. Seamstresses double up as fortune tellers in the summer; their winter trade is to fake "Florentine" embroidery. Neapolitan taxi-drivers are notorious for feigning charm while fiddling the meter. Windscreen-washing is second-nature to the shoe-shine boys but cigarette-selling and kite-making are also useful sidelines.

The Neapolitans' powers of persuasion are daunting. Impish bootblacks suggest polishing suede boots. The Corso Malta shoe market does not scorn *scarpe scompagnate* ("unaccompanied shoes" for one-legged people. Luciano de Crescenzo, the Neapolitan writer, records an attempt by a wily trader to persuade his customer to buy two odd shoes: "Once you start walking, they will look exactly the same – *tale e quale.*"

In Naples, even sex is deceptive: a Neapolitan naturally seeks to shroud his motives and enjoy the disguise. Napoli Centrale station and Corso Umberto teem with touts, traders, black marketeers, prostitutes and kerb-crawlers. But female prostitutes are losing out to male competition, notably to transvestites. The Camorra is indifferent since it shares in all immoral earnings regardless. In desperation, the average mountainous Neapolitan prostitute now advertises herself as *"una puttana vera"*, a genuine whore. In this city of deceptions, she may be one of the few not faking her craft. ∎

One of Naples' legendary transvestites.

families, many of whom were sent here as a penance, usually for an unsuitable love affair or other misdemeanour. As such, they were used to living well and food, furnishings and other comforts were lavish.

Harold Acton, in his book *The Bourbons of Naples,* gives an account of King Ferdinand's visit to such a convent and the culinary marvels he found there: "The company were surprised on being led into a large parlour, to find a table covered, and every appearance of a plentiful cold repast, consisting of several joints of meat, hams, fowl, fish, and various other dishes. It seemed rather ill-judged to have prepared a feast of such solid nature immediately after dinner; for these royal visits were made in the afternoon. The lady Abbess, however, earnestly pressed their Majesties to sit down; with which they complied. The nuns stood behind to serve their royal guests. The Queen chose a slice of cold turkey, which, on being cut up, turned out a large piece of lemon ice, of the shape and appearance of a roasted turkey. All the other dishes were ices of various kinds, disguised under the forms of joints of meat, fish and fowl…"

Christmas bazaar: The street on which San Gregorio Armeno stands is a rich source of tantalising aromas, particularly in the period before Christmas, when the *pastorai*, crib-makers, who commandeer the street, are at their busiest. Then the smell of pine resin blends with the scent of *struffoli* (tiny balls of deep-fried pastry glazed with honey and orange peel), a Christmas speciality. The brightly-lit shop windows crammed with crib figures, the voices of thousands of visitors, the melancholic strains of bagpipes and the smoke rising from the burning wood combine to create the unique atmosphere of a Mediterranean Christmas bazaar.

The local chamber of commerce estimates that over 300,000 crib figures are put on sale in the weeks before Christmas. The genuine articles are small

Market on the Via Biagio Librai.

works of art produced using the same methods and paints as in the 17th and 18th centuries; but, as with so many things in Naples, there are also fakes on offer, so goods should be examined closely before purchase. To be sure that the crib intended for the space under your Christmas tree is the bona-fide article, it is advisable to buy from one of the craft shops which sell throughout the year.

Slightly further north, between **Via San Paolo** and **Via Anticaglia**, modern department stores have been built on the remains of a large Greek theatre. It is estimated that the semi-circular auditorium had a diameter of over 330 ft (100 metres) and was built to accommodate some 11,000 spectators. The chronicles of the Latin writers Suetonius and Vitruvius repeatedly refer to *emmeleia* and *sicinnis*, tragic or satirical dances, which were performed by the most famous actors of that time, Apolaust, Pylades and Batillus.

Plutarch records that, after the murder of Julius Caesar, Brutus decided to come to Naples to persuade the famous actor Canuzius to perform in Rome, his aim being to defuse popular outrage at the the murder. And no lesser figure than Emperor Nero used this theatre to test his qualities as a poet and singer; the historical chronicles of the time record: "These were memorable days for the Neapolitan theatre. After news of this unique event had spread, crowds of people from all parts of Campania hurried to Naples to see for themselves. The Emperor arrived in Naples with a large entourage. His singing performances were accompanied by children wearing rings, curls in their hair and richly decorated costumes For their performance they earned 40,000 sesterces." Emperor Nero is said to have had a special love of monumental crowd scenes and the many Egyptian slaves who were living in the city at the time were obliged to serve as his extras.

A short distance to the northeast of here, on Via del Duomo, lies the

Dome by Lanfranco inside Naples cathedral.

cathedral. Recent restoration work has thrown some much needed light on the cathedral's confusing architectural history. It has been established beyond doubt that a Greek Orthodox as well as an early Roman Catholic church once stood on the site of the present building. Again, a member of the House of Anjou – Charles III – was responsible for the building of this Gothic cathedral, at the end of the 13th century.

The oldest part of the original church is the 5th-century Baptistry of San Giovanni at the end of the right aisle. Other important features include the marble statues, the frescoes and the floor. Of particular interest are the four chapels whose entrances lead off from the left transept, the most important of which is the chapel of San Gennaro, which was designed by the priest and architect Francesco Grimaldi and built between 1609 and 1637.

The interior of the chapel is a masterpiece of the Neapolitan baroque style. San Gennaro, the patron saint of Naples, is portrayed by a precious silver bust which was made by French silversmiths in 1306. It is this which contains the famous phials of the blood of San Gennaro, the object of a thrice-yearly miracle in the cathedral. On specified dates in May, September and December of each year the crusted blood is said to liquefy. According to legend, if this does not occur, the city will be struck by disaster (*see page 109*). This reliquary, an object of pilgrimage and said to be an oracle of good and evil, is framed by an enormous silver candelabra designed by Bartolemeo Granucci in 1744 and made by the goldsmith Filippo del Giudice.

Architectural connoisseurs may consider the neo-Gothic facade of the cathedral, completed at the turn of the century, as too massive and inappropriate. It was an attempt by the architect Enrico Alvino to forge a stylistic link with the original building of the Anjous. However, in many eyes the Gothic style, which Renaissance artists dis-

Piazza del Duomo.

missed as barbarian and vulgar, does not suit the character of the Neapolitans; in this context it appears far too overbearing.

A short detour north along Via Duomo leads to Via Foria and, after a few yards left, to Piazza Cavour and **Porta San Gennaro**. This city gate may not look as impressive as the other four remaining gates but there is every reason to believe that it is the oldest. Its existence was first documented in a notarial record from the year 928. One hundred years later the gate's *portatari*, as the guard and the tax collector were called, were mentioned in a contract with the monastery of San Gregorio Armeno. The gate was important because of its proximity to the cathedral.

The gate is remarkably preserved. Traces of a fresco by the 17th-century painter Mattia Preti can still be discerned. Apparently, Preti killed a sentry in a quarrel but instead of being condemned to death he was sentenced to paint the fresco. He chose as his theme the Virgin Mary and San Gennaro averting the plague from Naples.

Egyptian quarter: During Roman times the network of streets which spreads like a spider's web below **San Biagio ai Librai** near San Domenico Maggiore comprised the Egyptian quarter, inhabited by Alexandrians. The statue of Father Nile, the river god of antiquity, erected by the rich Alexandrian merchants who inhabited this area, can be found adorning a passageway to the university of Mezzocannone. The theory that the Greeks organised sports festivals here, on the space used by goldsmiths and armourers to sell their wares, is supported by the following inscription pertaining to the *Penterikon*, the games which took place every five years, which was unexpectedly revealed during excavations: "Titus Flavius Evanthes, who won the city boys' relay race at the XLIII Italian Games, and who dedicated the portraits of the Dioscuri to his brotherhood." The competitions, which took place in the **Elegant facade.**

stadium and on the neighbouring race-course, were so important that they were held under the presidency of no less a person than Emperor Titus. A memorial stone, written in both Greek and Latin, was erected to commemorate each of these games. The Romans granted the Neapolitans the privilege of using both languages and of continuing to foster Greek customs and practices.

Sublime athlete: Although nothing has been preserved of the one sports arena which existed in Naples at that time, a passage from a classical text tells of the Neapolitans' love of games and sport, specifically their admiration for the athlete Melanchoma. Crysostomos wrote of this famous athlete: "Standing on tiptoe we could see the youth's head and his raised hands; when we managed to push further to the front, we were able to see that while he was exercising so passionately his size and beauty were particularly graceful. During his exercises it appeared that he was fighting with his opponents and his grace and beauty could not be surpassed. From closer up he was comparable to a bronze statue." Eat your heart out, Diego Armando Maradona.

Proceeding east, to the southern part of Via Del Duomo, you come to the **church of San Giorgio Maggiore**, dating from the 18th century. It overlooks the **Piazza Crocelle ai Marmesi**, a square which received its name from the Brotherhood of Crucifix Bearers, whose monastery was situated in the *mandesi* (cart builders') quarter.

Almost opposite the church is a magnificent example of Renaissance architecture, a *palazzo* in which the **Filanfieri Museum** is now housed. Formerly the headquarters of the Monte della Misericordia, an aristocratic charitable organisation, it was built at the beginning of the Neapolitan baroque period. It is famous not only for its splendid octagonal chapel but also for its priceless collection of allegorical paintings by Caravaggio. These pictures represent the works of mercy, which, like the

A poorer abode.

deadly sins and the virtues, numbered seven.

Royal entrances: The area east of the Via del Duomo is the Forcella, stronghold of the Camorra and the site of some of the liveliest markets in town. A little distance above stands one of the loveliest gates in the city, **Porta Capuana**. The gate occupies a point where three densely populated quarters converge (Vicario, Duchessa, Annunziata), between the district court and the old Palace of Justice in Castelcapuano, at one time residence of the Swabian Hohenstaufens. The lovely Renaissance facade was commissioned by Viceroy Ferrante I and designed by the famous architect Giuliano da Maiano (the two Aragonese towers are symbols of honour and virtue). It is assumed that the original city gate was integrated into the old Norman fortress. The road through the gate led to Capua.

Porta Capuana was also the scene of many royal processions and triumphal entries into the city. It was an unwritten law that whenever the city was conquered – a regular occurrence right up until unification – the new rulers would present themselves to the Neapolitans through this gate. Roger the Norman, Henry VI, Charles I of Anjou, not to mention the Bourbons, all entered the city through here. An amusing story concerning Emperor Charles V's passage through this gate related in the notarial records tells how before entering the city his royal majesty stopped to attend to an urgent call of nature in the vegetable gardens of Campovecchio al Vasto. An old woman, who had not recognised the king with his trousers down, was so incensed at the sight of this uncouth behaviour that she attacked him with a pitchfork. It took the king's entire entourage to rescue him from the violent fury of the offended lady.

Porta Capuana was probably the most important gate in the city. It was invariably festooned with portraits of San Gennaro and Sant'Agnello and the open space in front of it was the site of public **Bikers...**

punishments. As a later edict of the viceroy expressed it: "The column of the royal province stood here, the place where debtors were forced to let their trousers down and display their naked debts for the scornful public to see." One aspect which has remained unchanged over the centuries is Porta Capuana's role as meeting place for street traders, shoppers and idlers. The jostling which Goethe enjoyed so much during his stay in Naples is unabated.

The same hustle and bustle dominates the scene in front of the **churches of Santa Caterina a Formiello** and **San Giovanni a Carbonara** (west along the street of that name). In the latter church the highly expedient liaison between Charles of Durres, the son of Sigismund and later king of Poland, and the Neapolitan noblewoman Bona Sforza was celebrated. It was here that the **Accademia Alfonsina** was founded by the Aragon rulers. The academy boasts one of the most famous collections of hand-written codexes. It was

also here that Ser Gianni Caracciolo, the steward of the upper house of the Neapolitan Empire and the lover of Queen Giovanna II, was stabbed in the back. The present-day quarter around Porta Capuana was built at the time of the Counter-Reformation, after the hostilities between Philip IV of Spain and King Louis XII of France ceased in 1659.

Porta Nolana lies south of Porta Capuana, beyond the massive **Piazza Garibaldi** and the Stazione Centrale (Central Station) at the end of Corso Umberto I. It marks the entrance to another working-class quarter, around the **Stazione Circumvesuviana**, the railway station linking Naples with Herculaneum, Pompeii and Sorrento. Again, like Porta Capuana, its Renaissance facade belies its true age. Archaeologists believe that this was the site of the antique Porta Furcillense, mentioned in the writings of the Latin historian Livy and believed to have separated the thermal baths from the **Regio**

...and cyclists.

Furcilensis. The relief on the Renaissance facade is of Ferdinand of Aragon, who commissioned the facelift; the two round towers symbolise faith and hope.

From here it is not far to the **Piazza del Mercato**. This is where Conradin of Hohenstaufen, the last of the Hohenstaufen dynasty, was beheaded under the orders of Charles I of Anjou in 1268, after his failed attempt to regain power. His sister Elizabeth tried, in vain, to have his remains transported to Bavaria. In the end he was interred behind the high altar in the **church of Bruna del Carmelo**. It was not until the last century, however, that King Maximilian of Bavaria gave him a monument appropriate to his status, the marble statue in the **church of Carmine al Mercat**o, designed by the Munich sculptor Peter Schoeps.

From here, it is only one block to the harbour and port.

Southern quarters: Over the other side of the harbour rises **Castel Nuovo**, or **Maschio Angioino** as it is now called in

recognition of Charles I of Anjou, the man responsible for its construction. Originally the site was occupied by a Franciscan monastery, but when Charles settled on it as the best possible place for a new fortress he evicted the monks and sent them to live in the church of Santa Maria la Nova. Thus his architect, presumed to have been Pierre de Chaulnes, was able to set to work. After Alfonso I of Aragon, the Spanish viceroy, came to power in Naples in 1442, he set about completely rebuilding the old castle and converting it into his private residence.

The appearance of the original version is shown in pictures of the time; for example, the castle forms the centre of the famous *Tavola Strozzi*, painted in 1464, one of the earliest views of Naples we have. It was two years after this view was painted that Alfonso I started his programme of reconstruction. As one of his prerequisites was that it should provide a high level of protection from attack, he had the battlements completely rebuilt. His other main concern was that it should be comfortable and in a style in keeping with the prevailing standards of other royal houses in Europe. He brought the Spanish architect Guillermo Sagrera to Naples to take charge of the work.

Sagrera's work, commited to the Gothic style, epitomised the current tastes of the Spanish court. The rebuilding was carried out over six years from 1446 to 1452. It included the addition of the five towers which form the heart of the castle today, all built with yellowish tuff stone with the exception of the **Torre dell'Oro**, which was built with a grey-coloured stone from Molara.

First impressions of the castle inevitably emphasise the **Renaissance Triumphal Arch**, built as a grand monument to Alfonso I's victory over Naples. It is a testimony to the cultural renewal of Naples by the House of Aragon. The fact that a triumphal arch, a reference to the Roman period, was built at all, shows that the Gothic was gradually

Left, Castel Nuovo. Below, young flower seller.

replacing the Renaissance style in Naples, even during the reign of Alfonso I.

Not only is the triumphal arch one of the first pieces of Renaissance architecture in Naples but it is also a very unusual work, for the four storeys which make up the arch were each designed according to different principles of composition. The entrance to the arch is framed on either side by two Corinthian double columns. Above this is a central panel commemorating Alfonso's triumphal entry into the city; it depicts Alfonso in his chariot surrounded by his court. In the upper part of the arch shell-shaped niches can be seen. These contain statues of antique iconography representing the four virtues of Ancient Rome: Justice, Temperance, Fortitude and Prudence (*Justitia*, *Temperantia*, *Fortitudo*, *Prudentia*).

Finally the gable at the top of the arch has the Archangel Michael watching over everything. Art historians' attempts to discover who was responsible for this unique work of art have so far failed. It is possible that it was the joint work of the architect Pietro di Martino from Milan and the Venetian Francesco Laurana.

In the 14th-century **Palace Chapel of Santa Barbara**, which is in the castle courtyard, some remains of works dating from the Anjou period can be admired (the best examples are the representations of the Virgin Mary by Andrea dell'Aquilas and Francesco Laurana). Unfortunately very little is left of the chapel's real masterpiece, a fresco carried out by Giotto between 1330 and 1331 called *Stories from the Old and the New Testament*. A victim of pillaging and destruction, the fresco has been reduced to a few fragments. None the less these are enough to indicate the importance which would have been given to this cycle of paintings had it survived in its entirety.

Centre of power: Official power in Naples still centres on Maschio Angioino. Its Sala dei Baroni is where the *Consiglio Communale*, the city

Pulling the crowds on the Piazza del Plebiscito.

council, holds its weekly debates on the city's ills: corruption and nepotism, mismanagement and financial deficits included. The hall derives its name from the successful conspiracy of the Neapolitan barons against Ferdinand I in 1485 which was hatched within its walls. When in the following year Ferdinand regained his ascendancy, his revenge on the barons was to have them arrested (in the very same hall), tortured and executed.

Here again, Sagrera's work is a symbiosis of Spanish influences and characteristics of the classical Roman style (inspired by his detailed studies of ruins around the Phlegraean Fields). The rounded windows and the round arch and vaulted ceiling of this square hall clearly show the Roman influence. The general structure of the hall, with its sober geometrical design, creates a dramatic contrast.

The Castel dell' Ovo, site of Virgil's vision.

The hall gives a wonderful impression of space. The remaining fragments of its original floor, made from exqui-site blue and white tiles brought from Valencia, are in the Museo Filangieri.

The Maschio Angioino dominates the large, tree-lined piazza in front of the **Stazione Marittima**.Likewise flanking this square is the **Palazzo Reale,** also known as **Palazzo San Giacomo**, one of the most important symbols of the city. It was built at the beginning of the 19th century and now serves as the city hall. The wheels of government turn exceedingly slowly in this centre of regional government. Campania is faced with a number of seemingly insurmountable problems: the traffic congestion created by the army of commuters that troops into the city every day, the insanitary conditions in many of the older quarters and the stranglehold organised crime exerts on the city.

The palace, which is of no particular architectural interest, was named after the **church of San Giacomo degli Spagnoli**, which stands next to it This church was originally built in the 16th

century at the behest of the Viceroy Don Pedro di Toledo, the man responsible for the proliferation of baroque architecture in Naples, but 200 years later it was rebuilt according to 18th-century tastes. It is worth entering the church to look at its paintings and sculptures. The atrium of the *palazzo* is also worth a closer look.

The flight of steps leading up to the palace is adorned by the marble bust of a woman. Opinions differ as to who this woman is supposed to be. Some claim she is "Donna Marianna", a symbol of Naples; others that the statue represents the Siren Parthenope; and some are convinced she is simply a goddess of beauty. Not in dispute is the antiquity of the statue; it is believed to have been sculpted at a time when life in Naples was under the influence of both the Greek and the Roman cultures. For over four centuries this statue stood on a pedestal overlooking one of the most overcrowded squares of the market. Thirty years ago it was moved to the shelter of the **Palazzo San Giacomo** to protect it from the ravages of wind, weather and air pollution.

It is only a few minutes walk from **Palazzo Municipale** to the massive **Piazza del Plebiscito**, the most harmonious and beautifully decorated square in the city. This piazza commemorates the incorporation of the Kingdom of Two Sicilies into the Italian national state in 1860, an event which resulted in Naples losing its traditional function as a capital. Between the Palazzo Reale, the royal palace (covered, along with the San Carlo Theatre, in more detail in the chapter on Via Toledo), built between 1600 and 1602 and extended in the 18th century, and the **Church of San Francesco di Paola**, a massive edifice built at the beginning of the 19th century and modelled on the Roman Pantheon, stands the **Prefecture Palace**. Next to this is the headquarters of the South Italian armed forces, similar in appearance to the Prefecture Palace.

This piazza is the heart of business,

Castel dell'Ovo: strategic look-out.

political and military activity in Naples, and Via Toledo (or Via Roma as it is now called), the ¾-mile (1.5-km) thoroughfare which is the favoured route of the evening *passeggiata*, is the main artery (again, covered in detail in the next chaper). As the style of architecture indicates, some of the buildings here date from the time of Fascism, when most of this area was redeveloped. Serried lines of dilapidated houses – still occupying the area to the west of the street – were cleared and replaced by the type of monstrous architecture which characterised the regime: the police headquarters, the tax office, the provincial administration and the post office are typical examples.

To the west, behind Piazza del Plebiscito and down the bustling Via Chiaia lies **Piazza dei Martiri**, which forms the centre of this elegant part of the city. The trader's association is housed in **Palazzo Migliaccio**, one of the monumental *palazzi* gracing the square. The original palace, named after the second wife of Ferdinand I of Bourbon, was built in the 18th century but it has been rebuilt several times since.

By turning south of the piazza you reach Piazza della Vittoria and the Via Partenope, lined by Naples' grandest hotels. Just to the east rises **Castel dell'Ovo**, engirlding the yachts of the Borgo Marino. This medieval castle built of tuff is steeped in more legends than all of Naples' other castles put together. Goethe described it disparagingly as a "badly situated monastery", but its period as an ecclesiastical institution was just one episode in its long and varied history.

The first documentary evidence of Castel dell'Ovo dates from 1278, but it is assumed that the original building was much older; many stories of antiquity, for example, cite the castle. One particularly widespread tale is that of Virgil, who is said to have had a vision on the site of the Castel dell'Ovo. According to this story, it was here that he encountered a magical *ovum*, the egg

Inside the Castel dell'Ovo.

which gave the castle its name. The Roman poet is said to have seen a rock in the form of an egg rising out of the waves of the incoming tide; the vision made such a powerful impression on Virgil that it changed his life. As is so often the case in mythological tales, the revelation is supposed to have happened on the night of a full moon.

There is, however, documentary proof that this rock was once called *Megaride*, the place which is supposed to have served as an outpost and a mooring place for the Siren Parthenope. Later, when the Romans ruled Naples, this outpost became a *castrum lucullanum*, a storage place for fine and costly groceries, which was kept under the strictest surveillance. After the fall of the Eastern Roman Empire, a whole series of different people lived or were imprisoned here. The first of these were not the barbarians (who never managed to conquer Naples during their invasion of Italy) but monks of the order of St Basil. At this time religious orders

tended to choose locations of strategic value for their settlements.

The monks replaced the store with a school for scribes. They made copies of many ancient literary works and philosophical treatises, thus preserving them for posterity. It was in this *insula sancti salvoris* (place of knowledge and salvation) that St Patricia locked herself up in a cell and starved to death.

However, the walls of Castel dell' Ovo have also witnessed more secular dramas, especially after Charles of Anjou began to use it as a prison. The last of the German dynasty of the Hohenstaufens, whose most famous family member was Barbarossa and whom Pope Innocent IV called "a clan of vipers", were imprisoned here. Prisoners were either incarcerated for life in the castle's dungeons or held until their execution on the scaffold in the central marketplace (the fate of both Conradin and Beatrice of Hohenstaufen). Under the rule of the Spanish House of Aragon the castle became a safe refuge for fleeing regents and popes: Queen Joanna I and the antipope Clement VII, for example, both sought shelter behind its impenetrable walls.

Up until half a century ago, when the water in the gulf was still relatively unpolluted and bathing here was still popular, Castel dell'Ovo was surrounded by the wicker beach chairs of guests staying in the swathe of grand hotels along Via Partenope, and its waters were patterned with the sort of fish traps used in mussel cultivation. Now the district of Santa Lucia, at one time a colourful but humble fishing community, has been redeveloped and the castle itself has been turned into a highly modern congress centre. The tip of the tongue of Pizzofalcone (the falcon's beak), the huge building dominates its surroundings and the promenade, as if it were guarding the mythological origins of Naples, the place where the defeated Siren Parthenope was washed up on the shore after failing to ensnare Odysseus.

Left, welcome refreshment. **Right,** eyewitness.

MARKETS

Almost anything, from antiques to washing powder, from groceries to computers, can be bought in the markets of Naples – if not in one of the city's dozens of legal markets, then at one of the many stalls which spring up without an official licence every morning and vanish at the first sign of a *vigile*, one of the traffic policemen also responsible for market stalls.

Unlike in other Italian cities, it isn't just the locals who are able to pick up bargains. Strangers stand as much chance as anybody else, for here economics are governed equally by the fight for survival and the laws of supply and demand, as the amount of energy that goes into making a sale demonstrates. A stallholder will wave his arms dramatically and extol the excellence of his goods with all the emotion of a La Scala opera star. The excited exchanges can even drown out the roar of the traffic.

The market which attracts most out-of-town visitors is the crib market, in Via San Gregorio Armeno, tucked into the labyrinth of Spaccanapoli. Although busiest, and therefore most atmospheric, at Christmas, it is worth visiting at any time of year. The crib figures are produced using the same methods and materials – hand-modelled terracotta clay baked in brick ovens – that were used in the 17th century.

The market suffered from the sudden popularity of plastic Christmas trees and crib figures in the 1970s, but is now enjoying unprecedented vitality. In keeping with the revived interest in handcrafted items, tourists are ignoring the kitschy plates decorated with pictures of Naples or Vesuvius, plastic miniatures of Castel dell'Ovo, dolls in tarantella costumes and other tacky souvenirs, and buying crib figures.

Another favourite among visitors is the large weekend flea market held twice monthly in the Viale Dohrn of the Villa Communale (next to Via F. Caracciolo). There is an astounding range of goods on offer, from the earliest types of smoothing iron, old petroleum lamps, engravings and richly inlaid chests to baroque cupboards and art nouveau bedside tables.

In any transaction, it is necessary to haggle: the rule of thumb for dealers is to ask double the price they expect to obtain. One way of speeding up the negotiations is to pretend to leave. (Remember that when negotiations have been concluded it is too late to quiz a dealer on the origins of the goods.)

The city's food markets are excellent places to buy daily supplies of food and drink, and the best place to go for specialities such as mozzarella cheese, fish (try the market at Porta Nolana) or spices. Food markets are also the places in which to absorb the rhythm of daily life. The most picturesque is the one in Pignasecca, where Via Toledo leads up to the hills of Vomero.

Left, lemon seller. Right, friendly exchange.

VIA TOLEDO

Naples' most glorious thoroughfare, its equivalent of the Ramblas, the Champs Elysées or the Grand Canal, is **Via Toledo**, the 2-mile (3-km) long thoroughfare heading north from Palazzo Reale. Like the east-west running Spaccanapoli, the south-north Via Toledo dissects the city. It is the spinal chord of Naples, linking the most important public buildings and flanked by the line of the old city wall to the east and densely packed alleyways rising steeply to the west. Always a lively, bustling place, it positively swarms in the late afternoon when Neapolitans gather for the evening *passeggiata*. Stendhal, visiting Naples in 1817, called Via Toldeo "the most populous and gayest street in the world".

The street has another, newer name, Via Roma, bestowed by politicians after the unification of Italy, but the Neapolitans prefer Via Toledo, after Don Pedro of Toledo who commissioned it in 1536. The fact that the Spanish viceroy financed the project with crushing taxes, in particular an unpopular tax on wine, makes no difference to the Neapolitans. The street and its name are seen as integral to Naples' history.

Imposing architecture: Via Toledo begins under the hill settled by Naples' earliest settlers, Pizzofalcone, at Piazza del Plebiscito, a square graced by the city's best examples of baroque architecture, a style which marked the transition from the rule of the Spanish viceroys to the Bourbon empire. On one side it is flanked by the Palazzo Reale, the Royal Palace, and on the other embraced by the twin arcades of the **church of San Francesco di Paola**, whose present facade dates from the beginning of the 19th century. The church was commissioned by Ferdinand IV of Bourbon after his return to the throne of Naples following the downfall of the French, in fulfilment of a vow. Ferdinand

is commemorated by one of the two equestrian statues gracing the square; the other is of Charles III of Bourbon.

The **Palazzo Reale** (also called Regio Palacio) opposite is considerably older. It was built in the middle of the 16th century on the site where the original royal palace had stood. The palace was improved and altered on numerous occasions over the centuries, for every ruler wanted to stamp his mark on the building; time and again mighty arcades were built only to be demolished later.

The palace has a relatively simple facade punctuated by niches containing statues representing the eight dynasties that ruled Naples: Roger the Norman, Frederick II the Swabian, Charles I of Anjou, Alfonso of Aragon, Charles V of Austria, Charles III of Bourbon, Joachim Murat, and Victor Emmanuel II of Savoy. But two names in particular are connected with this prestigious building, Don Pedro of Toledo (the instigator of Via Toledo) and Charles of Bourbon. The first, a Spanish nobleman, had the

Preceding pages: Galleria Umberto I: 19th-century shopping mall. **Left**, Joachim Murat strikes a pose on the Palazzo Reale. **Right**, the Palazzo Reale.

building converted into a royal palace in order to protect his family and guests from attack by the proletariat. The extensive alterations made by Charles of Bourbon, on the other hand, were designed to allow more light into the fortress-like building and make living conditions more comfortable.

The court architects did not count the costs of their work and their extravagance knew no bounds. The massive staircase, the Staircase of Honour, leading up to the royal chambers reserved for guests of honour is decorated with marble panels and 15th-century bas-reliefs. The palace's lavish embellishments are crowned by the statues of horses standing at the entrance to the banqueting hall. These, a present from Tsar Nicholas to Ferdinand II of Bourbon, were originally made of bronze. During the decades of Fascism, they were melted down to make cannons and replaced by plaster imitations.

The palace is crammed with huge gilded mirrors, vast tapestries, marble statues and pictures from the Neapolitan school of painting.

The history of the **San Carlo Theatre**, which is directly linked to Palazzo Reale by a corridor, is equally interesting. Italy's oldest and largest opera house – it can seat an audience of 3,000 – was commissioned by Charles of Bourbon and completed within just eight months. In the mid-18th century Naples was regarded as the capital of European music. Unlike in Rome, where the ecclesiastical authorities would not allow women to appear in public on stage, in Naples female singers were engaged and publicly acclaimed.

The official opening of the theatre was celebrated with a performance of the opera *Achilles in Sciro* on 4 November 1737. Charles was so flattered by the audience's calls of "Viva Carlos" that he felt obliged to bow his head several times in acceptance of his subjects' recognition. According to one source, His **San** Royal Majesty visited the theatre "to **Francesco** chat for half the performance and sleep **di Paola.**

the remainder – [which] must have been trying for the performers, since he reserved for himself the right of calling for encores." The theatre was an important social venue in 18th-century Naples and scandalous liaisons were formed in the comfort of its red velvet tiers.

There are several famous old cafés in front of the theatre where, at one time, the performances of customers rivalled those inside the theatre. Two of the most interesting are the **Caffé Europa** and the exclusive **Gambrinus**, an art nouveau café, which was a popular meeting place for artists and writers earlier this century.

The main entrance to the **Galleria Umberto I**, a glass-domed (185-ft/56 metre) arcade built in the late 19th century (restored in 1945), stands opposite the theatre. Somewhat run-down and reputedly an enclave for pickpockets and worse in the evenings, the *galleria* fails to create the grand impression intended by its architect.

Opposite the *galleria*, on Via Toledo,

is the tiny **Piazza Duca d'Aosta**, where you can catch a funicular to the Vomero, and just round the corner in Via Santa Brigida is the **church of Santa Brigida**, built in 1612 in honour of St Bridget of Sweden. St Bridget visited Naples in 1372 and was asked to use her influence to avert the plague rampaging through the city. Instead she vented her holy wrath upon what she found there, claiming the plague was due to pride, avarice and bestial sensuality. Two vices especially she denounced among the women, from the Queen downwards: the painting of their faces and the luxury of their dress.

Heading north: From there Via Toledo rises steadily northwards, passing the vast facade of the Banco di Napoli, to the site of the former barracks of the Spanish military garrisons and one of the most typically Neapolitan quarters of the city, **Pignasecca**, a name meaning dried pine tree, after an enormous pine which used to stand here.

Piazza della Carità has traditionally

Web of glass; roof of Galleria Umberto I.

served as a site for fruit and vegetable stalls, despite the fact that such trade was expressly forbidden by royal decree in 1802. A short distance to the northeast is the **church of Monte-oliveto** (or Sant'Anna dei Lombardi, as it is also called), containing a group of terracotta figures mourning the dead Christ by Guido Mazzoni, frescoes by Vasari and a wealth of Renaissance sculptures, all of which survived a bomb dropped directly on the church in 1944.

Some 150 yards (140 metres) further up Via Toledo, shortly after it crosses "Spaccanapoli", the other main artery of the old city, rises the **church of Spirito Santo**, whose interior is a fine example of the neoclassical style introduced under Charles of Bourbon and best exemplified in Naples by his official architect Luigi Vanvitelli, whom the king summoned from Rome.

In front of the church stands the **Palazzo d'Angri,** designed by Luigi and Carlo Vanvitelli and one time home of Giuseppe Garibaldi. It was from the balcony of this palace that Garibaldi proclaimed the annexation of the Kingdom of the Two Sicilies.

A little beyond Spirito Santo, a road running west of Via Toledo, Via Tarsia, leads to the **Cumana Station** (funicular to Montesanto) and the **church of Santa Maria di Montesanto**, where Alessandro Scarlatti is buried.

The splendour of Via Toledo begins to peter out at **Piazza Dante**, a circular piazza graced by a statue of the great poet. The original plan of the piazza's architect, Luigi Vanvitelli, was to build a Carolingian forum here in honour of Charles of Bourbon, but the project was never completed. North of here the buildings are a curious mixture of late Renaissance and baroque architecture, a trend which culminates in the Museo di Capodimonte at the very top of the hill, approximately 1 mile (2 km) further on, beyond the National Museum (*see page 189*).

It is worth taking a left turn just before the Museo di Capodimonte to visit the

Reading the news.

Catacombs of San Gennaro (entrance on Via Capodimonte). The tombs date from the 2nd century and are handsomely decorated with frescoes. It is here, at the spot marked by the church of San Gennaro, that the patron saint of Naples is buried. The Bishop of Beneventum, as he was then known, had come to Naples to lead resistance to persecution by Diocletian at the end of the 3rd century and had thus incurred the vengeance of the Governor Timotheus. The apparently indestructible bishop – he is supposed to have walked from a fiery furnace in Nola and been left unharmed when thrown to wild beasts in the amphitheatre at Pozzuoli – was finally beheaded by order of Timotheus. According to legend, on condemning Gennaro, the governor was struck blind but cured at the urgent prayer of the saint. Five thousand people are supposed to have converted at the miracle, but not, alas, Timotheus.

The **Museo di Capodimonte** was built on one of the last open spaces in the city, discovered by Charles of Bourbon on one of his many hunting expeditions. He immediately decided to build both a hunting lodge and a museum here, the first to satisfy his most passionate interest and the latter to house a large collection of art which he had inherited from his mother, Elizabeth Farnese, the last descendant in a long line of dukes and popes. In addition he had an extensive collection of valuable books and archaeological finds from Herculaneum also in need of a home.

The same court architect who had built the San Carlo Theatre in a record time of eight months was given the commission to build the Museo di Capodimonte. Such record-breaking speed could not be repeated here, however, for work was considerably delayed when an unexpectedly large number of tuff caves were discovered undergound. It was not until 1758 that the building was completed and part of the collection could be exhibited in the 12 rooms. The first visitors to the mu-

Market in
Piazza
Pignasecca.

seum included the German archaeologist and art historian, Johann Winckelmann, the Frenchman Fragonard and Goethe. The latter noted in his diaries that the exhibition seemed to be without a plan, but he nevertheless underlined its extraordinary value and importance.

Now, great attention has been paid to the presentation of the collection. The principal royal apartments on the first floor have been preserved and those rooms originally more modest (for example, the servants' quarters) have been adapted to provide a suitably spendid background for the art.

Among the many exhibits by Italian masters of the 16th and 17th century is one painting which, though a copy, has been the cause of heated argument among art historians: Marcello Venusti's copy of Michelangelo's fresco of *The Last Judgement*. Venusti's copy, which was finished shortly after the completion of the original fresco, provides conclusive proof that Michelangelo's original figures were nude. Their modest

covering was added to the fresco by another artist later.

Passion for porcelain: It was also King Charles who commissioned the building of a porcelain factory opposite the museum. He introduced to his court a number of porcelain makers from his father-in-law's factory in Meissen in honour of his wife, Maria Amalie Walburga of Saxony. The Capodimonte factory produced some notable work, including fine chinoiseries. However, when Charles III acceded to the Spanish throne, he had Naples' porcelain kilns destroyed and took the most important pieces of his collection with him. He continued his porcelain production in Buen Retiro in Spain.

His son and heir to the Neapolitan throne, Ferdinand IV, regenerated production in Naples in defiance of his father, by having a new porcelain factory build at Portici. But, in spite of some fine *biscuit* porcelain, the art failed to reach the same high standards. Ferdinand's removal of parts of the Farnese collection from Capodimonte to the archaeological museum, the National Museum, was also in defiance of his father, even though Capodimonte was in danger of collapsing and there was little else to be done.

Capodimonte Museum is well worth a visit. The exhibits provide an interesting cross-section of the Neapolitan school of painting of the 17th and 18th centuries as well as a representative collection of Tuscan and Flemish painting from the early Renaissance to the baroque period.

When satiated by Capodimonte's treasures, take time to enjoy the extensive park in which the museum is situated, landscaped by the German natural historian, Fredrik Denhardt. With its far-reaching views of Campania and Naples, it is an ideal place in which to relax from the noise and heat of the city, enjoy the shade of palms and the park's collection of exotic trees and contemplate the return journey, thankfully downhill, to the city centre.

Left, wedding belle. Right, painting by Marcello Venusti, Capodimonte Museum.

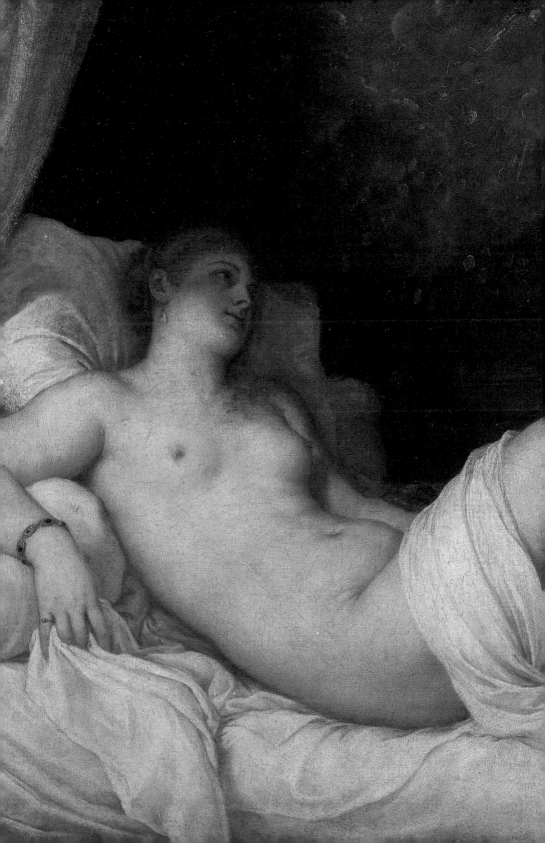

THE NATIONAL MUSEUM

When, in 1777, Ferdinand IV asked the Vatican for the immediate return of his Farnese collection of antiquities, it put a new strain on diplomatic relations between the Holy See and the Kingdom of the Two Sicilies. With the brand-new Real Museo, Ferdinand had, at long last, a suitable place for exhibiting the works which though borrowed (or in some cases stolen) by the Vatican the Neapolitan royal family believed belonged to them.

Others, however, considered the works of art to be part of the cultural heritage of the Vatican and were dismayed by their removal to Naples. Even Goethe expressed his displeasure; according to him, Rome was threatened with a great loss to its art history. Particularly contentious was the removal of the Farnese Heracles.

The Farnese collection: Before being exhibited in its entirety in Naples, the Farnese collection had been on a veritable odyssey through Italy. Charles III had inherited it from his mother, the noble Elizabeth Farnese of Parma, and had bequeathed it to his son, Ferdinand. The aristocratic Farnese family, to which Pope Paul III also belonged, was famous for its great love of art and archaeology, and had assembled a collection of antique and contemporary art unparalleled in Europe. It included, for example, the collection of sculptures found at the Caracalla thermal baths in 1547 – the Farnese bull, which is actually a group of four figures and animals and is the largest sculpture dating from antiquity; the Farnese Heracles, with his exaggerated muscularity; and the Farnese flora – as well as many paintings, in particular works by Titian.

For a long time part of the collection was housed in a palace on the Roman Palatine hill while another section was kept in Parma. Later additions to the collection were antique works of art uncovered during excavations in Pompeii and Herculaneum, which were at first inadequately housed in Villa Reale Vesuviana del Miglio d'Oro. These works include the beautiful bronze statues of dancing women known as *The Dancers of Herculaneum*, now numbering among the highlights of the National Museum.

When Ferdinand IV inherited the collection it was in such a chaotic state that a systematic reorganisation of the works became essential. Ferdinand requisitioned the old university building – formerly the Palazzo dei Regi Studi, an army barracks, which had been occupied by Naples University in 1599 – and commissioned the architect Ferdinando Fuga to convert it into the Royal Museum (its name until the unification of Italy). The Farnese library was the first part to be moved there, then the collection of paintings by 15th and 16th-century masters, and lastly the monumental antique statues from Rome and Herculaneum. In spite of

Preceding pages: painting by Tiziano Vecellio. Left, Farnese bull. Right, Athena.

occasional setbacks, Ferdinand's dream of establishing a "temple of wisdom and knowledge" was finally fulfilled in 1822, to official celebrations.

The Farnese collection is situated on the ground floor of the museum.(Also on the ground floor is the Egyptian collection, originally belonging to Count Borgia; it was acquired during the short period when Joachim Murat, a favourite of Napoleon, was on the Neapolitan throne.)

The Pompeii collection: In the period following acquisition of the Farnese collection, spectacular finds from Pompeii were added to the museum (they now occupy the mezzanine floor).The Romans were great collectors of art, particularly of Greek sculpture of the Hellenistic period, and Pompeii's wealthy patricians' houses contained some remarkably fine examples. They included *The Dancing Faun*, a lovely bronze sculpture which had originally adorned the grandiose entrance hall of the Casa del Fauno (named after the statue), a wealthy home in Pompeii, where it served as an indication of the pleasures within.

Dance and its attendant feelings of joy are embodied by the perfect figure of the young boy, whose arm and leg muscles are anatomically faultless. The faun was originally an ancient Roman deity of the woods and meadows and the protector of herds and agriculture. Later he became the Roman equivalent of the Greek god Pan and, like him, was portrayed with a goat's horns and hind legs. In art and literature he characterised uninhibited libido, expressing the exuberance of nature.

The same house in Pompeii was the source of many of the other masterpieces in the museum. The owner of this unique villa obviously favoured Greek mosaic art. One of the mosaics, *The Battle of Issus*, depicts one of Alexander the Great's legendary battles in his conquest of Persia. It shows Alexander as young and fearless before an army of terrified Persians. This masterpiece is **Bronze figures.**

thought to have been executed in a Sicilian workshop and installed in the villa towards the end of the 2nd century BC. It is a copy of a monumental Greek fresco painted, probably by Philoxenos, between 331 and 310 BC. At this time Greek decorative art had reached its peak as far as the use of colour was concerned. Unfortunately nothing is known about the artist who was responsible for this mosaic, but there is no doubt that he must have been familiar with Alexandrian culture.

Art historians believe that the person who commissioned the original fresco was an illustrious member of the Macedonian court. Both the original and the mosaic concentrate on a key scene in the battle between Alexander the Great and the Persian king Darius III. The main subject is not so much the battle itself but the conflict which arises between two contrasting worlds and their different traditions and cultures. The two commanders are depicted as the highest representatives of these worlds and

their differences are marked. Whereas Alexander is portrayed in the dress of a simple soldier without a helmet and armed only with a lance, Darius goes into action wearing splendid, flowing oriental robes. This contrast is also expressed in the men's behaviour; the mosaicist portrayed the human characteristics of the protagonists in exact detail.

Casa del Fauno was also the source of the frequently copied mosaic of a dog bearing the inscription *cave canem*, a warning to beware of the dog. Equally well known are the blue-coloured glass vase, the oil lamp made of pure gold and the so-called "Venus in bikini".

Some of the finest mosaics portray entertainment in ancient Pompeii. One, from the House of Cicero, shows two women, a man and a dwarf, masked and playing musical instruments. Other mosaics depict threatre masks. Also well represented are scene of wildlife. One particularly fine example depicts more than 20 species of marine life,

Detail from the Battle of Issus.

including a realistic looking octopus.

The first floor of the museum is dedicated to visiting exhibitions and finds from Pompeii and Herculaneum, particularly the Villa dei Papiri (excavated 1750–61) in Herculaneum. Highlights include the graceful *Young Satyr*, the light-hearted *Drunken Silenus*, a lamp holder from the House of the Marbles in Pompeii, and the elegant *Portrait of a Girl* (also known as *Meditation*), depicting a girl with a stylus raised to her mouth and a writing tablet in her hand.

Every detail of domestic life in Pompeii and Herculaneum, down to the food that was eaten, the soap that was used and the rope-sandals that were worn, has been meticulously documented. Particularly fascinating are the writing materials, musical and architectural instruments, weights and measures and surgical instruments.

Gallery of pornography: Under no circumstances should visitors miss the chance to see the many examples of Italian and Campanian fresco paintings.

These come mainly from Pompeii, Herculaneum and Stabiae and they are mainly depictions of mythological allegories, still-lifes of flowers and erotic scenes. The latter were found decorating the walls of brothels in Pompeii, their purpose being to stimulate the sexual appetites of the clients.

In line with the prevailing moral standards of his time, Francis I, the Duke of Calabria, criticised this display of erotic art and had them removed from the eye of the general public and placed in a special room. According to the duke, these frescoes were obscene and only "persons of mature age and reliable morals" should have access to them. In fact, in 1852, under the orders of Ferdinand II, this "gallery of obscene objects" consisting of over 100 exhibits was actually walled in. The aim of this drastic measure was, according to the director of the museum at that time, Sangiorgio Spinelli, "to wipe out all memories" of the collection.

John Stuart Mill, visiting Naples at the time of this censorship said: "The precious King has shut up the Venus Callipyge and the other Venuses on pretext of public decency. If these things are done in Italy what shall we come to next?" (Ferdinand's consideration for the morals of his subjects extended to ensuring that ballerinas in the theatre covered their nudity with tights of a colour unlikely to excite improper lasciviousness.)

It was not until 1860, when Garibaldi, who was for a time the self-proclaimed Dictator of Naples, had the frescoes brought out of their hiding place and catalogued, that the collection was properly exhibited. There is a plaque in memory of this bold action.

In 1931, during the Fascist dictatorship, the collection was again put under lock and key, for the same reasons as before, and it wasn't until 1972 that it was exhibited in its entirety. However, even today this fascinating collection is still not on general display and interested visitors must ask to be admitted.

Left, exhibit from Casa dei Veitti, Pompeii. **Right**, classic profile.

POSILLIPO

It is difficult to imagine that Posillipo was once considered to be a corner of paradise. These days first impressions are invariably spoiled by the long line noisy cars emitting smelly exhaust fumes as they edge slowly from the Riviera di Chiaia to Mergellina. The landscape which was once so admired is now crowded by unattractive Swiss-style chalets.

However, this was once an idyllic rural landscape and many people found peace and quiet here. The original Greek name for this area was Pausil-ypon, which roughly translates as "the soothing of pain". Nowadays, it is thought that Posillipo was the original location of the philosophical school of Epicureans, whose principle was the pursuit of pleasure. Their mentor Syron is said to have lived in a smart residence on the slopes of the foothills, a *villula*, which he bequeathed to his poetry student Virgil.

Enclave of privilege: There has been all manner of speculation as to the origins of the exclusive character of this area. What is known for certain is that the luxurious residences built here were part of the Phlegraean district rather than a suburb of Graeco-Roman Neapolis. The landscape here has two faces: away from the sea it is gently rural; while its coastline has been battered into steep, rugged cliffs.

There are many pointers to the original exclusivity of Posillipo, including the records of that time. One of the things they mention is that voracious moray eels – popular sustenance at banquets – were fattened on human flesh here. There were also a number of grandiose buildings in the area which were linked to the imperial court. One of its most famous villas was the one belonging to Vedio Polliones, infamous for its orgies and mentioned by Pliny in his *Naturalis Historia* (though by then it

belonged to the emperor Augustus). Further proof of privilege is the crypt built in the **Grotta di Seiano** which burrows into the foothills between Posillipo and the Phlegraean Fields and provides direct access to **Baia di Trentaremi**.

All that remains of the splendid Roman settlement, today marked by **Parco Virgiliano** (next to Piazza Sannazzaro), is the amphitheatre and its grotto. Unfortunately, because of repeated incidents of serious crime, the entrance to the grotto has now been walled up. Virgil is supposed to be buried here.

The best way to approach this area is from the Riviera di Chiaia where the rugged cliffs set against the gentle wooded slopes of the foothills can be seen to dramatic effect. In the 18th century the seashore bordered the front gardens of the aristocratic mansions as far as Mergellina. It was at this time that the promenade, where the Bourbon king was in the habit of taking walks,

Preceding pages: the promenade, Mergellina. Left, beaches too. Right, former grandeur, Mergellina.

was adorned with gardens and fountains and the famous *Farnese bull*, which is now displayed in the National Museum, was exhibited in the **Villa Comunale,** the elongated park running between the Riviera di Chiaia and Via Francesco Caracciolo on the seafront. It was here that, as a small child, the librettist W. S. Gilbert was kidnapped by bandits and ransomed, an incident which Gilbert later used in the *The Gondoliers*.

Also located in the Villa Comunale is the Aquarium, built by the German natural historian Anton Dohrn in the 19th century.

As in Roman times, in the 18th and 19th centuries rows of splendid mansions were built hereabouts, including the **Villa Pignatelli**, on the northern side of Riviera di Chiaia. The villa's history is closely associated with Sir Ferdinand Acton, an English baron, and is is furnished with antiques and works of art reflecting the English taste of that time. The villa became famous as a den of debauchery for Europe's aristocratic

circles. These days it enjoys a much quieter life as a museum for old horse-drawn coaches and a venue for cultural events.

Fish first: Mergellina, a bustling fishing community and the terminus for hydrofoils to the offshore islands, hidden among a jumble of boats and wicker beach chairs, was once an outpost of Posillipo. It remains a place worth visiting, if only for its excellent restaurants. Fish is still the speciality; the delicious *antipasto ai frutti di mare* and a fish soup particular to the region are highly recommended.

The Ciro, the Salvatore and the Giuseppone restaurants, whose fine cooking is much praised beyond Naples, are among the best.

At one time, or so it is said, Merg–ellina offered more than mouth-watering cuisine. Sexual appetites were also catered for in a number of bawdy, some secret, brothels.

Further along the coast is **Palazzo Donn'Anna**, built in 1642 as an enclave

Beside the seaside.

for latter-day epicureans. The Spanish viceroy built the palace, reminiscent of Venetian palaces on the Grand Canal, to show his gratitude to his lover Anna Carafa. On its completion – somewhat delayed, because the viceroy did not have enough money to complete the building, even though the Spanish monarch had agreed to act as guarantor for a loan of 150,000 escudos – the palace became a popular hideaway for clandestine lovers.

Among those who used the palace for amorous purposes were Joanna I of Aragon and Emma Lyon, better known as Lady Hamilton, who conducted episodes of her affair with Lord Horatio Nelson here. Richard Wagner stayed not far away, in the villa belonging to Princess Doria d'Angri, during his visit to Naples. It was here that he completed the last scenes of *Parsifal*. Other illustrious personalities visiting Naples were also in the habit of staying in Posillipo, whether aristocrats, industrial magnates or famous freedom-fighters. The street names give a clue to the large number of Anglo-Saxon visitors that decided to settle in the area.

The name of the Earl of Rosebury, Sir Archibald Philip Primrose, is closely associated with the art school in Posillipo, **Scuola di Posillipo**. The school achieved a high reputation, and helped make Posillipo and its surroundings world-famous.

The School's first painter of note was Gaspar van Wittel, father of the Neapolitan architect Vanvitelli who romanised his Dutch name. Others associated with the School were the German court painters Jakob Philip Hackert and Angelika Kaufmann, the director of the Bourbon Academy Wilhelm Tischbein and Kristopher Kneip.

They all contributed to the reputation of the Scuola di Posillipo as the epitome of European romantic landscape painting. The full development of the Posillipo School can be traced in the National Gallery of Naples (Capodimonte).

Community spirit.

VOMERO AND SAN MARTINO

Until the early decades of the 20th century Vomero was a rural idyll, a retreat for the aristocracy. After World War II, however, it became the receptacle for the affluent classes moving out of Naples' congested centre and was subject to extensive development programmes. The uncontrolled building ensured that little evidence of its past survived. Excluding the huge Carthusian Certosa di San Martino (Monastery of St Martin), the baroque neoclassical Villa Floridiana, and some relics from the art nouveau period the overwhelming impression of the district is of a thoroughly modern cityscape.

To see the few extant remains of ancient Vomero the best bet is to make a short detour to **Castel Sant'Elmo**. Here, in Via Antiniana, there is a branch of the Antignano settlement. In Gracco-Roman times this was the only link with the Phlegraean Fields. What used to be the centre of this antique settlement is now the site of a lively market where locals come to buy produce.

Undisturbed by the passage of time, the market enjoys a bustle reminiscent of Naples centuries ago. There is even some similarity between the items on offer here and the exhibits in the showcases of the Museo della Floridiana. The huge terracotta pots from which olives are sold are almost identical to the ones which are on display in the museum.

The park belonging to the **Museo della Floridiana** is rightly considered a botanical masterpiece. It occupies a spur commanding fine views over the sea. The man responsible for its landscaping was Fredrik Denhardt, the German director of the Real Orto Botanico, who was also in charge of the royal park of Capodimonte. Denhardt successfully exploited the natural amphitheatre of the site. Between the hedges and the rockeries lies the Bourbon villa. This

"baroque chocolate box with neoclassical touches", as it has been described, is an architectural masterpiece; the Bay of Naples in the background makes an ideal frame.

The villa was originally a wedding present from King Ferdinand I of the Two Sicilies (otherwise known as Ferdinand IV) to his second wife, Lucia Migliacco, the Duchess of Floridia. The king was not able to marry Lucia, who had been his long-term mistress, until after the death of his first wife, Maria Caroline of Habsburg, the daughter of the Austrian empress Maria Theresa. The wedding ceremony of this unusually late marriage was a small affair, attended by a select circle of friends in the relative seclusion of Sicily. (Ferdinand I and his court were forced to flee to Sicily after the failure of his attempted military attack on the Republic of Rome, which had been occupied by revolutionary French troops.)

Even during his lifetime it was well known throughout the city that the

Preceding pages: Castel Sant'Elmo. **Left**, Certosa di San Martino. **Right**, bronze statues inside Castel Sant'Elmo.

Bourbon monarch preferred the company of the Duchess of Floridiana to that of his Habsburg wife. Even before the death of Maria Caroline, he showered Lucia with expensive presents, including the Palazzo Coscia in the Piazza dei Martiri. A little later she exchanged this palace for the more secluded summer residence in the hills of Vomero, designed by the neoclassical architect Antonio Niccolini.

Lady Blessington, a British neighbour of the duchess, described the elegance of Villa Floridiana's bathroom in her book *The Idler in Italy*: "It is a small chamber, cased with white marble, and the bath occupies nearly the whole of it, leaving only a space sufficiently large for ottomans, formed of the same material, to be ranged around the room. A flight of marble steps, at each end, descends to the bath; whose dimensions would admit not only of bathing, but of swimming."

She goes on to describe the exquisite dressing-rooms, saying: "They look as if designed for some youthful lover, whose mind was imbued with the luxuriant and poetical fancies of Eastern climes; instead of the person for whom this fairy palace was created, who is a grandmother, and the lover who formed it, who is an octogenarian."

Nowadays the former summer residence is a museum housing a valuable collection of porcelain, pottery, ivory and china as well as a small group of Neapolitan paintings. Its most famous exhibit is a black Chinese vase. The only other pieces in Europe which are comparable are in the Victoria and Albert Museum in London. Other pieces of interest in the museum are the white porcelain *Pietà* made by the master of the craft, Gricci, and the *Oca* table service, which Ferdinand had specially made for his palace in Caserta.

The baroque found expression in many buildings in Vomero but two of its finest vehicles are the **Villa Belvedere** and the **Villa Patrizi**, made more delightful by the Mergellina panorama in **Vomero**.

the background. They prepare visitors for the **Belforte di Sant'Elmo** and the extravagant grandeur of the neighbouring Carthusian monastery. The castle stands on one of Naples' most beautiful hills. The Neapolitans owe the building, or rather rebuilding, of the castle to a whim of Robert of Anjou, the ruling king at that time, who liked to the magnificent view of the Bay of Naples from this spot. The Carthusian Monastery of St Martin was bequeathed to Carthusian monks by the son of Charles V.

According to records, it was on a beautiful day in the late summer of 1328 that the French monarch made the decision to turn his place of pleasant reflection into the site for his summer residence. It was his firm intention to have the *palatium in summitate montanae Sancti Erasmi* completed in the shortest possible time and with as little expense as possible. The building contract given to the curia of the royal province confirms that his strict orders were that not more than 1,000 ounces of gold should be spent on the building. However, the original plan was soon dropped when it struck Robert that the site would make an exellent place for a fortress. The rebuilding was organised by Tino da Camaino, an architect of the Sienese school, the same architect who, one year before, had designed the Monastery of St Martin.

The Norman influence on the fortress is unmistakable, not only in the elegant ground plan but also in the two square towers. In the summer the Aragonese used the fortress to hold extravagant banquets and parties, but it was for purposes of defence that the Spanish viceroy Don Pedro of Toledo had the fortress altered again. A new hexagonal ground plan and the addition of an earthwork made it almost impregnable.

Unfortunately, however, the castle's demise came from within: in 1587 an explosion in the powder magazine all but detroyed it. Later, after it had been completely rebuilt, the fortress was used as a dungeon. and many of those

Upmarket shops.

who took part in the Neapolitan revolution in 1799 were imprisoned and tortured here. Referring to the Austro-Hungarian plots and schemes of Queen Maria Caroline, the revolutionary leader Luigi Settembrini called the Castel Sant'Elmo a "castle of intrigues". Today, a large variety of cultural events take place within its walls. The fortress is easily reached from the city centre by the three funicular railways running to the top of the hill.

Grand finale: The *finale vomerse* of this excursion is without doubt the Carthusian **Certosa di San Martino** (Monastery of St Martin), which enjoys one of the loveliest views in the whole of Naples. The original monastery is somewhat older than the fortress and dates from 1325. Like the fortress it underwent considerable alterations under the Spanish viceroy Don Pedro. However, most of what you can see today dates from the 17th century and is the work of the architect and sculptor Cosimo Fanzago, who was commis-

sioned with the work by Severo Turboli, the prior at that time.

The baroque style is still predominant. It can be recognised in the marble ornamentation and the stucco work, in the sculptures by Bernini, Naccherino, Celebrano and Sanmartino, and in the emphatically religious paintings of the 17th-century Neapolitan school, in particular the work of Luca Giordano, Mattia Preti, Mícco Spadaro and José Ribera (known as *Spagnoletto*).

Visiting the monastery building is like taking a journey into a series of different architectural epochs. There is, for example, the huge **church** with its richly decorated chapels, the monks' chancel, the chapter and the sacristy with its inlaid walnut furnishings. Numerous paintings and other art objects known to have been here at the beginning of the 19th century were moved or disappeared in the prevailing confusion of later years, for example when plans were made to convert the monastery into a state psychiatric clinic.

The wealth of artefacts and paintings once housed in the **Museo di San Martino** suffered a similar fate to those in the church. Art historians have often expressed their astonishment at the poor range of exhibits left in the museum's 90 or so rooms – a few royal table services, some rock from Vesuvius, a Bourbon military uniform, a collection of ivory and precious stones. The main attraction of the museum is the *presepe napoletano*, a crib dating from the 18th century. Its hundreds of terracotta figures were made by the best Neapolitan sculptors of the 18th and 19th centuries.

Visitors to the museum are inevitably drawn to the Chiostro Grande, with its grey and white marble ornamentation. Although its design was conceived by Antonio Dosio in the 16th century, its present form is the work of Cosimo Fanzago in the 17th century.

The panorama from the top of the hill is breathtakingly expansive. But from here, alas, the urban decay afflicting the former royal city is all too visible.

Left, local lady. **Right**, *presepe* in the Museo di San Martino.

The region of Campania, like Naples, was born to soothe and disturb. Outside the sick heart of Naples stretches an astonishing array of archaeological sites, from the Phlegraean Fields, inspiration for Virgil's *Aeneid*, to Pompeii and Paestum.

Vesuvius, Goethe's "peak of hell rising out of paradise", is where the anguish began, embalming Herculaneum and Pompeii in ash for posterity. Neapolitans continue to appease the monster by chanting its pet name of *la buonanima*, "the good soul". Herculaneum has been a ghost town since the monster's wrath but retains its Neapolitan power to shock, from the figurine of the inebriated pissing satyr to the phallic symbols used then, as now, to ward off the evil eye.

Pompeii is the most vivid portrayal of life in classical times, from the sensuality of a wedding scene to the ruts of wagon wheels. Only the 2,000 years of graffiti recalls Naples; and the notice informing visitors that "the ancient environment is ruined beyond all measure of safetyness" (*sic*). Paestum, the Greek sacred city, was named after Poseideon but rechristened by the Romans. Set against austere mountains, the Doric temples are surrounded by violets and wild herbs, much as they were long ago. The Temple of Neptune is an atmospheric farewell to the ancient Greeks.

Yet Campania is a hymn to the living as well as a prayer for the dead. In Naples' heavenly islands, Capri, Ischia and Procida, there is no place for nostalgia. Capri, celebrated by poets and painters alike, has cornered a sophisticated clientele while Ischia has a monopoly on health. Procida is a country cousin, as yet uninvited.

Geologically, the islands have different origins. Strabo, the early Greek geographer, records that the eruption of a volcano on Ischia triggered an earthquake which caused Ischia and Procida to splinter from the Phlegraean Fields and then to split asunder. The same cataclysm may also have led to the severing of Capri from the Sorrentine coast. If so, the result is the haunting beauty the islands share with the Amalfi Coast.

Preceding pages: the Amalfi Coast; into the volcano; Positano. **Left**, ravishing Ravello.

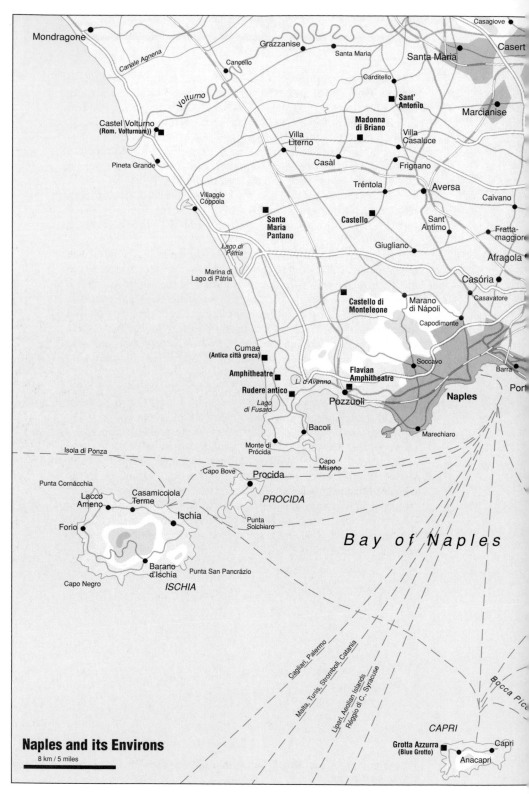

Naples and its Environs

8 km / 5 miles

216

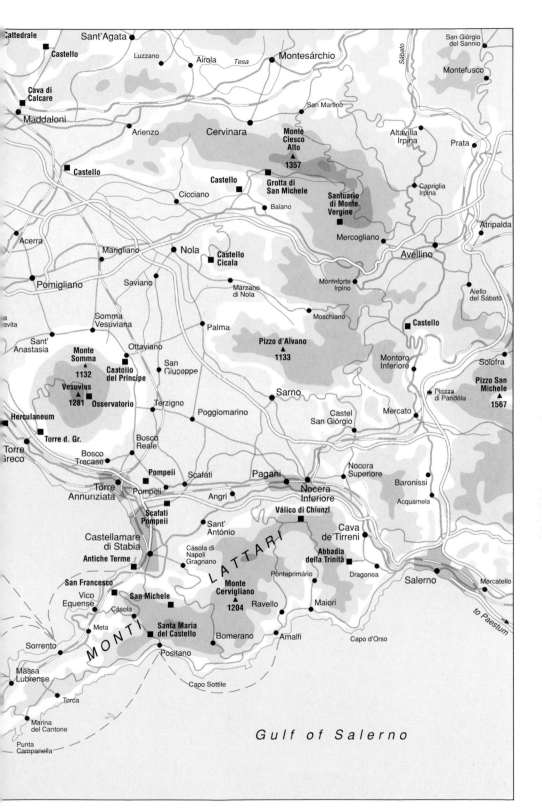

THE PHLEGRAEAN FIELDS

Campania has no shortage of mythical sites. Above all, the Phlegraean Fields, stretching from Agnano to Cumae, an area which evokes the poetry of Homer's *Odyssey* and Virgil's *Aeneid*. Pilgrims of the classical come here to experience the context of these ancient masterpieces.

The Phlegraean Fields can be reached via the districts of Fuorigrotta and Agnano (the smell of sulphur signals the geological structure of the area).

According to legend, in 1538, a mountain suddenly appeared here to stem a lava flow that had been running non-stop for two days. The farmers of Tripergoli, a village in the flow's path, prayed to the Phlegraean patron saint, St Proculus, to perform a miracle which would protect them from the volcano. They spent a whole day making offerings, but no sign came from heaven, and in desperation one of the village women turned for help to San Gennaro, the patron saint of Naples. Her cry was apparently heard, the mountain appeared and the village was saved.

The extinguished crater of the Agnano volcano is nowadays home to a modern racecourse and thermal baths fitted with all the latest facilities. The ancient Roman steam baths can still be seen; although they may look rather primitive compared with the modern complex, they were extremely efficient, exploiting the natural heat of the underground volcanic activity.

The burning fields: When the Euboeans, the first colonists of Magna Graecia (Great Greece), founded the oldest Greek settlement at Cumae in the 8th century BC, the area must have had a surreal, primeval countenance. The gigantic volcanic crater full of will-o'-the-wisps and tongues of fire must have seemed doubly threatening when reflected in the sea. At that time the volcano would have been extremely volatile, erupting suddenly and unexpectedly out of chasms in the slopes of the hills or from the many ravines between them along the coast.

For the people of the ancient world, the Bay of Naples, with its 19 volcanic craters in an area of around 25 sq. miles (64 sq. km), had such a sinister atmosphere that it was imagined to be the gateway to the land of the dead, the entrance to the underworld. The Latin poet Virgil (70 BC–AD 19) spent the last days of his life in Naples and found inspiration for his epic *Aeneid* here. Virgil believed that he had located the entrance to Hades in an underground passage near the Lago di Averna.

More than 1,000 years later a large elliptical crater from the Solfatara in Pozzuoli inspired Tuscan poet Dante Alighieri. The *inferno*, the hell of his *Divina Commedia* (which was written in vulgar Italian and thereby marked the beginning of the Italian language and literature) took its inspiration from this area around Naples.

Left, wreathed in steam. Right, Baia.

Despite such sinister associations, in the 1st century AD there was hardly another place in the Roman Empire which was so famous or so highly praised as the Campi Flegrei, the Phlegraean or "burning" Fields. Its "des res" villas, extensive complex of thermal baths and magnificent houses were considered to be the last word in luxury and splendour in ancient Rome. The leading members of Rome's literati, including Horace, Virgil, Suetonius, Ovid and Cicero, were among the Campi Flegrei's regular visitors.

Steaming pleasures: Now that this area has calmed down geologically, visitors can appreciate the unique natural attractions of the area in relative safety and great comfort. The sulphur vapours have been harnessed to the very latest in thermal technology; visitors can alleviate physical afflictions and enjoy excellent food and wine in the heart of ancient civilisation.

That said, like Vesuvius, the whole area of the Phlegraean Fields is under constant watch by scientists from the Centro Nazionale per le Ricerche (CNR) and by the Gruppo Nazionale Per La Vulcanologia (GNV). One phenomenon which has given the scientists cause for concern, especially in Pozzuoli, is known as Bradisism. This involves rises and then subsequent falls in the land level as a result of volcanic activity. Between 1982 and 1984 the increase was nearly 7 ft (2 metres). Part of the old city in Pozzuoli had to be evacuated as a precaution, and over 30,000 people were forced to move out against their will. This Bradisism is thought to have been responsible for the serious earthquake in November 1980 which left many homeless.

Dante's **Solfatara Crater** is situated on the way to **Pozzuoli,** whch confirms just how appropriate the ancient name Campi Flegrei was. Here it is still possible to recognise the *forum vulcani*, the description given to this area by the Greek geographer Strabo 2,000 years ago. Here, lava mud still bubbles up

Terme di Baia.

through innumerable small craters and sulphur vapours steam from holes in the earth's crust. Intrepid campers, unlikely to be bothered by the pervasive smell of sulphurous gases, can pitch their tents in one of the special camping sites located next to the crater.

Pozzuoli established Neapolitan domination of maritime trade in the Roman Empire. Nothing much is left from before this time, neither from the simple Greek settlements nor from the later Samnite settlements. Benefiting from an extensive area of thermal springs, it became one of the most famous and popular places in the Empire – in spite of its then being called *Puteoli* (the stench).

As well as boasting splendid villas, Puteoli had two amphitheatres where gladiatorial contests were regularly held. Only a few fragments remain of the first of these amphitheatres (dating from the Augustan era), but the **Anifeteatro Flavio** is fairly well-preserved. It was built in three large semi-circles and could hold up to 20,000 spectators; only the Colosseum in Rome and the amphitheatre at Capua were larger. During the summer months today the arena is used for open-air theatrical performances – though not, of course, of a gladiatorial nature.

The architecture at the harbour is no less splendid than that in the centre of Pozzuoli. As well as the gigantic supporting piers there are the pillars of what is now known to have been the market place, the erroneously named **Tempiodi Serapide** (the Temple of Serapia), half-submerged in the sea. These remains bear witness to the original size of the buildings. The **Macellum**, however, was almost certainly a sacred building; the Phlegraean example is much better preserved than the building at Pompeii.

The four pillars, which border on the large **Apsidiale cella**, are especially impressive. Beside these pillars are the most luxurious toilet facilities of the ancient world; the benches were made

Pozzuoli.

of marble and washing facilities were provided. The rectangular ground plan of the Macellum is similar to that of an oriental bazaar. The shops could be reached either by way of a gallery from outside or a colonnade inside. In the centre there was a circular pergola, still recognisable when the tide is out.

On crossing the old Via Consula the outline of the first Phlegraean lake comes into view. This lake was jokingly named after the Latin word for gain, *lucrum*, and is where Sergius Orata cultivated oysters and molluscs. Cicero lived on the shores of this lake in his Villa Academia.

The most magnificent view of the **Baia** and the anchorage where Odysseus moored in order to take part in the Baius funeral ceremonies can be gained from the top of the surrounding foothills. This is where the villas of many prominent Romans stood. Crassus and Caesar, Pompey and Hortensius, the consul Cornelius and the historian Livy, who tried to cure his arthritis with Cumaean water, all had houses here. The area is steeped in a rich mixture of legend and history: the thermal baths of Diana, Mercury and Venus were here; the Caesars had palaces built on its best viewpoints; and Emperor Nero had his mother Agrippina murdered and buried in the area. Nero's dungeons were also here; they consisted of a complex system of water wells.

These wells were originally the private water reserves of Hirrius's famous fish farm, which supplied the neighbourhood's sumptuous banquets with, among other things, 6,000 moray eels. A visit to the villa of the famous Roman gourmet Lucullus near Misenum gives a good idea of the extravagant lifestyle of that time. Lucullus, famous for his extreme wealth, paid 2½ million sestertia for his villa.

The fact that a large part of the Roman fleet spent the winter anchored in the double harbour of Misenum emphasises the strategic importance of this area for the Roman Empire. Originally water was supplied to the fleet from a well in the **Grotta della Dragonara**. Later the water came from the Piscina Mirabile, which was supplied with 12,000 cubic metres of water from the aqueduct, which in turn got its water from the Serino River. The aqueduct is well preserved and considered to be a masterpiece of hydraulic engineering.

Cumae, one of the marvels of Hellenistic culture, can be reached from Misenum by Via Domitiana. It was the northernmost outpost of the Magna Graecia, and successfully defended its supremacy against Etruscan invasions on several occasions. Its pre-eminence lasted until the Samnite invasion of Campania. It was in Cumae, which was rediscovered by Homer and Virgil and praised in their poetry, that two important tenets of religious faith began to take shape: the belief in the oracle and the belief in a life after death.

Antor della Sibilia played an important role in this development. This is a long gallery dedicated to the Cumaean sibyl who guided Aeneas through the underworld. It was excavated at the foot of the Cumae rocks and corresponds to the descriptions handed down by authors of that time. It is a long trapeziform *dromos*, a gallery of perfect Mycenean proportions built into a huge tuff rock and stretching for 426 ft (130 metres). It receives light from six side tunnels. At the end of the gallery the marks can still be seen where the *oikos* was closed off. Only the sibyl had access to this room; it was here that she made her prophecies.

Equally impressive is the view of the temple which stands on the **Cumae Acropolis**. This temple was dedicated to the cult of Jupiter and Apollo. The nearby **Lake Averno** is a ghostly place which birds are said to avoid.

The view of the lake takes us back to Acheron, one of the rivers in Hades over which the souls of the dead were ferried by Charon. Homer and Virgil both described the lake as the gateway to Hades in their epics.

Cumae.

VESUVIUS, HERCULANEUM AND POMPEII

The recommended way to ascend **Vesuvius** is up the asphalt road leading through the pine grove of **Torre del Greco** to the **Vesuvius Observatory**. From here the rest of the journey has to be made on foot as there is only a narrow footpath of lava scree leading up to the top. The effort is certainly worth it: those who make it to the crater of the now dormant volcano are rewarded by a spectacular panorama.

Weather permitting, the complete Gulf of Naples can be seen from here. The view stretches from Pozzuoli and the Phlegraean Fields, across the Sorrento peninsula and the islands of Ischia and Capri and, of course, over Naples itself.

At present Vesuvius, the most famous volcano in the world, lies dormant. Like a seriously ill patient who could fall victim to a terrible fever at any time, and whose temperature must therefore be measured on a daily basis, it has been under the auspices of the *Osservatorio Vesuviano* continuously since 1845. From this station, built at a height of around 1,970 ft (600 metres) on the Colle dei Canteroni, every change in the land or in the temperature and composition of the gases is recorded and analysed.

Consequently more data has been collected about Vesuvius than any other volcano and much of our knowledge about volcanic activity is based on it. Whilst we know that it has been active for at least 300,000 years, its geological history can only be reconstructed with any degree of certainty for the last 25,000 years. Today the skyline of the east side of the Gulf is dominated by a volcanic peak, which lies on top of a much older one, the Monte Somma. The peak's silhouette has a picture-book, conical shape, due to the fact that the main crater has remained virtually unchanged over the centuries and eruptions have smoothed out rough edges.

The oldest of the craters was formed at least 250,000 years ago. Since then it has been active irregularly but with the most devastating consequences. The violent eruption which first made Vesuvius famous took place in 79 BC, when the lava buried the flourishing Roman cities of Pompeii, Herculaneum and Stabiae under ashes. Pliny the Younger described the scene in his letters to Tacitus, and scientists have used these descriptions to reconstruct the various phases of the eruption.

The first explosion, which blew open the crater, created an enormous cloud of smoke, dust and pumice stone. The cause of the explosion was the pent-up gases produced by the magma. Pliny recorded that the lava and debris hurled out of the volcano, to a height of some 49,000 ft (15,000 metres) into the air, was shaped like a pine tree. On reaching Pompeii, the hot, gas-releasing pumice stone and ashes caused the immediate

suffocation of most of the city's population. The subsequent explosions buried the city under a layer of ash some 19–30 ft (6–9 metres) thick.

In Herculaneum, next to modern-day Ercolano, the eruption had quite different consequences. Although the city was much nearer to the volcano than Pompeii, favourable wind conditions meant that it escaped the deadly gases. However, heavy rainfall (which every volcanic eruption brings in its wake) cooled the ashes on the slopes of the Somma and turned them into an enormous avalanche of mud, which proceeded to bury Herculaneum. The volcanic tuff reached a height of some 65 ft (20 metres).

The most recent eruption of Vesuvius occurred in March 1944. For many days vast carpets of glowing lava unfurled down the slopes, reaching the villages of San Sebastiano and Massa and taking the cable railway celebrated in Neapolitan songs with it. The disaster, an infernal combination of earthquakes and explosions, reached apocalyptic proportions. It finally came to rest when the crater swallowed up the cone.

Since then Vesuvius has been dormant, but it is a fitful sleep. The vulcanologists pay particular attention to the seismic movements and changes in the electromagnetic fields. On the basis of annual measurements, they have established that the main crater is continually cooling down. This may appear to be good news, but in the opinion of the experts it is actually a cause for concern. Although the danger of a new eruption is getting increasingly smaller, the danger of an earthquake rises as the magma seeks another way of escaping to the surface.

But nothing is certain; all that exists are predictions and estimates. Nobody can say with absolute conviction that the volcano won't erupt in exactly the same manner. The extent of the magma which has accumulated since the last eruption in March 1944 is estimated to be around 50–100 million cubic metres.

Vesuvius from Castel Sant'Elmo.

In the event of an eruption the plug would blow open like the cork in a bottle of champagne. "We have to be prepared for this possibility," says Giuseppe Luongo, the head of the Osservatorio Vesuviano. If it does erupt, lava will stream down the mountain at speeds of up to 60 mph (100 kph), and the ash and vapours will reach a temperature of some 300°C (572°F).

HERCULANEUM: The descent down the lava slopes of Vesuvius, somewhat spoilt by the concrete blocks of the suburbs, leads to the site of the once prosperous town of **Herculaneum**.

In contrast to Pompeii, Herculaneum was a small town inhabited largely by farmers and craftsmen before it was swallowed up by the all-consuming lava mud. The houses here do not have the elegance or extravagant grandeur of the houses in Pompeii. The ancient town was excavated by an Austrian, the Marquis d'Elbocuf, in 1709. His servant came across the town petrified in tuff stone while he was sinking a well.

As well as the many houses, the excavators found a wealth of tools and materials used in everyday life, such as fabrics, ship's rigging and timber. What's more, unlike in Pompeii, such items did not immediately crumble on being subjected to light and air, for the mud acted as a natural preservative.

According to the conclusions of one of Italy's most celebrated archaeologists, Amedeo Maiuri, who led the excavations in Herculaneum from 1927, the majority of Herculaneum's inhabitants must have had time to flee from the disaster, unlike in Pompeii. Maiuri wrote: "The houses were left behind with all their contents in order that citizens could reach safety as quickly as possible by fleeing to Naples or to the beach. We return there after nearly 2,000 years with all our painful experience of survival with the wish to pick up the thread of antique life."

Since Maiuri's time, however, doubts have arisen about this version of events. Such doubts are mainly based on the

Herculaneum.

depiction of the catastrophe by Pliny, who wrote: "The rain of ashes was beginning to fall onto the ships, and it became hotter and denser the nearer one came to it. With the ash fell pumice stone and pebbles which had been calcified and split by the fire. The sea, which had drawn back, was no longer deep enough, the rubble which was raining down from the mountain made the shore impossible to walk on."

It was on this very beach that, eight years ago, the first horrifying evidence was found of a thwarted mass exodus from Herculaneum. Under the arch of the fortress on the outskirts of the town were found tangled groups of human corpses, people who, in desperation, had been trying to escape certain death. It was like a bas-relief, dreadful in its realism and reminiscent of Picasso's *Guernica*. The last moments of terror in Herculaneum, the gestures of despair, have been preserved in a state of petrification in the lava: the agony of the soldier with his dagger and purse, the Roman lady richly decked with jewellery, the old man with his fur hat, the baby whose mother was trying to protect it, the frightened horse and the shipwrecked sailors beside their capsized vessel.

Art thieves: The town plan of Herculaneum is like a version of the Hellenistic Neapolis, but on a much more modest scale. The humble and the grand stand side by side. Most astonishing is the excellent condition of the furniture and wooden tools and the intact upper floors of many of the houses. In contrast to the houses in Pompeii, where the roofs collapsed under the weight of the hailstorm of ash and pumice stone, these homes managed to withstand the catastrophe.

Among the villas, those worth visiting most are the **Casa del tramezzo di legno**, whose functioning pair of doors can still be admired, and the **Casa a graticcio** with its wooden staircase. The techniques of half-timbering, which spread throughout Europe and reached its peak centuries later, is thought to have been developed in Herculaneum.

Unfortunately, since excavations began many of the art objects have been secretly removed, some of them smuggled abroad. One master in the art of ruthless plunder was the discoverer of Herculaneum himself, the Austrian Marquis d'Elboeuf, whose villa on the **Mole of Granatello di Portici** still stands. He was extremely generous with his loot and made presents of it to many other European aristocrats. This was stopped in 1738 when Charles of Bourbon put Alcubierre, from Spain, and later Weber, from Switzerland, in charge of the excavations. Weber was responsible for handing down the ground plan of the famous **Villa dei Papiri**. This villa was not only home to the celebrated bronze statue of *The Dancers of Herculaneum* but also of the carbonised texts called the *papiri*. These were philosophical treatises from the school of Epicurus and probably

Villa in Herculaneum.

belonged to the domestic library of Lucius Calpurnius Piso.

A visit to Herculaneum should also include a visit to the **Miglio d'oro**, the Golden Mile, a collection of splendid buildings dating from the 18th century. They were built at the foot of Vesuvius under the reign of the Bourbons. One building in particular stands out in this collection of architectural masterpieces – the Villa Campolieto. This magnificent building was a source of inspiration for many visitors to Naples. Goethe, Saint-Non and Winckelmann were among those bowled over by the classical beauty of the house and its lovely location.

POMPEII: The Roman town of Pompeii has been described as the Hiroshima of the ancient world. In fact, as the destruction of Pompeii was the result of a natural disaster and not the work of man, this is a misleading description. One thing, however, is sure – the ruins of Pompeii are the most famous and most impressive ancient remains in the world. Certainly no other ancient city captures the imagination of the modern world as Pompeii has done.

Before the eruption of Vesuvius completely buried it under the layer of ash and pumice stone which was to preserve it so uniquely, Pompeii was a flourishing city with a population of 20,000 inhabitants, the largest along the whole of the west coast of Italy. In contrast to Herculaneum, the other Roman town buried by the outpourings of Vesuvius, whose architecture shows a strong Hellenistic influence, Pompeii's geometrical city plan points to its Roman origins.

Viewing Pompeii from the city walls or the Fortress of Mercury, which still bears evidence of the damage caused by the Roman general Sulla's violent occupation of the city, it is hard to imagine the violent and immediate end to the city's life. Everything in this most extraordinary of open-air museums seems to have remained just as it was on 24 August, AD 79, when the tumultuous eruption took place. It was not until

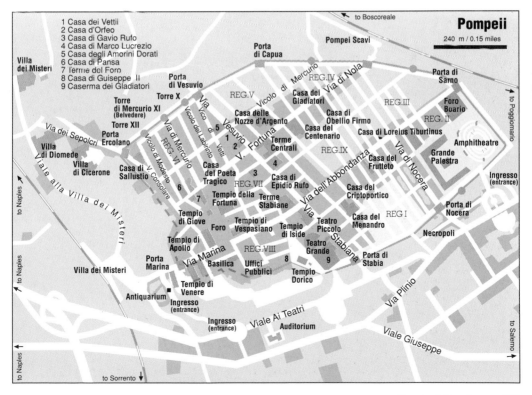

1748 that the archaeologists of the Bourbon court of Charles III uncovered the first finds from Pompeii. After the discovery of Herculaneum, 40 years before, extensive searches were made to uncover Pompeii. Unfortunately many of the finds from the original excavations mysteriously disappeared. It is thought that a large part of these lost pieces were used in the building of houses and villas.

Right from the beginning of the excavations the main problem was where to exhibit the uncovered objects. This problem was not solved until the building of the **Regio Museo** in Naples.

Tour of the city: Our tour begins at Porta Marina, which leads directly to the Forum. The Forum is graced by the Temple of Jupiter and the Temple of Apollo as well as the most important public buildings. Unlike other antique cities, however, the forum does not represent the heart of the city but is merely part of an urban complex; only in the city's early days is it likely to have formed the real centre. It is triangular in shape and in one corner stands a **Doric temple** whose pillars dominate the forum. Other buildings include the city treasury, the basilica, the law courts and the **Macellum**, the market hall. At the other end of the Macellum is the richly-decorated portal of the **building of Eumachia**.

From the Forum, the Via di Mercurio leads to a number of wealthy patricians' villas. One of the most famous is the **Casa del Fauno**, named after the bronze statue of a faun (exhibited in the National Museum), which was found here. The famous Mosaic of Alexander, which shows a fearless Alexander defeating the Persians, was also found in this patrician's villa. The original (the one here is only a copy) is presumed to have been completed in AD 311 and shows how skilled mosaic artists had become both in the decoration of rooms and in the use of colour. Like the bronze faun, the original mosaic is now found in the National Museum in Naples.

The amphitheatre, Pompeii.

Also well worth seeing among the villas is the **House of Labyrinths,** in which the mosaic-like **Fresco of the Minotaur** was found, and **Casa dei Vettii.** The entrance hall of the latter, named after its owner, used to be graced by a **priapic phallus**, a huge penis. Now, its main attraction has been locked away, along with other erotic works, in a small room which is opened on request for adults only.

Street of shame: Most of the *tabernae*, the taverns or inns, are found in **Via dell'Abbondanza**. The **Vicolo Storto**, an inn-cum-brothel, provided archaeologists with a fascinating picture of aspects of Roman life which, under normal circumstances, later civilisation would have destroyed. Graffiti found on the walls of the brothel's private booths belong to the most expressive erotic literature to have survived from ancient times.

Graffiti graces many of the buildings, including the sacred buildings and the galleries of the thermal baths, richly decorated with frescoes and stucco. It tells a lot about the inhabitants of Pompeii and their way of life, from advertising, philosophical observations – "Nothing lasts forever: the shining sun disappears into the ocean, the moon which was full wanes and the strong south wind becomes but a light breeze" – to declarations of love. It frequently displays a sense of humour – "It surprises me, O Wall, that you have not long since collapsed under the weight of so much boring prattle" – and, as the following examples illustrate, displays an enjoyment of bawdy jokes and references to sex: "Euplia lay here with very strong men and put them all out of action" and "We have made the bed wet. I admit my wrong, O Host, but if you ask me why, then I must answer that there was no other place where we could have done this."

Graffiti also helps provide information on what the Romans ate and drank. By all accounts, one of Via dell'Abbondanza's most popular watering holes

Relief in Pompeii.

was the famous Asellina's tavern. Here the citizens of Pompeii could enjoy the best *garum* in the city, a piquant sauce made from marinaded cuttlefish famous as far away as Gaul. Another speciality was *mulsum*, a tasty dish made of beaten eggs and sliced onions and seasoned with wine. The landlord Modestus, whose inn was near the Vicolo Storto, also offered *moretum*, a long flat dumpling made from wheat and served hot from the oven – a forerunner, one might hazard to guess, of the Neapolitan pizza.

Antique theatre: Plays were performed as well as concerts and poetry readings in Pompeii's two theatres, the large **amphitheatre** and, next to it, **the odèion**. Pompeii's poetry reading contests were highly-competitive championships, almost as cut-throat as the gladiatorial challenges. The latter were very popular with the people of Pompeii, as can be seen from the size of the amphitheatre (it could seat 15,000 spectators), the prominence given to the Samnite **sportsground** at the Forum, the **Grande Palestre** (Great Gymnasium) with its colonnades on three sides, and the *natatio* where the gladiators practised.

Combat wasn't confined to the arena; hooliganism on the terraces was a frequent problem. In AD 59 fighting broke out of such violence between spectators from Pompeii and Nuceria that it was recorded in a painting. As a result, under orders of Emperor Nero himself, the arena was placed out of bounds for a period of 10 years.

Life in the villas of the suburbs of Pompeii was no less luxurious than in the city itself. This is documented in the small and perfectly wrought objects of everyday life which were found there. These include fine bracelets, pieces made of obsidian, silver dishes and pomade containers, all on view in the Antiquarium.

Examples of the splendid buildings which can be found on the outskirts of Pompeii include the much-admired Villa of Diomedes, with its large covered colonnade, and the Villa dei Misteri (Villa of Mysteries), which contains a cycle of frescoes depicting initiation ceremonies in the rites of Dionysius. It is not known whether the flagellation scenes were realistic or merely symbolic.

Shortly after the catastrophe which blotted out all human life in Pompeii, the Latin poet Martial described the bleak and tragic scene of loss: "There stands Vesuvius which was once covered with fertile vineyards and produced the most excellent wine. It is the mountain which Bacchus loved more than the hills of Nysa. Choruses of satyrs danced on its slopes.

"And there stood Pompeii, the favourite city of Venus which she loved more dearly than Sparta. And there stood Herculaneum whose name was dedicated to the great Hercules. Look, now everything is blackened and buried under fire and ashes. The gods regret what they have done."

Below and **right**, Pompeii's vivid frescoes.

SORRENTO AND THE AMALFI COAST

"Paradise of exiles" was Shelley's term for the colonisation of Italy. Later, Victorian polite society decanted subversive elements abroad. Climate and culture made the South a magnet for moral exiles in flight from repressive sexual norms. While Naples attracted wealthy English adulterers, Capri was a homosexual haunt and **Sorrento** was favoured by divorcees. When Lady Lismore eloped with an officer from the guards, it was Sorrento she chose as her new home. There she luxuriated in a grand villa, attended decadent parties and swanned around on her yacht.

The scenery and tolerance of sexual solecisms were not the only attractions. Victorians travelled in expectation of classical models of beauty. In Sorrento in 1864, J. A. Symonds was entranced by Hellenic visions of loveliness: "Girls carrying pitchers on their heads have the neck or bust of a statue, and the young men look like Athletes with deep ardent eyes." The romanticisation of the South continues.

The travel writer Norman Douglas admired the "half naked, Praxitelean shapes of men and boys" working in Sorrento's olive mills. There too, he cast off "outworn weeds of thought with the painless ease of a serpent" under the tutelage of an illiterate peasant boy named Amitrano. Sex in Sorrento remains a preoccupation of visitors today. Not for nothing is the city advertised as "sizzling Sorrento" in British brochures. Since 80 percent of the city's tourists are British, expectations are high. Lurid T-shirts proclaim "Sex-Instructor – First Lesson Free".

Piazza Tasso, the town centre, spans a ravine with, at the foot, a ruined watermill. The Piazza looks down over **Marina Piccola**, the embarkation point for boats to Capri and Naples. Sorrento is a good base from which to visit the Bay of Naples and the Amalfi Coast.

Boat trips also explore the classical ruins on the coast, including Grotte delle Sirene, the fabled cave from which Sirens lured sailors to their deaths by the beauty of their songs. Odysseus was forced to lash himself to the mast of his ship after plugging the ears of his crew with wax so that they could hear neither the songs of the Siren nor his own entreaties to be released.

On the capes, the winds have carved arches into the rocks. The central beaches lie at the foot of steep cliffs and are reached by lifts. **Marina Grande** offers a tiny strip of sand but further west, the beaches are cleaner, larger and less crowded. For better beaches, press on to Amalfi and Positano.

From Piazza Tasso, follow the Corso Italia west to the **Sedile Dominova**, a Renaissance loggia which was the summer meeting place for the Sorrentine nobility. Virtually next-door is the **Duomo**, the 15th-century cathedral. The choir is a tribute to Sorrentine craftsmanship, with marquetry and

marble bas-reliefs in evidence. Church ceremonies combine drama and sentimentality, an unchanging Neapolitan blend. In 1851 Cato Lowes Dickinson walked among the corpses in the crypt of Sant'Angelo near Sorrento and emerged "sickened, and with a blessing on my lips that we were saved in England such religious ceremonies as these".

Behind the cathedral, the remains of 16th-century ramparts incorporate a Roman gateway. From here, Via Tasso leads to the seafront and **Villa Comunale**, a terrace with views over Vesuvius, Procida and the Bay of Naples. In the lush grounds glints **San Francesco**, a baroque church with an onion-domed bell-tower. Summer classical concerts are held in the medieval cloisters. The capitals are decorated with aquatic symbols and foliage while the pointed arches reflect Moorish designs. Further east lies the **Museo Correale di Teranova**, a museum set in a lemon grove. This period *palazzo* captures the patrician ambience of 18th-century Naples, complemented by gracious Neapolitan furniture and classical sculptures.

Hemmed in by three ravines, Sorrento sprawls along the ridge of its legendary cliffs. It is famed for its sunsets, rose gardens and *belle époque* villas. This once genteel resort drew celebrated visitors from Byron and Sir Walter Scott to Wagner, Nietzsche and Goethe. Alexandre Dumas and Stendhal made long visits; but its most famous resident was Ibsen, who wrote part of *Peer Gynt* here. The orange and lemon groves, the balmy climate and the seductive light still work their magic. In Sorrento, the *passeggiata*, the evening stroll around Piazza Tasso, remains an Italian seduction ritual. Even in this cosmopolitan city, the *tarantella*, the whirling southern Italian dance, has not been confined to folklore.

J. A. Symonds felt "a continual, unsatisfied desire" by the splendours of Sorrento, a sense of coming too late into a world too old. This mortified sensibil- **Festivities in Sorrento.**

ity has disappeared with mass tourism. The bustling crafts quarter near Piazza Tasso reflects the materialism of latter-day visitors. Lace, coral and *intarsio* (marquetry) are the prize. Norman Douglas felt that Sorrento enabled him to renew contact with "elemental and permanent things". In their inimitable way, today's tourists feel the same passion for sultry Sorrento.

A stroll west from Via del Capo leads to **Capo di Sorrento**, the spot for swimming or sunset gazing. En route is the villa Maxim Gorky occupied from 1924 to 1933. From here, a track goes to the sea and the **Roman Villa of Pollio Felix**. Views of the villa's Roman *nymphaeum* fade to a smoking Vesuvius. Round the cape are glimpses of Capri before the road turns inland to the village of **Massa Lubrense**, built on the slopes of Monte San Costanzo. From Massa, a choice of routes unfolds: the scenic harbour descent; the coastal path to the headland at Punta della Campanella, the site of a Greek temple, to Athena; or the high road through olive groves to Sant'Agata sui Due Golfi.

The Amalfi Coast (Costiera Amalfitana): The mountain village of **Sant'Agata** commands views of the Gulfs of Naples and Salerno. The church houses a Florentine altar of inlaid marble. The village high road, known as the **Strada di Capodimonte**, is also the beginning of the glorious cliff-top drive along the Amalfi Coast. The Amalfi Coast is 30 miles (50 km) long to Salerno and much of the hair-raising drive is without guard rails. From Salerno, the mountains recede but the appeal of Greek temples at Paestum carries one on. To avoid the crowds, it is best to do the Amalfi drive on weekdays in the early morning or at lunchtime.

From Sant'Agata, follow signs to Positano and the **Strada Amalfitana**, the dramatic coastal road. This narrow ribbon winds its way up and down the mountains, allowing vertiginous glimpses of the sea and promontories guarded by ancient Saracen towers. The

Room with a view.

rocky coast has been carved into weird shapes by the elements. The road threads through olive groves and sandstone tunnels and makes sudden appearances beside steep terraces and pastel-coloured villages wedged between the mountains and the sea. Forsythia, roses and bougainvillaea bloom along the limestone cliffs all year.

On first sight, **Positano** could be a village in the Andes rather than a chic resort. The name is a derivation of Poseidon and the settlement was supposedly founded by the Greek inhabitants of Paestum, further down the coast.

Positano's appeal lies in flowery gardens, Moorish houses and the majolica-domed church. Sugar-cube pastel houses rise in ordered ranks, clinging to the cliffs. The harshness is softened by the clusters of camellias, bougainvillaeas, oleanders and almond trees. Writer John Steinbeck and director Franco Zeffirelli are two famous residents who have fallen under Positano's spell. "Positano bites deep," said Steinbeck. "It is a dream that isn't quite real when you are there and becomes beckoningly real after you have gone."

From the foot of the cliffs, two roads snake their way through the town. The domed church of Santa Maria Assunta houses a Byzantine Black Madonna but otherwise the village offers atmosphere rather than culture. By day, visitors flock to the pottery shops and beaches. By night, the cosmopolitan élite hire boats to take them to the best fish restaurants along the coast. Steinbeck believed that tourism could never destroy his hide-away: "In the first place there is no room. The cliffs are all taken – and the Positanese invariably refuse to sell."

Between Positano and Amalfi is the fashionable hamlet of **Praiano** and its popular beach. A short boat trip away is the **Grotta di Smeralda**, the Emerald Grotto. Although similar to Capri's more celebrated Blue Grotto, it is more dramatic. The emerald water is punctuated by deep gorges; weird submerged stalagmites reach towards the stalactites above. The soaring cliffs and plunging valleys continue to **Amalfi**, a medieval city clustered in a ravine.

The Maritime Republic: In its heyday, Amalfi rivalled Pisa Genoa and Venice. By the 7th century the city was ruled by Doges, as at Venice, and was recognised as the greatest naval power in the West. Its naval expertise led to the invention of the compass and the codification of the earliest maritime laws. In the 12th century, this great maritime republic had a population of 100,000 who masterminded regional trade with the East. Shortly afterwards, the Normans from Sicily vanquished Amalfi and the city was repeatedly sacked by Pisa, its greatest rival.

Amalfi merchants established trading posts in Byzantium, Asia Minor and Africa. In the Holy Land, they founded the Hospital of St John of Jerusalem, from which the Crusader Knights of St John developed. Their symbol, the Maltese cross, is still carved on Amalfi's street corners. Webster's brooding re- **Cafersa.**

242

venge drama, *The Duchess of Malfi*, was based on the tragic life of Joanna of Aragon, the Duke of Amalfi's consort in the 15th century.

The Regatta of the Four Ancient Maritime Republics, complete with galleons, is a magnificent evocation of the past, held in Amalfi every four years. Since the collapse of the republic, Amalfi sunk into oblivion until Edwardian times. As a favoured winter resort, it was then a genteel haunt for foreigners who tired of the excesses on the French Riviera. Amalfi today, with a population of 6,000, is a shadow of its former self but retains an air of faded elegance. Horse-drawn carts still ply the Lungomare dei Cavalieri for visitors' amusement, much as they did in Edwardian days.

The **Duomo**, the glittering Cathedral, is viewed from down below. The steep walk up is a chance to appreciate the spindly Moorish archways and geometric facade, inlaid with vivid mosaics. While looking authentic, the facade was

Positano.

reconstructed in the 19th century, based on the medieval model. Henry Swinburne, the 18th-century traveller, was not sympathetic to the Arab influences, calling the cathedral typical of the "barbarous ages, when Grecian rules and proportions were forgotten". Yet, framed by mountains and monasteries, the Norman-Saracen bell-tower presents a striking vision to visitors.

The baroque interior leads to a crypt containing the remains of St Andrew the Apostle, moved here from Constantinople in 1208. Like the miraculous liquefaction of San Gennaro's blood in Naples, the cult of St Andrew attracts fanaticism amongst locals. The Manna of St Andrew, a mysterious oil, is said to seep from his bones. Even St Francis of Assisi declared himself a devotee.

To the left of the church is the **Cloister of Paradise**, a medieval patrician cemetery which was later incorporated into the church. It is now a museum of Amalfian art, from Etruscan sarcophagi to Renaissance frescoes. Classical concerts are held in the Moorish cloisters in summer. The covered streets nearby are reminiscent of a souk, as are the arcaded piazzas on either side of Via Genova. The Tavole Amalfitane, the Latin book of naval law, is visible in the **Municipio**, a sombre *palazzo*. The laws applied until 1570.

Around every corner is a converted monastery or a crumbling convent, a sign of earlier cultural riches. On this coast, the hotels are often the sights, laden with literary history. Ibsen wrote much of *The Doll's House* in Room 15 of **Hotel Luna**. Hotel Cappuccini Convento was once a Capucin monastery.

Margaret Drabble's meditation on Amalfi feels true: "Amalfi clusters, the cliffs aspire, the sea extends. It is a living view, of living rock and living light. It changes… like a moving painting, like a wall of slowly evolving time, a perfect composition of safety and danger, distanced, marginally landscaped by man, inviting the artist." On a

more mundane note, the Guardia Finanza, the police arm of the tax authority, recently made a routine check in search of tax evaders. They were astonished to find that many of the yacht-owners who had declared meagre incomes were living in luxury.

Ravello spills down the steep hillside, "closer to the sky than it is to the seashore," mused André Gide. The setting is dramatic: azaleas and vines grow to the edge of the cliff and come to a dramatic standstill; below the scarred cliffs are isolated coves. Its uncompromising location meant that Ravello was often besieged but never conquered. In medieval times, it had a population of 30,000 but shared the fate of Amalfi, for good and ill. Between the 11th and 13th centuries, Ravello traded with Sicily and the Orient. The wealthy merchants imported the Moorish artefacts and architectural styles which remain one of Ravello's glories. Perhaps as a result, the inhabitants have a haughty air.

However, a number of celebrities have entered this magic circle. D. H. Lawrence worked on *Lady Chatterley's Lover* here. Gore Vidal, who lives in the Villa Rondaia, the "swallows' nest" overlooking the bay, has been made an honorary citizen of Ravello. As a controversial and spunky writer, Vidal would appreciate Boccaccio's choice of Ravello as the setting for the bawdier stories in *The Decameron*.

The **Duomo di San Pantaleone** is an 11th-century church dedicated to St Pantaleone, whose blood is also supposed to liquefy twice a year. Its austere facade is emboldened by Romanesque bronze doors. Inside, the nave is supported by classical columns and adorned with marble busts. The exotic 13th-century Arabo-Byzantine pulpits are richly decorated: in one, dragons and birds are held aloft by fierce lions; the other pulpit is a mosaic of St Jonah and the Whale. The crypt contains a small collection of medieval sculpture and goldsmiths' work. The custodian, a wily old shark, claims to be a friend of

Jacqueline Kennedy, Vidal's half-sister. Connections are everything in incestuous Ravello.

Palazzo Rufolo, in the shadow of the cathedral, was built in seductive Moorish style by the Rufolo dynasty, the richest family in medieval Ravello. The atmospheric tower is adorned with a Norman-Saracen vault and four statues depicting the seasons in the corners. The courtyard of the ruined villa resembles cloisters, with its richly-decorated columns and glorious gardens. Here Wagner found inspiration for the magic garden in *Parsifal*, his last opera in 1880. In the former chapel is a small collection of classical sculpture.

Villa Cimbrone was designed by the eccentric Lord Grimthorpe at the turn of the century. The gardens enjoy glorious views of the mountain ridge and bay. Sadly, the villa itself is mostly closed to the public but there are tantalising views of the courtyard and chapel cloisters. Nearby, flower-hung courtyards and crooked stone walls are a prelude to

clambering along the *scalinata*. These steep passageways are the only way to walk through Ravello.

As in Amalfi, the hotels are some of the sights. **Hotel Palumbo**, in particular, has a Romanesque *cortile* and baroque frescoes. Famous names in the Visitors' Book include E. M. Forster, Tennessee Williams, Ingrid Bergman and François Mitterrand. Wagner was naturally the most revered guest and, as a tribute, the hotel helps sponsor Wagnerian concerts in the Villa Rufolo every summer.

Hotel Caruso, the converted *palazzo* next-door, boasts an equally venerable cast, from the royal families of Italy and Hungary to Toscanini, Humphrey Bogart and Gina Lollobrigida. The star is undoubtedly the enigmatic Greta Garbo who spent one long hot summer here with conductor Leopold Stokowski. Greta Gasse, the pseudonym, fooled no one. The world's press descended on Ravello and anyone in dark glasses was accosted.

From Ravello are **lovely walks** to Fontantelle, Torca and the slopes of Monte Rotondo and San Costanzo. Shepherds trails pass through Mediterranean *maquis*, myrtle and heather. The skyline is fret-worked with peaks and cols, the foreground sliced by chasms. Bleached rocks, Saracen towers and classical ruins are all part of the scenery. Ravello swathed in mist is unforgettable, its sombre Saracenic architecture framed by brooding mountains.

Scala, the next village, offers a church with a fine Romanesque doorway while **Maiori** boasts the widest beach on the Amalfi Coast. At any of the villages on the Amalfi Coast, it is worth sampling the **local dishes**. *Sfogliatelli*, light pastries stuffed with spinach and ricotta, make tasty snacks. *Linguine all'arragosta* is a lobster and pasta concoction while *agnello pasquale*, roast lamb with sage, is a traditional Easter dish, now eaten throughout the year.

Salerno, the major city at the end of the Amalfi Coast, is initially unappeal-

Villa Cimbrone, Ravello.

ing. The grim industrial suburbs come as a particular shock after the beauty of the wild coastline. Hotels and restaurants in Salerno are distinctly inferior to the grand affairs on the Costiera Amalfitana. The old quarter was damaged by the Allied invasion in 1943 and has only been half-heartedly restored. Visitors who wish to savour the romance of the Amalfi Coast should ignore Salerno and proceed to the Greek ruins at Paestum.

In its favour, shabby Salerno claims to be a living, working city rather than a museum piece. Its claim to fame is as the capital of the Norman empire in the 11th century. It also lays claim to the oldest medical school in Europe, supposedly founded by an Arab, a Jew, a Christian and a Turk. Apparently, William the Conqueror's son came here to treat a wound he received as a Crusader in the Holy Land.

Garden of delights.

Follow signs to the *centro storico*, the historic city centre. The **Duomo**, the cathedral, was built by Robert Guiscard, the Norman leader in 1085. It is Salerno's main attraction, with a grand courtyard and a loggia supported by classical columns plundered from Paestum. The Byzantine bronze doors open on to a disappointing interior which was clumsily restored after the 1688 earthquake. None the less, the 12th-century pulpits are a satisfying combination of Arabo-Sicilian and Moorish design.

The dark streets around the cathedral reveal curious sights, from sculpted *palazzi* to Moorish arches. The bustling traders' quarter in Via dei Mercanti is still the place for leather-making. From the Lungomare and sea wall are views of fishermen's cottages, the rugged Amalfi Coast and the sombre old town. Behind the city are two stern Norman castles perched on the mountains. Any fleeting gloom is dispelled by Salerno's Sunday evening *passeggiata*, a livelier and more spontaneous affair than the one in Sorrento.

Paestum is the site of an ancient

Greek city situated along the coastal road, 25 miles (40 km) south of Salerno. Unlike other classical ruins in the region, Paestum languishes in atmospheric solitude. It is set in an open field amidst flowers, herbs and wild artichokes. Ovid and Virgil sang the praises of Paestum's sweet-scented roses and violets. Founded in 7 BC, Paestum remains the closest we can come to sensing the completeness of a Greek colony in the West. The overgrown site was only discovered in the 18th century during the building of a coach road through the forest.

Paestum's name derives from Poseidon, the legendary sea god. As Poseidonia, the city guarded the crossroads of three trading empires: Greek, Etruscan and Latin. Its prosperity coincided with the decline of the Etruscan civilisation but Poseidonia inevitably fell to the Romans in 273 BC. In the Middle Ages, the population, threatened by floods, settled around the oldest temple but was eventually forced to flee.

The Via Sacra first passes **Basilica of Hera**, the oldest temple, dating from 565 BC. As the protectress of Jason and the Argonauts, Hera had special status in Greek mythology. Compared with the majestic Temple of Neptune, the taper of the Basilica's fluted columns is a touch crude. Beside it is a sacrificial altar and a pit into which entrails were cast. The **Temple of Ceres**, originally dedicated to Athena, was used as an early Christian church. Greek fertility rites were absorbed into local lore. Even after the citizens of Paestum fled to the hills, Ceres' pomegranate became a Christian symbol.

The **Temple of Neptune**, arguably the loveliest Doric temple in the world, is certainly the only rival to Agrigento in Sicily and Theseus in Athens. It too was dedicated to Hera but was the inspiration behind the Temple of Zeus in Olympia. Its grace and harmony make it the perfect embodiment of Greek classicism. Looking over the golden ruins at sunset, Goethe felt in touch with the **Salerno.**

eternal. Little remains of the sunken Roman forum and baths, still less of the Greek agora and theatre. Yet Goethe is not alone in finding Paestum the most enchanting experience in Italy.

The sombre plain, stark temples and jagged mountains in the background create a romantic juxtaposition. Shelley found the view "inexpressibly grand". In 1883, Baedeker's guide praised these "temples adorned with a luxurious growth of ferns and acanthus, enlivened solely by the chirping grasshopper, the rustling lizard, and the gliding snake". Compared with the blatant commercialism of Pompeii, Paestum is an oasis of tranquillity.

Paestum's small **museum** contains a remarkable collection of terracotta pots and tomb paintings. Metopes, fragments of Doric friezes, depict Homeric myths. Sculpted satyrs in flight accompany the trials of Hercules, Orestes and Sisyphus. Yet the merest half-smiles in repose reveal the Italian softening effect on Greek sculpture.

The ancient Greeks considered painting the noblest of arts. So, as the only extant Greek murals, Paestum's are unique. These tomb paintings depict a funeral banquet and the farewell to earthly pleasures. The **Tomb of the Diver** (*Tomba del Tuffatore*) is the masterpiece. A tense figure dives into space. The symbolism is ambiguous: academics may see a Platonic meditation on immortality. We simply see the deceased diving into the underworld, paradise or oblivion.

Diving diversions: Paestum is a place for pleasure rather than morbid reflections. Endless beaches offer good diving opportunities. **Agropoli**, a town just south of Paestum, provides pleasant bathing as well as a crumbling Byzantine castle. **Acciaroli**, further south, is part of the Cilento Coast. The scenery is less dramatic than on the Amalfi Coast. Hemingway adored the orange groves, lush vegetation and solitude. The Cilento remains unspoilt, a far cry from sophisticated Capri.

Temple of Neptune, Paestum.

Ischia cannot compete with Capri in glamour. Instead, it offers charm: tiny white houses, domed churches and appealing wine-growing villages. Ischia is the largest island in the Bay of Naples, with a population of 40,000 and a circumference of about 28 miles (46 km). Unlike Capri, Ischia and Procida form part of the submerged volcano of Campano, which once stretched from the Pontine islands to the Aolian islands. The volcanic soil is conducive to thermal cures and to the production of excellent wine. There are fewer sights than on Capri but compensations lie in the rural culture, sensuous atmosphere, volcanic scenery and varied beaches.

Blessings and disasters: In 8 BC Ischia became a Greek colony, the first in the Western Mediterranean. As a Greek outpost, it was a pivotal trading link between East and West and a base from which to colonise Campania. Archaeological excavations at Lacco Ameno, in the north of Ischia, reveal a Greek settlement and necropolis.

The Romans flocked to Ischia's spas but less than a century after Pompeii was buried under lava, Ischia's Monte Epomeo erupted, destroying all life on the island. Ischia is pitted with ancient craters, the result of volcanic eruptions. In 1883 an earthquake virtually destroyed Casamicciola, killing 3,000 residents in the space of 15 seconds.

In the days of the Grand Tour, Ischia was a playground of the European aristocracy but that exclusiveness faded in Edwardian times. Compared with Capri, modern Ischia attracts a health-conscious clientele: Italians and Germans throng the thermal establishments. The hottest spring, at the resort of Casamicciola, gushes forth at a temperature of 82°C (180°F). Water sports

Preceding pages: Ischia. **Left,** exploring Sant Angelo.

enthusiasts and walkers are also in their element. Capri's tiny coves may masquerade as beaches but, on Ischia, beaches embrace long golden sands and darkly volcanic rocks. Ischia is "the green island" because of its olive groves, pine woods and vineyards.

Boats from Capri and Naples arrive at **Ischia Porto**, a town clustered around the harbour. This ancient crater lake only became a port in 1854 when a canal opened it up to the sea.

Ischia Porto, the bustling commercial quarter, is linked to the more peaceful Ischia Ponte, a former fishing village. The avenue is bordered by boutiques, bars, sandy beaches and a pine grove. Summer transport includes jokey canopied tricycles, run by rapacious touts who are in league with local hoteliers. A trip by horse and carriage feels equally touristy but infinitely more sedate: the horses peer sleepily from under widebrimmed straw hats.

A small archaeological museum in Corso Vittoria Colonna displays Greek and Roman finds but classical ruins are not central to the island's charm. Even so, **Ischia Ponte** offers considerable historical interest. A narrow causeway leads to the imposing ruin of the medieval **Castello Aragonese**, the site of the original Greek settlement. The causeway was built by Alfonso of Aragon in 1438 to link the old quarter to the castle. Vittoria Colonna, the Renaissance poet and friend of Michelangelo, grew up in the castle and retired there after the family estates were confiscated by Pope Alexander VI. Vittoria's husband, Francesco Ferrante, was killed shortly after their marriage and Vittoria was left to rule Ischia wisely for 50 years. The Castello encloses churches and twisting alleys as well as the castle.

The cathedral was destroyed by the British but retains its 14th-century frescoes in the crypt. The Baroque Immacolata church and the Renaissance San Pietro are also mere shells.

The highest building is the tumbledown 15th-century castle. Staying in Il Monastero, the only hotel in the Castello, is an opportunity to enjoy magnificent views from the terrace and to haunt the castle grounds after daylight. At dusk, doves and bats fly in and out of the roofless churches. The dark Convent de Clarisse contains an eerie cell in which the bodies of dead nuns were left to putrefy in small seats.

During the July festival of Sant' Anna, the *N'drezzata*, a ritualistic dagger dance dating from Vittoria's time, is performed by villagers in front of the Castello.

The hilly hinterland: From Ischia, a clockwise route leads west through the hills and hugs the coast at Sant'Angelo and Forio before returning to Ischia via Lacco Ameno. If driving rather than taking the bus, follow Via de Luca and Via Mazella into the countryside. After passing pine woods and a Roman aqueduct, the road winds through vineyards to the Monte Epomeo. Guided hikes can be arrranged in the resorts.

In **Buonopane** and other hillside vil-

Left, coastal café. Right, beached.

lages, traditions are deeper than on the coast. Although dying out, folklore is a genuine legacy of the peasant culture. Amongst the farming community of Buonopane, *N'drezzata* is a popular tradition: this boisterous Greek-style male dance has been passed on from father to son for centuries here. It is a male-oriented culture: at sunset, the scene is of women working in the vineyards, children picking tomatoes and, in the cafés, men drinking Epomeo. This heady white wine is iodine-scented, as if the sea air had swept through the mountain vineyards.

Just north is the village of **Fontana**, the base for a donkey ascent of **Monte Epomeo**, an extinct volcano. Pliny the Elder dreaded an eruption of this 2,600-ft (790-metre) high volcano and Epomeo later fulfilled his fears. The mountainous terrain is sparsely populated; lush sub-tropical vegetation soon gives way to scrubby Mediterranean *maquis*. Since local roads peter into steep, tiered paths, donkeys are still an

essential form of transport and are bred in Fontana. After hiring one from a weather-beaten peasant, allow time for idle munching and for detours through the volcanic scenery. As the summit looms, a remote hermitage appears on the horizon, followed by rugged views over Casamicciola Terme.

Sant'Angelo, a fishing village perched on the southernmost tip of the island, is a delightful spot. This self-conscious community lives in pastel cottages stacked on the slope. Poetic fishermen refer to the aesthetic clutter as swallows' nests. Marina dei Moronti, the nearby beach, is noted for its hot springs and fumaroles gushing gases and vapour. The surrounding hills are pitted with ancient cave dwellings. Just west of Serrara and Sant'Angelo is **Succhivo**, a village with whitewashed cottages and neatly-tended gardens.

Forio, a wine-growing village at the foot of the mountains, makes a good base, even for those taking a cure. The spa town was once encircled by 16 tow-

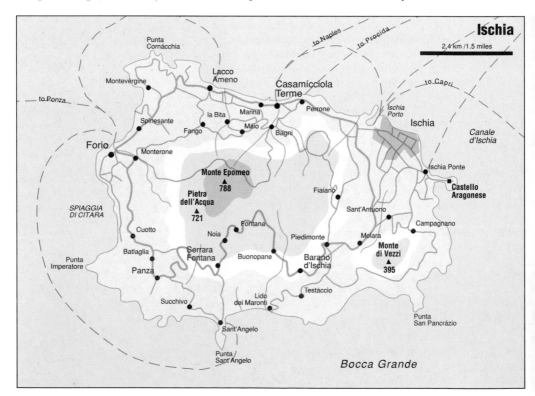

ers to protect it against pirate invasions and retains a sturdy Saracen's tower. Forio has a foreign colony of artists and potters who are responsible for much of the inferior ceramics on Ischia.

At the end of the headland is the white, Greek-looking church of Santa Maria del Soccorso with views over the bay. The radioactive beaches near Forio are allegedly good for backache but, in return, leave one with a headache.

From here, it is a short drive north to the wild **Monte Caruso** promontory, one of Ischia's most romantic spots. Twisted rocks and burnt *maquis* alternate against the shoreline. Lacco Ameno and **Casamicciola Terme**, popular spas, lie just east. Henrik Ibsen worked there but, if *The Doll's House* is anything to go by, neither the scenery nor the spa cured his melancholy.

Prison colony: The island of **Procida** feels surprisingly remote, despite its proximity to Naples. Still, its notoriety as Italy's Alcatraz plays some part in this isolation. Procida has housed a prison colony since Ferdinand IV's time. As a result, the island lives off fishing, sailing and agriculture, leaving tourism to glamorous Capri and Ischia.

The island's history is linked to the Benedictines and the Bourbons. A Benedictine community flourished here from the 11th century but suffered attacks from the Saracens and the pirate Barbarossa. After the abbey church was burnt down in 1544, local fishermen donated a third of their income to rebuild it. As a special dispensation, the Pope granted them permission to fish on Sundays to survive. Under Bourbon rule, the island became a royal hunting estate with the forbidding Castello d'Aragona transformed into a prison. Today's 10,000 islanders are resolutely traditional, religious and rural. Tourism is confined to cheerful restaurants lining Marina Grande and to the island's sole craft industry, the production of carved models of ships.

As the wildest island in the Bay of Naples, Procida boasts undiscovered coves, empty sands and luxuriant vegetation. The rich volcanic soil is ideal for citrus fruits, melons and grapes. Procida's lemons are reputedly the tangiest in Italy. The coast is pitted with craters but, apart from a rocky promontory, is flatter than Ischia. The pace of life is slow, with scenes of fishermen mending nets on the quayside or tomato-laden donkeys plodding uphill.

Tranquil sights: Beside the busy harbour at **Marina Grande** is Santa Maria della Pietà, a flowing baroque church decorated in luminous colours. Over the hill is the ancient church of San Rocca in **Corricella**, the most traditional village on the island. The community has a Moorish feel, echoing Sicily rather than Naples. This stone warren hugs a sheltered cove in the shadow of Terra Murata, once an impregnable citadel. Via San Rocco winds to the island's centre at **Piazza dei Martiri** and yet another colourful domed church, Madonna delle Grazie. A short climb leads to the ruined citadel.

Pastel-painted Procida.

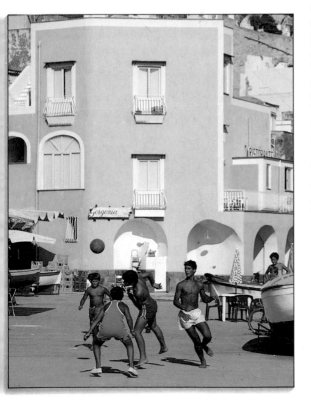

Looming over the medieval walls are the triple domes of **San Michele Arcangelo**, the abbey church. Its exotic Saracen allure from afar gives way to an austere facade. The interior is eclectic, with an array of relics, trinkets and amulets. A fresco on the domed ceiling depicts St Michael defeating Lucifer but the finest painting is of his expulsion of the Saracen hordes from Procida in 1535. Outside are scenic views from the terrace beside the **Castello**, the grim prison which is home to 100 inmates.

Procida has a shabby charm unlike the neat purity of Capri. The interior is dotted with isolated farmhouses and terraced wine growers' homes. In the villages, honeycombs of alleys are linked by ancient arcades; once grand *palazzi* are slowly crumbling. On the coast, pastel-painted cottages are reminscent of those on the Venetian island of Burano. The fishermen's and gardeners' cottages are often domed and painted white, yellow, ochre or pink. From the quayside are views of blue and white fishing boats bobbing in the bays.

Boats and beaches: A boat trip around the island takes about three hours and is an idyllic way to appreciate the secluded coves and headlands. The beaches at **Lido di Procida** and **Marina di Chiaioella** are more attractive than those near Marina Grande. The Marina was once a volcanic crater while the Lido borders a Roman necropolis. Procida's most peaceful spot is the rocky islet of **Vivara**, off the south coast, a haunt of wild rabbits which tend to end up in tasty stews.

After a storm off Procida in 1811, Lamartine, the Romantic French poet, was marooned on the island. The fickle poet fell in love with Graziella, a fisherman's daughter, but forgot her on his return to Paris. She died, heartbroken, two months later. To make amends, Lamartine immortalised her in his bestselling novella *Graziella* and dedicated a poem in *Harmonies* to her. Procida recalls the tragic affair in an annual Miss Graziella beauty contest.

Left, faith in healing powers.

TAKING THE WATERS

According to legend, Ischia's magical springs were a consolation from the gods for the constant misfortunes the island suffered as a result of earthquakes and volcanic eruptions.

In imperial times, generals and legionaries were sent to Paestum and Pompeii for the Roman equivalent of rest and recreation. The volcanic lakes and bubbling baths were prized for their therapeutic powers and were often adorned with elaborate mosaics or even marble temples. Ischia, however, was the favoured haunt of patrician Roman patients. Its gushing hot springs and radioactive mud baths were considered particularly beneficial in the treatment of arthritis.

The hot springs are praised in the *Iliad* and the *Aeneid*, but Homer, Virgil, Pliny and other addicts of thermal cures did not anticipate the popularity of the future spas. Campania is still Italy's foremost region for thermal cures and Ischia is its commercial centre. In the 6th century, Casamicciola Terme was home to the first medical school specialising in thermal cures. Today, Casamicciola remains a prestigious resort. Between May and September, Italians, Austrians, Germans and Swiss pour into Ischia's thermal establishments, combining a holiday with doing something constructive about their health.

Spa culture is enshrined in modern Italian medical practice. In Ischia, a wide programme of thermal cures has been developed for those suffering from rheumatism and arthritis to liver or gynaecological complaints. The prescribed treatment ranges from wallowing in mineral-rich mud or steam baths to the imbibing of sulphuric water. A local doctor's certificate is often necessary for visitors contemplating bathing in Ischia's highly radioactive waters.

The *stazioni termali* are situated all around the coast but over half of Ischia's hotels offer health cure programmes. Thankfully, they don't all look like hospitals: several elegant hotels are redolent of past glamour, with marvellous art nouveau marble sculptures and stucco decoration.

The neighbouring resorts of Casamicciola Terme and Lacco Ameno are the only spas of any size outside Ischia Porto. Casamicciola Terme, a characterless modern spa, has little to recommend it apart from water cures, extensive sea views and several less healthy night clubs. Lacco Ameno is slightly more appealing, overlooking a mushroom-shaped rock naturally known as "*il fungo*". In Ischia Porto, the Antiche Terme Comunali, the former communal baths, are a real tribute to the spa culture.

To devotees, the spas represent a virtuous retreat. Critics should not be deterred by the blend of commercialism and blind faith that underpins the spa culture. Even for visitors sceptical of water cures, a short session at a spa is a memorable and certainly relaxing experience. Massage, mud packs and "anti-stress experiences" are also on offer. Price determines whether one gets the pampered atmosphere of an expensive health farm, complete with celebrity guests, or the brisk professionalism preferred by the German middle classes.

The resorts also have a growing reputation as elderly match-making bureaux. "A radioactive relationship is for life," laughs Dr Meconceli. ∎

Right, taking the waters, Spaggia di Citara.

CAPRI

The island of Capri is known as *un pezzo di cielo caduta in terra* (a piece of paradise fallen from the skies). Legend has it that Capri is the Paradise Lucifer stole and transplanted in Italy. Mythical Capri lives up to its name: it is captivating, capricious and cute. For a sophisticated summer élite, Capri is a three-storey St-Tropez.

Yet its commercialism, crowds and self-conscious chic can disappoint. In the height of summer, when outdoor cafés are heaving with the season's visitors, few notice the play of light and shade on domes and arches. However, Capri is saved by sublime scenery, dramatic rocks and shimmering coves. It has the magic of a wild garden perched on a rocky mountain.

A foreign affair: Capri has long been romanticised, anglicised and germanised by an illustrious foreign colony. When John Dryden sailed around the island in 1700 he coined a term for its wild beauty: *romantique*. Exalted by German Romanticism, Capri has drawn Nietzsche and Rilke, the Austrian lyric poet, as well as the less lyrical munitions manufacturer, Alfred Krupp. After the abortive St Petersburg uprising in 1905, Lenin found exile in Capri along with Maxim Gorky and the Russian singer Chaliapin. Amusingly, Gorky ran a school for revolutionaries in this idyllic setting.

Capri is celebrated by writers, playwrights and poets, from Turgenev and Alexandre Dumas to Joseph Conrad, George Bernard Shaw and D. H. Lawrence. Hans Christian Andersen even transplanted one of his Nordic tales to the island. This literary tradition flourishes: Alberto Moravia, the great Italian novelist, has a house here, as did Graham Greene.

Preceding pages: Capri at twilight. **Left,** holiday idyll.

Capri has been notorious for louche living since Roman times, when the Emperor Tiberius's penchant for sado-masochistic practices became a source of scandal. Visits by the infamous Marquis de Sade did little to quell public prurience.

As a homosexual haunt, Capri later attracted Oscar Wilde and the inevitable newspaper headlines. At the turn of the century, Baron Adelsward Fersen infused "the gay Nineties" with its modern meaning: the Swedish millionaire's orgies at Villa Lysis drew the cosmopolitan Côte d'Azur crowd. Norman Douglas's scandalous novel, *South Wind*, captured the Capri jet-set before World War I spelt an end to the sybaritic old order. One homely island dweller who does not fit the pattern is Gracie Fields. The beloved English variety star chose Capri over her native Rochdale as a retirement home.

The Caprese would like to think that the island's name comes from *capra* (goat), a nickname given to Emperor Tiberius for his hairiness and sexual appetite. More mundane is the view that the name derives from *kapros*, the Greek word for wild boar. The discovery of wild boar fossils supports the Greek interpretation. Still, lusty Caprese prefer the reflected glory of Tiberius and proudly name snack bars after their Emperor. Although the Roman influence is more pronounced, Capri was originally a Greek colony. Linked to Sorrento in 6 BC, the island played a minor role in the empire as a maritime trading centre. Locals might deny the influence, but the traditional costumes and female faces look distinctly Greek.

Trading settlement: The island, only 4 miles long by 2 miles wide (6 by 3 km), is essentially an extension of the Sorrentine peninsula. The shape of the island determined its development, with the maritime community based on Capri and the trading settlement on Anacapri. To gain access to the sea, the citizens of Anacapri built the Scala

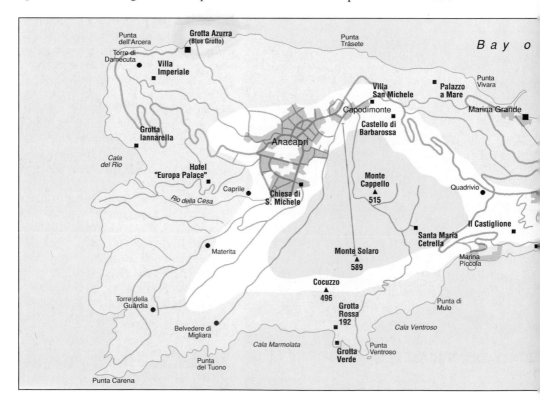

Fenicia, a so-called Phoenician path carved out of the rock. This tumble-down mountain staircase was the only link between the two sides of the island and it remains an evocative symbol.

Today's population of 12,000 is mostly based in the centres of Capri ("low town") and Anacapri ("high town"), a natural geographical and social divide that has existed since antiquity. Capri Town nestles betwen the mountains of San Michele and Castiglioe while Anacapri is dominated by the Monte Solaro. The main bays are Marina Grande and Marina Piccola.

On arrival in 29 BC, Emperor Augustus witnessed an oak burst into leaf beforc his eyes and read it as a portent of renewal for the decadent republic. He promptly negotiated with Naples to exchange fertile Ischia for exquisite Capri: aesthetics won out over economics. Graced by the gods, Capri came to resemble a Roman holiday camp. In return, Augustus built the aqueducts, roads and villas which dot Capri. His successor was the melancholy Tiberius. According to Tacitus, Tiberius covered the island with palaces. He even moved the imperial capital here for the last 10 years of his life. During this voluntary exile, he allegedly learnt of the trial and death of Christ.

Thanks to Tiberius, Capri acquired a fame that survived the fall of Rome. Given his reputation for vice, notoriety would be more accurate description. The tales of debauchery at his Villa Jovis invite comparison with Villa Lysis of the 1890s or San Francisco of the 1970s. Tiberius died aged 78, either from a fever or suffocated by a rival. Caligula, his jaded camp follower, was standing by to take his place. In medieval times, Capri was pillaged by Saracens and pirates and sank into political oblivion. However, during the Napoleonic Wars, it regained its defensive role, occupied and fortified by the British.

Today, Capri still deserves cachet as the "pearl of Naples". In a warm May or

Piazza Umberto I.

mild September it is arguably the most beautiful island in the Mediterranean. Even in the height of summer, visitors can abandon the crowds in Capri Town and head for the fragrant hills. The mountainous terrain offers dramatic cliffbound scenery, plunging views and lush vegetation.

Dusty tracks wind through olive and lemon groves, deep pine woods and chestnut plantations. Mediterranean and semi-tropical plants abound, from myrtle and acanthus to cacti and bougainvillaea.

Island approaches: From Marina Grande, the touristy and slightly tacky port, a rickety funicular leads past banks of flowers to **Capri Town**. Alternatively, the road winds through olive groves, orchards and sloping vineyards. Past a steep bend is San Costanzo, a 10th-century church with a Byzantine dome and views of the Scala Fenice staircase. Capri Town developed as a bastion against Saracen raids and, despite splendid views, gives a sense of enclosure. Narrow alleys, immaculate pastel facades and minuscule squares present themselves at every turn.

The most charming of these *piazzette* is Piazza Umberto I, celebrated as "the drawing room of the world". At sunset, it is a magnet for visitors who want to sip cocktails and watch the *beau monde* go by. This outdoor salon lies in the shadow of San Stefano, a church designed in Byzantine baroque style, topped by an oriental dome.

Capri Town is a natural departure point for lovely walks. A coastal walk explores **Punta Tragara** and its curious rock formations. From Via Vittorio Emanuele, a turning left along Via Tragara leads to Punta Tragara, the promontory in the southeast of the island. Nearby are the weird **Faraglioni**, a trio of pierced rocks which are home to the rare blue lizard. A stroll along Via Emanuele leads to **Certosa San Giacomo**, a 14th-century Carthusian charterhouse. The honey-coloured church is topped by a baroque tower. **Easter procession.**

Although sacked in the 16th century, the church and cloisters radiate a cool Gothic air. The smaller cloisters show clear Byzantine influences while the grander 15th-century cloisters once served the monastic cells. In summer months concerts are held in the adjoining conservatoire.

From Certosa San Giacomo a gentle stroll leads down to the fishing village of **Marina Piccola**. From the charterhouse, turn right along Via Matteoti and follow it to the Giardini di Augusto, Imperial terraced gardens overlooking the sea. From here, a twisting path leads to Via Krupp and rejoins the main road linking Capri to Marina Piccola. En route, there are stunning glimpses of Monte Solaro before Marina Piccola comes into view. The village is stacked on the flower-carpeted slopes of Monte Solaro and Castiglione.

From here, a bus goes back to Capri Town while boat trips leave for the Grotta Verde and various other mysterious caverns.

Boat trips: Capri is an island of kaleidoscopic caves, often named after their colours, embracing blue, green, white and red. Apart from the world-famous Grotta Azzurra, the loveliest are the Grotta Verde, Bianca, dei Preti and Meravigliosa. It is worth haggling with grasping boatmen to visit the grottoes and find a secluded cove for a swim. The appeal of a boat trip also lies in the limestone coves, sheer slopes and wonderful rock formations. Ochrecoloured rocks are matched by houses in the same shade. Small, dark boys dive off rocks into the turquoise waters.

Villa Jovis, an hour's walk from Capri, is an enticing experience. From Piazza Umberto, take Via Botteghe through the old crafts quarter and follow the signs to "Villa Iovis" (there is no J in Italian). Walled gardens and olive groves give way to views of Marina Grande and an ancient lighthouse dating from the time of Augustus. The palace is one of 12 Tiberius had built on the island. The isolation and grandeur of

Card sharks.

the spot reflect his inward-looking, misanthropic disposition. The overgrown villa has four huge cisterns and the remains of an open-air gallery, private quarters and thermal baths. Sadly, nothing remains of the original observatory and mosaics. This and the other Roman residences on the island were destroyed by the same Vesuvius eruption that buried Pompeii in AD 79. But in true Italian style, some of the mosaics have found their way into private homes.

Death leap: The view from the terraced gardens lives up to what Italians call a *"panorama stupendo"* over the Bay of Naples and the neighbouring islands of Ischia and Procida. On the highest point is a tiny chapel and the infamous Salto di Tiberio (Tiberius Leap). The Emperor's love of solitude and his low boredom threshold led him to hurl enemies and unsatisfactory lovers over the precipice. Centurions and fishermen alike were tossed to the bottom of the cliff after a night of debauchery. Sailors were stationed below to whack the plummeting bodies with oars until they were indisputably dead. Still, the Salto di Tiberio is a magnificent way to go.

The **Grotta Azzurra** (Blue Grotto) is the island's greatest moneyspinner but has a grace and dignity which transcend the false folklore of the experience. It is reached by bus from Anacapri or by boat from Marina Grande. The water trip involves a change of boat at the entrance to the cave, an opportunity for Capri's boatmen to dress as fishermen and over-charge. The legendary light in this marine cavern is best between 11am and 1pm. The effect is caused by the sun entering the cave through the water and the refraction of light from the walls. The vaulted chamber is bathed in an intense aquamarine light while shapes on the sandy bottom assume a silvery glow. The scene has been compared to a candle held at the back of a bowl of copper sulphate.

The Romans knew the grotto and recent excavations have unearthed broken busts and heads. Mosaics on the island show water nymphs dancing in the grotto's silvery light. Even so, the boatmen's story, that the pool once served as a *nymphaeum* for Tiberius, stretches credulity. Still more dubious is the information that, from his villa above, Tiberius entered this swimming-pool through a passage at the back of the cave. As Norman Douglas wrote in *Siren Land*: "Tiberius and his frail cortège, after scrambling on their stomachs for half a league through this dank and dismal drain, certainly deserved, and perhaps needed, a bath."

The experience evokes the ancient journey to the Underworld with Charon who, like today's boatmen, expected to be paid highly for his services. The writer André Gide loathed it.

Anacapri, the rival centre to Capri, can be reached by mini bus or boat. Anacapri has a more rustic atmosphere and a stark Moorish presence. Critics call it "Capri without the chic" but it can be a refreshing change. It is greener,

quieter and less self-consciously cute. The Sicilian influence is present in the whitewashed houses. These Moorish-looking cubes are a legacy of the Arab invasions.

In the nearby Piazza San Nicola is the church of **San Michele**. Built in 1719, the church is renowned for its vivid Neapolitan majolica floor, viewed from a gallery. The 18th-century mosaics depict the Expulsion from Paradise, with Adam and Eve accompanied by unicorns, cats and wild birds.

Above Piazza della Vittoria and its tawdry craft shops lies the whitewashed **Villa San Michele**. Axel Munthe, a Swedish physician, built this gleaming villa in an idyllic spot and lived here until his death in 1933. He immortalised the island in *The Story of San Michele* but, unlike the usual run of pleasure-loving writers, he also made a humanitarian contribution to the region. He willingly forsook his villa to sleep on the streets of Naples and to tend the Neapolitan plague victims. His lumi-nous house is now a museum combining ancient Roman busts with eclectic furnishings. Many exhibits are vulgar copies but the dramatic Medusa head is authentic.

The magnificent gardens, best seen at sunset, have sweeping views over the Bay of Naples to Salerno.

Anacapri walks: From here, charming strolls lead to Barbarossa's castle, Villa Damecuta and **Monte Solaro**, the highest point on Capri. From Piazza della Vittoria, Monte Solaro can also be reached by cable car. After climbing through terraced gardens, chestnut groves and vineyards, there are panoramic views over the Bay of Naples.

A walk or mini-bus ride leads to the ruined **Villa Damecuta**, one of Tiberius's homes, and from there to the Grotta Azzurra. Follow the main road west through olive groves and turn right after a mile or so (2 km) for the villa. Alternatively, carry straight on for the Blue Grotto. The villa, perched on a rocky cliff, overlooks a 12th-century tower. Not far away, the ruins of **Barbarossa's castle** occupy an atmospheric spot, set amongst pine trees and rocks in a gorge. This is the only Byzantine fortification on the island but was partly destroyed by Kheir-ed Din Barbarossa, the Algerian pirate who gave the castle its name.

Capri is still the haunt of the sophisticated and the would-be famous. Modest visitors come on day trips but at night Capri is quiet and exclusive, the preserve of *le tout Capri*. Yet ordinary visitors can still share the fun of the fashion circus and enjoy the charade of stardom vicariously.

Boisterous taxi-drivers offer an entertaining tour of the stars' villas in pidgin English. Against a background of vertiginous views and squealing brakes, they point out: "Villa of Jackie O, no good lady, Graiyam Greener down there; quick, *panorama stupendo* of Napoli, *palazzo* of Tiberio – a man *molto virile*." In Capri, Tiberius is never far away.

Left, gone fishing. **Right**, a long wait.

TRAVEL TIPS

GETTING THERE

BY ROAD

As the city of Naples is situated right on the *Autostrade del Sole*, it can be reached quite conveniently via motorway (toll required), though during the holiday seasons roads become heavily congested and the going is slow. The combined cost of tolls, petrol, insurance, overnight accommodation (and, for British travellers, cross-Channel ferries) makes travel by road an expensive and time-consuming option and only really worth it if there are at least three or more in the car.

Anyone entering Italy by car must carry a valid driver's licence, car registration papers and an International Green Insurance Card.

Petrol in Italy is expensive, but it is possible to buy petrol coupons at the Italian border (or in advance through motoring organisations such as Britain's AA and RAC) which entitle you to a 15 percent discount.

BY AIR

There are several European as well as international and charter airline companies which fly into Capodichino Airport, located in Naples. Included among these are Lufthansa (flights leave daily from Frankfurt via Genoa), British Airways (flights depart from London 5 times per week), and Air France (flights leave Paris 4 times a week).

There are also a good many Alitalia flights which depart daily from all major European cities including Frankfurt, Paris, London, Dusseldorf and Brussels.

In addition to international flights, Alitalia, Ati and Alisarda all offer domestic connections to Bari, Bologna, Brindisi, Cagliari, Catania, Florence, Genoa, Lampedusa, Milan, Olbia, Palermo, Pantelleria, Pisa, Rome, Trieste, Venice and Verona. Helicopter and private jet services are also available at the airport.

The following is a list of airline companies which maintain offices in Naples:
Alitalia-Ati, Via Medina 41–42. Tel: 081-542 5111.
Air France, Via San Carlo 34. Tel: 081-552 1547.
British Airways, Capodichino Airport.
Tel: 081-780 3087.
Lufthansa, Piazza Municipio 72. Tel: 081-551 5440.
Swissair, Piazza Francese 3. Tel: 081-551 1440.

BY RAIL

The three railway stations in Naples are **Stazione Centrale** (Piazza Garibaldi), **Napoli-Mergellina** and **Napoli-Campi Flegrei** (located somewhat outside the city).

Information pertaining to timetables and destinations is available from the Stazione Centrale on Piazza Garibaldi. Tel: 081-553 4188.
Two other phone numbers which may also be useful for rail travellers are:
Lost and Found: Tel: 081-286 200
Railway Police: Tel: 081-553 4152

TRAVEL ESSENTIALS

VISAS & PASSPORTS

For visits up to three months, no visas are required by members of EC countries, the US, Canada, Australia or New Zealand. A valid passport (in the case of EC members, a valid personal identification card) is sufficient.

For a list of foreign consulates in Naples, *see Useful Addresses*.

MONEY MATTERS

The unit of currency in Italy is the lira. There are 1,000, 2,000, 5,000, 10,000, 50,000 and 100,000 lire bills and 10, 20, 50, 100, 200 and 500 lire coins. The exchange rate is determined daily by the Italian stock market.

Prior to bringing large sums of money into Italy, visitors are advised to enquire about current policies pertaining to the importation of currency. Regulations introduced in the 1970s to prevent money being taken from one country to another without being subject to national control are still partially in effect today. Travellers can exchange money at border crossings, in many banks and at many travel agencies and hotels.

Banks: are open from 8.30am–1.20pm Monday–Friday; some maintain afternoon business hours between 2.30–4pm or 3pm–4.30pm. Because bank employees are considered to be members of the more privileged, professional classes customer service tends to be slow and leisurely. In view of this, it's a good idea to arm yourself with plenty of time and patience when you enter a bank to cash traveller's cheques or Eurocheques. The exchange offices in train stations and in places frequented by tourists are usually open all day and on weekends. Most hotels and restaurants accept Eurocheques and credit cards.

HEALTH

The standard of hygiene in Naples doesn't always meet Central European requirements. Public lavatories are few and far between, and should you happen to find one, chances are its condition will leave much to be desired.

When travelling in Italy it's a good idea to bring along an international medical insurance record. This will ensure that any medical attention you receive from a public health system doctor (much better than their reputation) will be free of charge. However, it is first necessary to exchange this record for a treatment certificate at a local Italian health insurance office. If, despite all this, the doctor still insists on being paid in cash, it's important that you receive a detailed bill, which you can present to your medical insurance company back home.

GETTING ACQUAINTED

TIME ZONE

Italian Standard Time corresponds to Central European Time; Daylight Saving Time (Central European Time plus 1 hour) is in effect during the summer.

CLIMATE

Naples and its surrounding area enjoy a sunny, Mediterranean climate. The average temperature is about 63°F (17°C), and even in January temperatures rarely falls below 50°F (10°C).

Keeping this in mind, visitors can confidently pack a suitcase full of lightweight clothing for both summer and winter holidays.

The Neapolitans have always been known for their tolerance and hospitality. Nevertheless, during summer visitors should take care to avoid wearing garments intended for the beach while sightseeing in the city and especially when visiting churches. The most pleasant months for travelling (in terms of average temperatures) are May, September and October.

LANGUAGE

As elsewhere in the country, the people of Naples are more or less "bilingual". On the one hand, Italian is spoken and on the other, Neapolitan. Linguists refer to the latter as a Southern Italian dialect.

To the uninitiated ear, Neapolitan, with its tendency to run sounds together and simplify everything, is almost incomprehensible. Even the Northern Italians are hard-pressed to understand it. Despite this, it is an extremely musical and expressive language. As a visitor, you will probably fall back on the tried and tested way of making yourself understood – by using your hands and feet liberally. In the main tourist areas many Italians also speak English and German.

BUSINESS HOURS

The arbitrary business hours of national museums and churches in Italy cause many travellers to shake their heads in incomprehension and irritation (the main reason for discrepancies is the lack of sufficient supervisory staff).

Generally speaking, most museums in Naples – with the exception of national museums – are closed on Mondays. On other days they are usually open 9am–2pm, and on Sundays and holidays 9am–1pm. In addition to these regular hours, during the months of August and September the most important museums, for instance Naples' National Museum of Archaeology, remain open throughout the day, from 9am–7.30pm; other museums are open all day only on certain days of the year.

The excavation sites at Pompeii and Herculaneum are also open all day, from 9am–1 hour before sunset, though these too are closed on Monday. For the exact hours of specific museums, your best bet is to consult the local newspaper.

Offices are accessible to the general public in the mornings only and in many cases just for a few hours.

Shops are generally open 9am–1pm and 4pm–8pm Monday–Saturday, but keep in mind that exact business hours may differ from store to store.

For bank opening times see *Money Matters*.

NATIONAL HOLIDAYS

1 January	Capodanno (New Year's Day)
Easter Monday	Lunedì dell'Angelo
25 April	Liberazione (Liberation Day)
1 May	Festa del Lavoro (Labour Day)
15 August	Assunta (Day of the Assumption of the Virgin Mary)
19 September	San Gennaro (festival of the patron saint)
1 November	Ognissanti (All Saints' Day)
8 December	Immacolata (Day of the Immaculate Conception)
25 December	Natale (Christmas)
26 December	Santo Stefano (Feast of Stephen)

In just about all large and small Italian cities you can find something interesting going on, and this certainly holds true for Naples. Numerous religious, historical and commercial festivals take place throughout the year. Although they are not officially recognised as holidays, they are invariably celebrated as such. There are also innumerable cultural events, exhibitions and trade fairs. The following is a list of the most important events:

17 January: Carnival commences at the St Antonio Abate Church, Naples. Lively, colourful parades take place in other areas of the city.

Settimana Santa (Holy Week): Good Friday processions are organised in many surrounding communities from Thursday evening until Easter Saturday.

1st Weekend in May: The celebration of San Gennaro in Naples cathedral.

17–19 May: The celebration of Santa Restituita, followed by a procession of boats.

15–16 July: The celebration of Madonna del Carmine. During this festival the "fire" in the tower of the Santa Maria del Carmine Church is commemorated by a magnificent fireworks display.

15 August: Festival of the Assumption of the Virgin Mary.

7–9 September: This festival, in honour of the Madonna di Piedigrotta, is considered by many to be the most significant and gloriously colourful celebration in Naples. It is accompanied by lively parades and the *canzone napoletana*, a music festival.

19 September: The birthday of San Gennaro, Naples' patron saint. Processions are followed by the famous "blood miracle" in the cathedral.

COMMUNICATIONS

The most popular daily newspaper in Naples is *Il Mattino*, whose pages are mainly devoted to local and regional reporting. Since the spring of 1990, however, the daily Roman paper *La Repubblica* has provided strong competition.

In the local sections of both newspapers you'll find opening times for museums, exhibitions, tours, theatre performances and cinema programmes, as well as the departure and arrival times of the ferries and hydrofoils to the various islands. The most important rail connections and a schedule of flights at Capodichino are also listed here. Other helpful tips can be found in the brochure *Qui Napoli*, published by the *Azienda Autonoma di Soggiorno, Cura e Turismo* (in both English and German).

In most large hotels it is possible to get private cable and satellite programmes in addition to the regular Italian and innumerable local Neapolitan programmes.

The **Postal Centrale** is open all day long. The only time you'll really need to visit it, however, is when you want to send a letter by certified mail, a telegram or parcel. Stamps can be purchased in any tobacco shop designated with a black sign sporting the letter "T" (*Tabacchi*).

It is possible to pick up mail sent *poste restante* at the main post office; all letters must be clearly marked with *fermo posta*.

In Italy you can't make a telephone call from the post office; all telecommunications are operated by the company *SIP*.

There are telephone booths located on almost every corner in the city. In addition to these, you'll find pay phones in nearly all bars, restaurants and other eateries, which can be operated either by inserting *gettoni* (telephone tokens) or by using special calling credit cards.

The dialling code for Naples is 081 (omit the zero when calling long distance). The international code for Italy in general is +39.

EMERGENCIES

In some of the slum areas of Naples the incidence of petty crime is especially high. If you want to take measures to protect yourself from pickpockets (otherwise known as *scippatori* and exceptionally adept at snatching jewellery and purses with lightning speed) and car thieves, it's absolutely necessary to take basic precautions.

Here are some important telephone numbers:

Carabinieri, tel: 112 (for emergencies only).
Polizia, tel: 081-794 1111 (Questura Centrale); tel: 081-794 1435 (mobile task force for car theft).
Polizia Stradale, tel: 081-293 748.
Vigili del Fuoco, tel: 115 (Fire Brigade).
Vigili Urbani, tel: 081-751 3177 (Traffic Patrol).
Medical Emergency Service, tel: 081-751 3177 (in service only at night and on holidays; for emergencies occurring at other times, contact the *Pronto Soccorso* in every public hospital).

ANTI-THEFT PRECAUTIONS

Unemployment in Naples is running at over 30 percent. In addition, the city has a big heroin problem so most crime is drug-related. As a precaution, keep a record of credit card numbers. Leave most travellers' cheques, currency, passport, camera and your handbag in the hotel safe.

Avoid looking like a tourist – cameras, if carried, should be kept out of view. Avoid wearing jewellery – especially anything flashy – except for a wedding ring. A necklace is an invitation to steal so if you must wear jewellery, keep it concealed. Ideally, don't leave a car in Naples unless staying in one of the few (expensive) hotels that have parking facilities.

PRECAUTIONS FOR WOMEN TRAVELLERS

Sexist advice though it is, play the little woman and be above reproach in perceived moral behaviour – avoid doing anything that could be misconstrued as flirtation; dress down or dress formally. If travelling alone, wear a wedding ring and refer to your husband as if he were travelling with you – but at a conference at that precise moment. Avoid sitting in parks alone and reject offers of lifts or guides.

Avoid walking through central areas alone at night. Ask the hotel frankly about the safety of that particular area – they're usually helpful. If at risk, appeal to other women who may intervene; as a last resort, appeal to the Neapolitan respect for married women and mothers! If blonde and fair-skinned, expect hassles. At worst, it's see Naples and die.

POSSIBLE DANGER ZONES

Station area: Avoid all hotels and restaurants in the area – the hotels are either sleazy or operate as brothels. Petty thieving is not uncommon in these hotels. Corso Umberto (Piazza Garibaldi end) is the red-light area, the place for kerb crawlers and prostitutes as well as blackmarket racketeers. The Umberto I arcades are fine by day but should be avoided at night, when pickpockets and drug dealers are at large.
Spaccanapoli – the old quarter, including the poor Quartieri Spagnoli (the Spanish Quarter): Reasonable during the day if one is sensible but best avoided at night, especially if you are alone.

Markets: Markets are one of the joys of Naples. Even so, be on your guard against pickpockets, especially in the Forcella market.
Fontanella Cemetery and Catacombs Quarter: This is a fascinating area and fairly safe during the day if one takes the anti-theft precautions mentioned, but avoid at night.
The Suburbs: As a driver, be heartless if your help is sought. The following is a common ploy used to rob unsuspecting drivers: someone appears to be in trouble (eg lying in/near the road or with a friend trying to flag your car down). Drive on.

THE COAST & ISLANDS

As far as casual crime is concerned, the rest of Campania is generally safe. However, avoid the impoverished (and ugly) Camorra-controlled towns to the north of Naples.

GETTING AROUND

TOURS

Different travel agencies offer a wide selection of day trips within the city itself as well as excursions into the surrounding countryside and islands. Further information pertaining to exact tour destinations, prices and services can be obtained from the following travel agencies:
Cit, Piazza Municipio. Tel: 081-552 5426.
Cima Tours, Piazza Garibaldi 114.
Tel: 081-554 0646.
Tour Car, Piazza Matteotti 1. Tel: 081-552 3310.

PUBLIC TRANSPORT

The public transport system in Naples consists primarily of a well-developed bus network, trams, an underground system, four funiculars and countless small, privately-run services. The vehicles operating in the latter category are prone to be rather dilapidated, but because they do not not need official clearance before setting off on a route they often manage to beat the buses to the waiting customers. Not infrequently, drivers of these conveyances overload their vehicles to the point where it is dangerous. Despite these drawbacks, travelling in this fashion is sure to be an adventure and provide closer contact with the Neapolitans themselves. (Beware of pickpockets.)

Tickets for the various forms of public transport are relatively cheap. The only problem is knowing where to purchase them. In many cases they can be bought at newspaper stands, tobacco shops and bars in the vicinity. There are special discount prices for all-day and multiple-journey tickets. Free timetables and route descriptions are available at the Azienda Autonoma di Soggiorno (Palazzo Reale).

TRAMS

Line 1 (Poggioreale – Piazza Garibaldi – Piazza Municipio – Riviera di Chiaia – Fuorigrotta – Bagnoli).
Line 2 (the same route as Line 1, but only during peak traffic hours and as far as Fuorigrotta).
Line 4B (Sperone – Corso San Giovanni a Teduccio – Via Reggia di Portici – Via Marina – Piazza Municipio – Galleria Vittoria – Piazza Vittoria).
Line 29RB (operates only on regular working days; Sperone – Corso San Giovanni a Teduccio – Via Reggia di Portici – Via Vespucci – Corso Garibaldi – Piazza Nazionale).

FUNICULAR

Funicolare centrale (Via Toledo – Piazza Fuga).
Funicolare di Chiaia (Via del Parco Margherita – Via Cimaros).
Funicolare di Montesanto (Piazza Montesanto – Via Morghen).

You can reach Vomero, the highest part of the city, in just a few minutes by any of these funiculars.
Funicolare di Mergellina (Via Mergellina – Via Manzoni).

UNDERGROUND

The *Metropolitana*, run by the National Italian Railways, travels both under and over the ground at 5–10 minute intervals. Another municipal underground system is currently being built, but it will take some years before it is fully operational.

BUSES IN THE SURROUNDING AREA

Napoli–Caserta: Departures from early in the morning until late at night every 20 minutes on regular workdays and every 40 minutes on Sundays and holidays. The journey takes about 1 hour and the end of the line is at the Piazza Porta Capuana. The name of the transport company is Consorzio trasporti pubblici Napoli. Tel: 081-700 5091.
Napoli-Avellino: Departures from early until late every 20 minutes on regular workdays and every 40 minutes on Sundays and holidays. The end of the line is at the Piazza Porta Capuana. The name of the transport company is Consorzio trasporti irpini. Tel: 081-553 4677.
Napoli–Salerno: Departures from early until late every half hour on regular workdays and every 2 hours on Sundays and holidays. The end of the line is at Via Pisanelli (near the Piazza Municipio). The name of the transport company is Sita (Via Pisanelli 3-7). Tel: 081-552 2176.
Capodichino Airport–Sorrento: Departures in the morning and afternoon. The journey takes about 1 hour. The name of the transport company is Curreri. Tel: 081-879 8524.

TAXIS

If you happen to be in a hurry, you can always take a taxi. Keep in mind, however, that they are little quicker than other forms of public transport, but at least you'll be spared the discomfort of being squashed in with a lot of passengers.

The meter initially registers 2,300 lire. This sum increases by 100 lire every 395 ft (118 metres). Standing still also has its price: 100 lire for every 33 seconds. In addition to these basic costs, you may or may not be charged extra for diverse services.

There's no point in trying to calculate the final fee yourself; the saying "control is good, but trust is better", which has become axiomatic in Naples, also holds true for taxi rides.
Taxi/Radiotaxi: Tel: 081-556 44 44 or 081-556 43 40.

CAR RENTAL

The nationally known car rental agencies all have offices at Capodichino Airport as well as in the city of Naples itself. The driver must be over 21 years of age and have been in possession of a full driving licence for at least one year. The following is a selection of the largest of the car rental companies:
Avis
Via Partenope 32. Tel: 081-764 56 00
Piazza Garibaldi. Tel: 284041
Capodichino Airport. Tel: 081/7805759
Europcar
Via Partenope 38. Tel: 081-40 14 54
Capodichino Airport. Tel: 081-7805643
Bisin Tour
Via Carducci 35. Tel: 081-41 30 66
Hertz
Via Partenope 29. Tel: 081-764 55 33
Piazza Garibaldi. Tel: 081-20 62 28
Capodichino Airport. Tel: 081-7802971
Maggiore
Via Cervantes 92. Tel: 081-55 21 900
Piazza Garibaldi. Tel: 081-28 78 58
Capodichino Airport. Tel: 081-7802963
InterRent
Via Partenope 14. Tel: 081-764 63 64
Capodichino Airport. Tel: 081-7802963

In case of **breakdown** – either in Naples or anywhere else in Italy for that matter – assistance from the Automobile Club d'Italia (ACI) can be obtained by dialling the number 116. In Naples the following garages also provide emergency services at night:

Autoservizi Lux, Via Ponza (Casoria). Tel: 081-584 45 89.

Autosoccorso del Sud, Corso Amedeo di Savoia 307. Tel: 7413777.

Giovanni Parlato, Via Pontetti Sanseverino. Tel: 081-75968 02.

PETROL STATIONS OPEN AT NIGHT

In the City Centre:
Piazza Carlo III (Mobil)
Via Foria (Mobil)
Piazza Municipio (Mobil)
Piazza Mergellina (Agip)
Posillipo:
Via Manzoni (Esso)
Fuorigrotta:
Via Caio Duilio (Agip)
Via Terracina (Agip)
Vomero:
Via Falcone (IP)
Corso Europa (Agip)
Viale Michelangelo (Esso)
North of the City:
Via Caserta al Bravo (Fina)
Via Janfolla (Agip)
Viale Maddalena (Agip)
Via Nuova Miano (Mach)
Quadrivio Arzano (Esso)
Santa Maria a Cubito (Mobil)
East of the City:
Via Argine (Mach u. Mobil)
Via Ferraris (Esso u. Mobil)
Ponte di Casanova (Esso)
Via Repubbliche Marinare (IP)
Via Stadera (Agip)

MULTI-STOREY CAR PARKS

Since trying to find a parking spot on Naples' streets is pretty much a lost cause from the beginning, you may as well head for one of the multi-storey car parks. An additional advantage here is that your car will be more protected from thieves.

The following is a list of multi-storey car parks:
Grilli, Via Galileo Ferraris 40. Tel: 081-26 43 44. (Near the main railway station.)
Mergellina, Via Mergellina 112. Tel: 081-761 34 70.
Morelli, Via D. Morelli 65. Tel: 081-40 53 68.
Sannazzaro, Piazza Sannazzaro 142. Tel: 081-68 14 37. (Near the Mergellina railway station.)
Supergarage, Via Shelley 11. Tel: 081-551 31 04.
Turistico, Via Alcide De Gasperi 14. Tel: 081-552 54 42.

WHERE TO STAY

HOTELS

Many hotels have "representatives" at ports and main cities who try to talk you into staying in particular hotels. Expect to be told that all other hotels in the area are full/bad etc. The touts invariably offer to drive you to the hotel but if, on arrival, you refuse the accommodation you have to make your own way back or pay for the drive. This is also a feature of Capri and Ischia. At best, you will pay slightly over the odds; at worst, you will be ripped off for inferior or over-priced accommodation. Tourist offices are not above suspicion in that they will sometimes send visitors to a (reasonable) hotel in which they have a vested interest.

In Naples itself there is an overwhelming assortment of hotels and pensions to choose from. During the peak seasons it's a good idea to reserve rooms well in advance. The following is a brief list of hotels, arranged according to location.

NAPLES

LUNGOMARE

Excelsior, Via Partenope 48. Tel: 081-41 71 11. This five-star hotel offers the classiest accommodation in Naples and the prices here reflect this luxury. Restaurant.
Continental, Via Partenope 44. Tel: 081-76 44 636.
Miramare, Via Nazario Sauro 24. Tel: 081-42 73 88. A 4-star establishment with a magnificent view of the sea.
Royall, Via Partenope 38. Tel: 081-764 48 00. Restaurant.
Santa Lucia, Via Partenope 46. Tel: 081-41 65 66.
Canada, Via Mergellina 43. Tel: 081-68 20 18.
Vesuvioo, Via Partenope 45. Tel: 081 41 70 44. This is an especially tastefully decorated and comfortable establishment. The boast that Enrico Caruso spent his final days here is still exploited by the hotel management. Restaurant.
Rex, Via Palepoli 12. Tel: 081-41 63 88
Bella Napoli, Via Caracciolo 10. Tel: 081-66 38 11. Restaurant.
Galles, Via Sannazaro 5. Tel: 081-66 83 44.
Le Fontane al Mare, Via Tommaseo 14. Tel: 081-764 34 70.
Muller, Via Mergellina 7. Tel: 081-66 90 56.

WITH PANORAMIC VIEWS

Britannique, Corso Vittorio Emanuele 133. Tel: 081-7614145. Restaurant.
Paradiso, Via Catullo 11. Tel: 081-761 41 61. Restaurant.
Parker's, Corso Vittorio Emanuele 135. Tel: 081-7612474. Restaurant.
Belvedere, Via Tito Angelini 51. Tel: 081-578 81 69. Restaurant.
Splendid, Via Manzoni 96. Tel: 081-64 54 62. Restaurant.
Camaldoli, Via Iannelli 586. Tel: 081-546 68 36.
Oasi, Via Mariano D'Amelio 69. Tel: 081-36 05 61.

IN THE CITY CENTRE

Jolly Ambassador's, Via Medina 70. Tel: 081-41 60 00. Restaurant.
Majestic, Largo Vasto a Chiaia 68. Tel: 081-41 65 00.
Mediterraneoo, Via Nuova Ponte di Tappia 25. Tel: 081-5512240. Restaurant.
Oriente, Via Armando Diaz 44. Tel: 081-551 21 33.
Casa Betania, Via Settembrini 42. Tel: 081-44 48 33.
Lago Maggiore, Via del Cerriglio 10. Tel: 081-522 24 10.
Pinto-Storey, Via Martucci 72. Tel: 081-68 12 60

NEAR THE RAILWAY STATION

Terminus, Piazza Garibaldi 91. Tel: 081-28 60 11. Restaurant.
Cavour, Piazza Garibaldi 32. Tel: 081-28 59 29.
Mexico, Via Rosarolli 13. Tel: 081-26 63 30. Restaurant.
Nuovo Rebecchino, Corso Garibaldi 356. Tel: 081-26 80 26. Restaurant.
Palace, Piazza Garibaldi 9. Tel: 081-26 70 44. Restaurant.
Prati, Via Rosarolli 4. Tel: 081-26 88 98. Restaurant.
Bristol, Piazza Garibaldi 61. Tel: 081-28 17 80. Restaurant.
Charlie, Via Milano 82. Tel: 081-20 57 41.
Cristal, Via Torino 108. Tel: 081-26 65 44. Restaurant.
Eden, Corso Novara 9. Tel: 081-28 56 90. Restaurant.
Esedra, Piazza Cantani 12. Tel: 081-553 98 68.
Europa, Corso Meridionale 15. Tel: 081-26 75 11. Restaurant.
Gallo, Via Spaventa 9. Tel: 081-28 60 09.
Garden, Corso Garibaldi 92. Tel: 081-26 84 13.
Guiren, Via Bologna 114. Tel: 081-28 65 30.
Mignon, Corso Novara 7. Tel: 081-554 88 93.
Pugliese, Via Pica 14. Tel: 081-26 97 66. Restaurant.
San Giorgio, Vico III Duchesca 27. Tel: 081-28 16 02.
San Pietro, Via San Pietro ad Aram 18. Tel: 081-553 59 14.

Sayonara, Piazza Garibaldi 59. Tel: 081-554 03 13. Restaurant.

FUORIGROTTA

San Gennaro, Via Beccadelli 41. Tel: 081-570 54 22. Restaurant.
Delle Terme, Via Agnano Astroni. Tel: 081-570 17 33. Restaurant.
Domitiana, Viale Kennedy 143. Tel: 081-61 05 60.
Pasadena, Via Terracina 159. Tel: 081-61 63 17. Restaurant.
Serius, Viale Augusto 74. Tel: 081-61 48 44. Restaurant.
Miravalle, Via Astroni 380. Tel: 081-726 17 81. Restaurant.
Montespina, Ortsteil Agnano Terme. Tel: 081-570 29 62. Restaurant.
Nuovo Diana, Via degli Scipioni 13. Tel: 081-61 98 41.
Oltremare, Via Cintia 14. Tel: 081-767 23 27.

POZZUOLI & DOMIZIANA

American, Pozzuoli. Via Scarfoglio 15. Tel: 081-570 65 29. Restaurant.
La Perla, Castelvolturno. Tel: 0823-509 31 66. Restaurant.
Solfatara, Pozzuoli. Via Solfatara. Tel: 526 26 66. Restaurant.
Tennis, Pozzuoli. Via Righi 5. Tel: 570 90 33. Restaurant.

SORRENTO

Cocumella, Via Cocumella 7. Tel: 081-878216. Expensive, period villa outside town. Elegant restaurant and pool.
Excelsior Vittoria, Piazza Tasso 34. Tel: 081-8781900. Atmospheric hotel-restaurant in Art Nouveau style. Pool. The celebrated opera singer Enrico Caruso stayed here and a room is dedicated to him.
Villa Garden, Corso Marion Crawford. Tel: 081-8781387. Mid-range hotel-restaurant with lovely views. Situated in the less touristy Sant'Angelo edge of town.

THE AMALFI COAST

AMALFI

Santa Caterina, Strada Amalfitana. Tel: 089-871012. Sumptuous hotel perched on the cliffs. Terrace. Pool.
Cappuccini Convento, Amalfi. Tel: 089-871877. Atmospheric but expensive hotel-restaurant set in a former monastery.
Hotel Luna, Amalfi. Tel: 089-871002. Expensive hotel-restaurant where Ibsen wrote part of *The Doll's House*.

POSITANO

Il San Pietro di Positano, Via Laurito. Tel: 089-875455. Very expensive hotel. Magnificent cliffside location. Antiques and bougainvillaea everywhere. Best cuisine on the Amalfi coast. Restaurant, pool, tennis courts.

La Sirenuse, Via C Columbo 30. Tel: 089-875066. Very expensive hotel. Gracious period villa with terrace. Pool.

Palazzo Murat, Via dei Mulini. Tel: 089-875177. Mid-range hotel in heart of town. A period *palazzo* with walled garden.

RAVELLO

Palazzo Palumbo, Via Toro 28. Tel: 089-857244. Very expensive. Charmingly furnished with antiques. Cosy restaurant.

Hotel Caruso Belvedere, Ravello. Tel: 089-857111. Mid-range hotel. Nostalgic villa where Greta Garbo once stayed.

SALERNO/PAESTUM

Albergo Italia, Piazza Ferrovia, Salerno. Tel: 089-224477. Comfortable, unexceptional mid-range hotel in town centre.

THE ISLANDS

CAPRI

Quisisana, Via Camarelle, Capri Town. Tel: 837 0788. World-class hotel. Sumptuous. Elegant ambience and rooms dotted with antiques. Terrace, enclosed garden with pool.

Scalinatella, Via Tragara 8, Capri. Tel: 837 0633. Expensive but sophisticated hotel set among terraced gardens. Overlooks the Certosa (domed charterhouse). Pool.

La Floridana, Via Campo di Teste, Capri Town. Tel: 837 0101. Fairly expensive but great views and friendly service.

San Michele, Via G Orlando, Anacapri. Tel: 837 1427. Charming, mid-range villa hotel with fine views.

ISCHIA

Excelsior Belvedere, Via E Gianturco 19, Ischia Porto. Tel: 991 522. Expensive hotel with pool and garden. Central but quiet.

Mare Blu, Via Pontano 40, Ischia Ponte. Tel: 982 555. Mid-range hotel on the waterfront. Views of the castle.

Il Monastero, Castello Aragonese, Ischia Ponte. Tel: 992 435. Inexpensive *pensione* with romantic location high up in the castle precincts. Views over the bay. Friendly owners.

Punta del Sole, Piazza Maltese, Forio. Tel: 998 208.

Expensive hotel linked to a thermal establishment.

San Montano, Via Monte Vico, Lacco Ameno. Tel: 994 033. Expensive hotel with pool, thermal baths and tennis courts.

Romantico Terme, Via Ruffano, Sant'Angelo. Tel: 999 216. Mid-range hotel with spa, pool and tennis court in Ischia's most charming fishing village.

PROCIDA

L'Oasi, Via Elleri 16. Tel: 081-8967499. Quiet mid-range villa hotel with restaurant and garden.
This is the only hotel open all year but rooms can be booked in private homes through the tourist office in Procida.

CAMPSITES

NAPLES

Most of the campsites are located in Pozzuoli, in the northern part of the city. For visitors wanting quick and easy access into the city centre, the following sites are good choices:

Vulcano Solfatara, Via Solfatara 161. Tel: 867 34 13. This campsite is situated 1 km (about half a mile) from the beach and also has a number of bungalows for rent. Open: 1 April–10 October.

Averno, located near the 55 kilometre-marker on the Domiziana secondary road and situated just a few hundred metres from the beach. Tel: 866 12 02. Also has bungalows to rent. Open: all year.

Marina di Licola, located near the 49.2-kilometre marker on the Domiziana secondary road and situated just a few hundred metres from the beach. Tel: 867 81 19. Also has bungalows to rent. Open: 1 May–30 September.

YOUTH HOSTELS

Generally speaking, in Italy youth hostels are few and far between and this certainly applies in Naples. In fact, there is only one youth hostel in the city, located in Mergellina. The address is: Salita della Grotta 23. Tel: 081-761 23 46.

FOOD DIGEST

Italian food has a fine reputation and Neapolitan cuisine is no exception, with numerous and excellently-prepared specialities. This region also has the reputation of being the birthplace of Mozzerella cheese, made from water buffalo milk, which is increasing in popularity by leaps and bounds. There are also quite a few excellent fish dishes in the local culinary repertoire. (*See chapter on Food.*)

NAPLES

RESTAURANTS WITH A VIEW

Belvedere, Via T. Angelini 51. Tel: 081-578 81 69.
La Sacrestia, Via Orazio 116. Tel: 081-66 41 86. Closed: Wednesdays.
D'Angelo, Via A. Falcone 203. Tel: 081-578 90 77. Closed: Tuesday.
Le Arcate, Via A. Falcone 249. Tel: 081-68 33 80. Closed: Tuesdays.
Renzo e Lucia, Via T. Angelini 13. Tel: 081-36 50 04. Closed: Mondays.

LUNGOMARE

Bersagliera, Borgo Marinaro. Tel: 081-764 60 16. This is an old, venerable and well-maintained dining establishment. The fish is especially good. Closed: Tuesday.
Zi Tore, Piazza della Repubblica. Tel: 081-66 37 07. Although "Uncle Salvatore" is no longer slaving over the hot stove himself, the quality of the food here is as good as ever.
Da Peppino, Via Palepoli 6. Tel: 081 41 55 82. Popular with office workers in the neighbourhood. The lunch menu is especially highly recommended. Closed: Sundays.

POSILLIPO

A fenestella, Via Marechiaro 23. Tel: 081-76 900 20. This restaurant is famous for its incredible view and the fish specialities here are truly exceptional. Closed: Wednesdays.
Le Castellane, Via Posillipo 176. Tel: 081-769 68 89. A superb establishment which offers a variety of international dishes. Closed: Mondays.

CITY CENTRE

A Canzuncella, Piazza S. Maria La Nova 18. Tel: 081-551 90 18. Serves a variety of hearty, tasty dishes originating in the hinterland.
Dante e Beatrice, Piazza Dante 44/45. Tel: 081 34 99 05. In addition to an assortment of well-known specialities, excellent fish appetisers are served. Closed: Wednesdays.

PIZZERIAS

The home of the pizza still has many restaurants which prepare it in the authentic and traditional manner. Here is a choice:
Port'Alba, Via Port'Alba 18. Tel: 081-45 97 13.
Bellini, Via Santa Maria di Costantinopoli 80. Tel: 081-45 97 74.
Lombardi e Santa Chiara, Via Benedetto Croce 59. Tel: 081-552 07 80.
Trianon, Via Colletta 46. Tel: 081-553 94 26.
Brandi, Salita Sant'Anna di Palazzo 1. Tel: 081-41 69 28.

CAFES

Because it is customary in Naples to drink *espresso* while standing at a bar, the city has no tradition of coffee houses.

In spite of this, there are a number of cafés where you can sit down and enjoy a leisurely cup of coffee and a piece of cake. The following is a list of the best establishments:
Caflish, Via Toledo 253. Tel: 081-412466; or Via Chiaia 143. Tel: 081-40 45 88
Gambrinus, Piazza Trieste e Trento. Tel: 081-41 75 82.
La Caffettiera, Piazza dei Martiri. Tel: 081-40 44 17.
Motta, Via Toledo 152. Tel: 081-552 06 20.
Verdi, Via Verdi 23. Tel: 081-552 08 35.

SORRENTO

Don Alfonso, Sant'Agata. Tel: 081-8780026. Set in the hills above the town. Expensive traditional Campanian cuisine.
Kursaal, Via Fuorimura 7. Tel: 081-8781216. Chic restaurant perched on a gorge. Try the *pesce al cartoccio* (baked fish).
O'Parruchiano, Corso Italia 77. 081-8781321. Very popular restaurant. Greenhouse-style dining room. Try the *scallope alla sorrentina* (escalope with mozzarella and tomatoes).

THE AMALFI COAST

AMALFI

La Caravella, Via M Camera 12. Tel: 089-871029. Mid-range restaurant under arches. Specialities:

THE COLOUR OF LIFE.

A holiday may last just a week or so, but the memories of those happy, colourful days will last forever, because together you and Kodak Ektachrome films will capture, as large as life, the wondrous sights, the breathtaking scenery and the magical moments. For you to relive over and over again.

The Kodak Ektachrome range of slide films offers a choice of light source, speed and colour rendition and features extremely fine grain, very high sharpness and high resolving power.

Take home the real colour of life with Kodak Ektachrome films.

LIKE THIS?

OR LIKE THIS?

A KODAK FUN PANORAMIC CAMERA
BROADENS YOUR VIEW

The holiday you and your camera have been looking forward to all year; and a stunning panoramic view appears. "Fabulous", you think to yourself, "must take that one".

Unfortunately, your lens is just not wide enough. And three-in-a-row is a poor substitute.

That's when you take out your pocket-size, 'single use' Kodak Fun Panoramic Camera. A film and a camera, all in one, and it works miracles. You won't need to focus, you don't need special lenses. Just aim, click

and... it's all yours. The total pictur

You take twelve panorami pictures with one Kodak Fun Pan ramic Camera. Then put the camer in for developing and printing.

Each print is 25 by 9 centimetre Excellent depth of field. True Kodak Gold colours.

The Kodak Fun Panoramic Camera itself goes bac to the factory, to be recycled. So that others too can capture one of those spectacular phooooooooootoooooooooooooos.

scialatelli (pasta in a shellfish sauce) and *pesce al limone* (fish in a lemon sauce).

Taverna degli Apostoli, Largo Augustariccio Tel: 089-872991. Atmospheric vaulted restaurant close to the Duomo. Try the *acqua pazza*, fish cooked with vegetables.

THE ISLANDS

CAPRI

La Pigna, Via Roma 8, Capri Town. Tel: 837 0280. Expensive but lovely setting in the pine trees. Try *fettucine alla Sophia Loren* – named after the local star.

La Capannina, Via Botteghe 14, Capri Town. Tel: 837 0732. Vine-hung courtyard. *Antipasti* include fried ravioli, *melanzane* (aubergines) and stuffed peppers. Chicken dishes.

Da Gemma, Via Madre Serafina 6. Tel: 837 0461. Intimate and friendly. *Fritto misto* (mixed seafood) and *spaghetti con cozze o vongole* (with mussels or clams) are recommended.

Da Gelsomina la Migliera, Via Migliera 6, Anacapri. Island specialities including mushroom dishes.

ISCHIA

Da Ciccio, Via Porto 1, Ischia Porto. Risotto dishes, especially *risotto alla pescatore* (with fish).

Giardini Eden, Via Nuova Cartoromana 50, Ischia Ponte. Tel: 993 909. Fish and lobster eaten beside the castle.

La Meridiana, San Francesco Beach, Forio. Lobster and seafood specialities.

Padrone d'o Mare, Lacco Ameno. Good fish dishes.

Dal Pescatore, Piazza Troia, Sant'Angelo. Fish dishes.

PROCIDA

Crescenzo, Via Marinara, Chiaiolella. Restaurant with a few rooms to let. Try *Spaghetti ai frutti di mare* (with seafood).

CULTURE PLUS

In Pompeii, and many other archaeological sites and churches, you will need to tip the custodian to see certain "closed" rooms/exhibits. Exhibits undergoing restoration (*sotto restauro*) can sometimes be miraculously restored if the price is right. Bargain if the bribe seems unreasonable.

MUSEUMS

At present there are 14 museums in Naples, covering subjects as diverse as archaeology, fine arts, minerology and crafts. Some of them are internationally famous. Admission at many museums is free.

Museo Archeologico Nazionale, Piazza Museo. Tel: 081-44 01 16. Many people think this is the most important archaeological museum in Europe. Exhibits from the 8th century BC until the 5th century AD vividly portray the life and artistic accomplishments of those times. Highlights include parts of the Farnese Collection, which Charles of Bourbon inherited from his mother, Elisabeth of Farnese, and finds excavated at the sites of Pompeii and Herculaneum.

The artifacts found in Cumae and throughout Campania are also exhibited here. Of special interest are the Etruscan and Egyptian collections of Borgia, and the famous Santangelo Collection of antique coins.

Hours: 9am–2pm and 9am–1pm on holidays. During August and September the museum is open all day 9am–7.30pm. Admission: charge for visitors between the ages of 18–60; for all other visitors admission is free.

Museo e Gallerie Nazionali di Capodimonte, Parco di Capodimonte. Tel: 081-741 08 81. This museums includes the National Gallery, founded on the Farnese Collection (with its numerous paintings by Titian) bequeathed by the House of Bourbon; the 19th-Century Gallery, and the porcelain and majolica collection. The grandiose museum buildings are surrounded by an enormous park.

Hours: 9am–2pm and 9am–1pm on holidays. Admission: charge for visitors between the ages of 18 and 60; for all other visitors admission is free.

Museo Nazionale di San Martino, in the city district of Vomero, next to the Castel Sant'Elmo. Tel: 081-578 17 69. This splendidly situated museum was originally a monastery of the House of Anjou. Displays trace the history of the Neapolitan Kingdom, and the region's festivals and customs. The museum also contains an important collection of paintings done by members of the Neapolitan School of Painting.

Hours: 9am–2pm and 9am–1pm on holidays. During the months of August and September the museum is open all day on Tuesdays, Thursdays and Saturdays until 8pm. Admission: charge for visitors between the ages of 18–60; for all other visitors admission is free.

Museo di Palazzo Reale, Piazza Plebiscito. Tel: 081-41 38 88. The great halls and salons of the former royal palace are furnished with paintings, sculptures, porcelain and furniture as if still inhabited by the Bourbons themselves. The exhibit "Arte sacra di Palazza" is on permanent view in the chapel.

Hours: 9am–2pm and 9am–1pm on holidays. During August and September the museum is open all day until 7.30pm. Admission: charge for visitors between the ages of 18–60; for all other visitors admission is free.

Museo Pricipe di Aragona Pignatelli Cortes, Riviera di Chiaia. Tel: 081-66 96 75. In this museum visitors will primarily find collections of carefully selected pieces of 19th-century furniture and porcelain. There are some magnificent carriages on display in the garden.

Hours: 9am–2pm and 9am–1pm on holidays. The museum is closed on Mondays. During the months of August and September hours are 9am–2pm Monday; on Wednesday, Thursday, Friday and Saturday the museum is open all day from 9am–8pm. Admission: charge for visitors between the ages of 18–60; for all other visitors admission is free.

Museo Duca di Martina, In the city district Vomero, in the Villa Floridiana. Tel: 081-578 84 18. An extensive collection of European, Chinese and Japanese porcelain, majolica and other *objets d'art*.

Hours: 9am–2pm and 9am–1pm on holidays. Closed: Mondays. In the months of August and September the museum is open 9am–2pm Monday and on Tuesday, Thursday and Saturday throughout the day until 8pm. Admission: charge for visitors between the ages of 18–60; for all other visitors admission is free.

Museo Civico di Castel Nuovo (Maschio Angioino), Piazza Municipio. This museum contains valuable sculptures and frescoes from the 14th and 15th centuries, as well as a collection of paintings dating from the 15th right up until the 20th century. The museum is closed on Mondays.

Museo Civico Filangieri, Via Duomo 288. Tel: 081-20 31 75. Here you'll find art, weaponry, furniture and porcelain collections, as well traditional ethnic costumes and the Filangieri Archive.

Hours: 9am–2pm and 9am–1pm on holidays. Closed: Mondays. Admission: charge.

Museo di Mineralogia, Via Mezzocannone 8. Tel: 081-20 68 01. The museum houses an extensive collection of Vesuvian rocks, meteorites and minerals from the Phlegraean Fields, and quartz crystals.

Hours: 9am–2pm and 9am–noon Saturday. Closed: Sundays. Admission: free.

Museo Ferroviario Nazionale, Corso S. Giovanni a Teduccio. Tel: 081-47 20 03. This museum is housed in the restored workshop halls of Pietrarsa. The star exhibit is a steam locomotive.

Hours: workdays 9am–2pm. Admission: free.

Cappella Sansevero, Via De Sanctis 19, near the Piazza San Domenico Maggiore. Tel: 081-551 84 70. Masterpieces of sculpture dating from the 18th century. Giuseppe Sanmartino's sculpture of the Veiled Christ is especially worth seeing.

Hours: 10am–1pm and 5pm–7pm (open only during the morning on Tuesday), and from 10am–1pm on holidays. Closed: all day Wednesday. Admission: charge.

Museo di Etnopreistoria, Castel dell'Ovo. Tel: 081-764 53 43. This museum is located in the headquarters of the Club Alpino Italiano. The museum is open for visitors by pre-arranged appointment only. Admission: free.

Pinocoteca dei Girolamini, Via Duomo 142. Tel: 081-44 91 39. The old collection housed here primarily contains works from the 16th and 18th centuries.

Hours: workdays 9.30am–12.30pm and 2pm–5.30pm. Admission: free.

THEATRE

The most important theatre in Naples is the **Teatro San Carlo** (Via San Carlo; tel: 081-797 21 11), located just behind the Palazzo Reale. It is one of the most famous music theatres in Europe and was built in 1737 by Charles of Bourbon. The oldest ballet school in Italy divides its time between this theatre and the Scala in Milan.

There are several other interesting theatres in Naples, including the **Sannazaro** (Via Chiaia 157. Tel: 081-41 17 23) and the **San Ferdinando** (Piazza Teatro San Ferdinando. Tel: 081-44 45 00).

Plays written by the most significant Neapolitan playwright of the 20th century, Eduardo De Filippo, are chiefly performed in San Ferdinando.

CINEMA

In order to be able to enjoy going to the cinema, a fluent understanding of Italian is essential; foreign films are shown only during special film festivals.

NIGHTLIFE

Where nightlife is concerned, things do not get going until after the clock has struck midnight. The best places for carousing are in Chiaia, where you'll come across a number of establishments offering live-music shows. The following is just a small selection of recommended venues:

Airone, Via Petrarca 123. Tel: 081-575 01 75. Exclusive piano lounge with restaurant.
Cachaca, Via Petrarca 29. Tel: 081-769 04 90.
Chez moi, Parco Margherita 13. Tel: 081-40 75 26. Piano lounge serving good French food.
Boomerang, Via Giotto. Tel: 081-36 51 85.
Il Gabbiano, Via Partenope 26. Tel: 081-41 16 66. Piano lounge with a superb restaurant.
La Tongue, Via Manzoni 207. Tel: 081-769 08 00.
Shaker Club, Via N. Sauro 24. Tel: 081-41 66 66. Piano lounge and restaurant.
Zeppelin Club, Via Manzoni 176. Tel: 081-64 09 23.
Le Grotte, Vico Vasto a Chiaia 28. Tel: 081-40 05 01.
Kisskiss, Via Sgambati 47. Tel: 081-54 66 566. Newly-renovated jazz music bar.

SHOPPING

The city centre in Naples is a veritable paradise for both casual strollers and shoppers alike. There is an incredible variety of goods for sale and there are plenty of bargains.

Business hours reflect the Neapolitan lifestyle in general – individualistic and often dependent on personal commitments – so don't be surprised to find a *torno subito* ("be right back") sign hung in the doorway of a shop. Generally speaking shops are open 9am–12.30pm and again from 3.30pm–7.30pm Monday–Saturday.

In smaller, family-run shops as well as markets you can ask for a discount (*uno sconto*) for almost any reason and often get it if you seem serious.

Bargaining is a part of the daily business routine.

For many Neapolitan shopkeepers a rule of thumb when dealing with foreign tourists is to ask double the normal price, thus leaving both parties with room to bargain.

Most markets, where you can get good deals, take place in the side streets around Corso Umberto, Corso Garibaldi, in the Forcella and in the Via della Sanità. Flea markets are held every Sunday morning in the Via Foria, located near the National Museum.

When doing business with itinerant salesmen, it pays to keep the following advice in mind: if the price seems incredibly cheap, be suspicious. Invariably there is something wrong with the goods. Another ploy of unscrupulous vendors is to switch the article you have bought with rocks while it is being wrapped.

The following is a list of some of Naples' more important second-hand book, arts and crafts, and antique shops in which the careful browser is sure to make some interesting discoveries.

SECOND-HAND BOOKSHOPS

Barisio, Via Port'Alba 28. Tel: 081-554 76 39.
Casella, Via Carlo Poerio 92. Tel: 081-764 26 27.
Cassitto, Via Port'Alba 10. Tel: 081-45 90 68.
Grimaldi & C., Via Bausan 61. Tel: 081-40 60 21.
Colonnese, Via S. Pietro a Maiella 33. Tel: 081-459858.
Fiorentino, Calata Trinità Maggiore 36. Tel: 081-55 22 005.
Guida, Via Port'Alba 20. Tel: 081-44 63 77.
Lombardi, Via Costantinopoli 4 bis. Tel: 081-21 19 21.
Milano, Via Benedetto Croce 60. Tel: 081-551 65 55.
Regina, Via Costantinopoli 51. Tel: 081-45 99 83.
Nearly all these bookshops will also buy or exchange books.

ARTS & CRAFTS

Baracca e burattini, Piazza Museo 2. This unique shop, located among the arcades of the Galleria Principe across from the National Museum of Archaeology, makes masks, puppets and dolls.
Bottega artigiana del libro e della carta (bookbindery), Calata Trinità Maggiore 4. Tel: 081-55 11 280. Books are bound by hand according to traditional methods.
Costumi teatrali Napoli, Via Serra 75. Tel: 081-42 57 11. Shop selling Neapolitan theatre costumes. You can commission new garments to be made or purchase second-hand ones.
Sagittario, Via Santa Chiara 10 A. This shop specialises in making masks, sculptures and paintings out of leather.
Il cantuccio della Ceramica, Via Medina 63. Tel: 081-552 58 57. Sells a variety of ceramic items.
La Soffitta, Via Benedetto Croce 12. Tel: 081-20 74 97. A ceramic studio.

Legatoria Villa di Chiaia, Riviera di Chiaia 202. Tel: 081-40 04 75. A bookbindery.

Ospedale delle bambole, Via S. Biagio dei librai 81. Tel: 081-20 30 67. A shop specialising in dolls and puppets.

ANTIQUES

Most of Naples' antique shops are located in the area around the Piazza dei Martiri-Santa Lucia and the National Museum of Archaeology.

Affaitati, Via Morelli 45. Tel: 081-764 33 10.

Alabardieri antiquariato, Via Alabardieri 28. Tel: 081-40 21 86.

Bianchi D'Espinosa, Via dei Mille 18. Tel: 081-41 45 01.

Uberto Bowinkel, Via Santa Lucia 25. Tel: 081-41 77 39.

Brandi, Via Morelli 11. Tel: 081-764 36 60.

British trade, Via Morelli 39/41. Tel: 081-764 30 20.

Catalano, Via Chiatamone 35. Tel: 081-42 28 27.

Galleria Ferdinando IV, Via Morelli 6. Tel: 081-764 36 99.

Maison d'art , Piazza dei Martiri 18. Tel: 081-40 78 64.

Sessantasei, Via Bisignani 58. Tel: 081-40 15 08.

Affaitati, Via Santa Maria di Costantinopoli 18. Tel: 081-34 96 22.

Bugli, Via Santa Maria di Costantinopoli 34. Tel: 081-34 83 26.

Napoli nobilissima, Via Broggia 20. Tel: 081-45 97 02.

Rapuano, Via Sapienza 12. Tel: 459702.

OUTSIDE NAPLES

Campania has more to offer than the ubiquitous coral. Amalfi has been famous for its paper since medieval times, even though manuscripts have now given way to headed notepaper. *Intarsio* (marquetry) is a long tradition in Sorrento, just as leather is in Salerno. Pottery has been produced in Vietri since the classical era. The *ceramiche* shops cluster around the main square offer colourful tiles, plates and pasta bowls as well as pottery figurines and copies of 17th-century majolica designs. Capri style is synonymous with contemporary ceramics yet the designs reflect Neolithic pots discovered on the island.

SPORTS

Soccer maintains absolute rule in Naples. Those wishing to experience the excitement of a match at the Stadio San Paolo in Fuorigrotta, should be sure to reserve tickets well in advance from the SSC Napoli office (Piazza dei Martiri 30. Tel: 40 74 77; telex: 720 250).

Enthusiastic racegoers can indulge their passion at the race course in Agnano (tel: 760 16 60). For sport fans more inclined towards active participation, there are numerous tennis courts and swimming pools. Keep in mind, however, that it's not a wise idea to swim off Naples' beaches.

FURTHER READING

The Gallery, by John Horne Burns. A description of World War II through the eyes of an American resident in Naples.

Thus Spake Bellavista, by Luciano da Crescenzo (Picador). Romanticised short tales about Neapolitan life.

Siren Island, Summer Islands, South Wind and *Old Calabria*, by Norman Douglas. Atmospheric travel books on Southern Italy.

The Decameron, by Boccaccio. Some stories are set in Southern Italy. "The Sixth Tale of the Fifth Day" is a raunchy story set on Ischia.

Graziella, by Alphonse de Lamartine (AC Mclurg, Chicago). The Romantic French poet's affair with a fisherman's daughter on the island of Procida.

The Story of San Michele, by Axel Munthe. Based on Capri.

Italian Journey, by Johann Wolfgang Goethe. Vivid descriptions of Naples.

Rome, Naples and Florence, by Stendhal (published 1817).

The Mediterranean Passion, by John Pemble (OUP). Descriptions of the travels of Victorians and Edwardians to the South.

The Mafia, by Clare Sterling (Grafton). The book includes information on the links between the Mafia and the Camorra.

Christ Stopped at Eboli, by Carlo Levi. Story of a year spent in a poverty-stricken community of Southern Italy.

Naples '44, by Norman Lewis. Fascinating account of the author's experiences in Naples between 1943–44.

SPECIAL INFORMATION

TOURIST INFORMATION

NAPLES

Azienda Autonoma di Soggiorno, Cura e Turismo, Palazzo Reale, Piazza Plebescito. Tel: 081-41 87 44.

The Tourist Information Centre on the Piazza del Gesù. Tel: 081-55 23 328 or 55 12 701. Hours: 9am–7pm Monday–Saturday and 9am–3pm on holidays.

The Tourist Information Centre at the entrance of the Borgo Marinari, Castel dell'Ovo. Tel: 081-76 45 688. Hours: 9am–7pm Tuesday–Saturday, 9am–3pm Mondays and holidays.

Ente Provinciale per il Turismo, Via Partenope 10. Tel: 081-76 44 871; At the Main Railway Station. Tel: 081-26 87 79.

Associazione Albergatori (Hotel Association), Piazza Carità 32. Tel: 081-55 20 205.

ENIT, the Tourist Information Office located at Capodichino Airport. Tel: 081-78 03 050.

Automobile Club Napoli, Piazza Tecchio 49. Tel: 081-61 45 11.

Associazione Alberghi per la Gioventù (The Association of Hotels for Young People), Piazza Carità 40. Tel: 081-55 13 151.

Centro Turistico Studentesco e Giovanile, Via De Gasperi 35. Tel: 081 55 20 074.

Agriturist Campania, Via Santa Lucia 90. Tel: 081-41 24 62.

Consorzio Regionale Aziende Turistiche, Via Marino Turchi 31. Tel: 081 41 53 06.

TOURIST OFFICES

THE COAST & ISLANDS

Sorrento: Via De Maio 35. Tel: 081-878-2104.
Amalfi: Corso Roma 19. Tel: 089-871107.
Positano: Via del Saracino 2. Tel: 089-875067.
Salerno: Via Velia 15. Tel: 089-224322 (and at station).
Capri: Piazza Umberto 19. Tel: 081-837-0686; 081-8370686.
Ischia: Carso Colonna 116. Tel: 081-991464.
Procida: Via Rodia. Tel: 081-8969624.

USEFUL ADDRESSES

TOUR OPERATORS

Below is a list of British travel companies operating to selected destinations in the Bay of Naples and on the Amalfi Coast.

Chapter Travel, 102 St John's Wood Terrace, London NW8. Tel: 071-722 9560. Operates to Positano.

Citalia, Marco Polo House, 3–5 Lansdowne Road, Croydon, Surrey. Tel: 081-686 0677. Operates to Ischia.

Highways Holidays, 63 Gray's Inn Road, London WC1. Tel: 071-405 1368. Specialises in pigrimage holidays, which in Campania means to Capri, Naples, Pompeii and Rome.

Italian Interlude, 91 Regent Street, London W1. Tel:071-494 2031. Operates to Positano, Ravello and Sorrento.

Italian Jewels, 18 Hammet Street, Taunton, Somerset. Tel: 0602-322 805. Operates to Positano, Ravello and Sorrento.

Magic of Italy, 227 Shepherd's Bush Road, London W6. Tel: 081-748 7575. As well as operating resort holidays to Naples, Amalfi, Positano, Ravello, Sorrento, Capri and Ischia, Magic of Italy offers a Bay of Naples Tour, taking in Pompeii, Herculaneum, Ischia, Caserta, Naples, Sorrento, Pozzuoli, Baia and Cumae. Also arranges bespoke holidays and tours for the more independent traveller.

Major and Mrs Holt's Battlefield Tours, Golden Key Building, 15 Market Street, Sandwich, Kent. Tel: 0304-612 248. Battlefield tours to Salerno and Sorrento, and archaeology tours to Pompeii, Herculaneum and Naples.

Special Tours, 81a Elizabeth Street, London SW1.

Tel: 071-730 2297. Garden and Villa tours to Naples, Capri and Amalfi.

Swan Hellenic, 77 New Oxford Street, London WC1. Tel:071-831 1616. Archaeology tours, accompanied by an expert lecturer.

Villa Italia, Hillgate House, 13 Hillgate Street, London W8. Tel:071-831 1616. Operates to Positano.

Voyages Jules Verne, 10 Glentworth Street, London NW1. Tel:071-221 4432. Botany holidays to Campania.

CONSULATES

Austria: Corso Umberto I, 275. Tel: 081-287 724.
Belgium: Via Depretis 78. Tel: 081-551 0535.
France: Via F. Crispi 31. Tel: 081-761 2275.
Germany: Via Crispi 69. Tel: 081-664 647.

Great Britain: Via F. Crispi 122. Tel: 081-663 511.
Greece: Via Da Marcone 2. Tel: 081-761 1075.
Spain: Via del Parco Margherita 23.
Tel: 081-411 157.
Sweden: Via Cervantes 55. Tel: 081-551 5049.
Switzerland: Via Pergolesi 1. Tel: 081-761 4390.

ART/PHOTO CREDITS

289

INDEX

THE KODAK GOLD GUIDE TO BETTER PICTURES.

Good photography is not difficult. Use these practical hints and Kodak Gold II Film: then notice the improvement.

Move in close. Get close enough to capture only the important elements.

Frame your Pictures. Look out for natural frames such as archways or tree branches to add an interesting foreground. Frames help create a sensation of depth and direct attention into the picture.

One centre of interest. Ensure you have one focus of interest and avoid distracting features that can confuse the viewer.

Use leading lines. Leading lines direct attention to your subject i.e. — a stream, a fence, a pathway; or the less obvious such as light beams or shadows.

Maintain activity. Pictures are more appealing if the subject is involved in some natural action.

Keep within the flash range. Ensure subject is within flash range for your camera (generally 4 metres). With groups make sure everyone is the same distance from the camera to receive the same amount of light.

Check the light direction. People tend to squint in bright direct light. Light from the side creates highlights and shadows that reveal texture and help to show the shapes of the subject. If shooting into direct sunlight fill-in flash can be effective to light the subject from the front.

CHOOSING YOUR KODAK GOLD II FILM.

Choosing the correct speed of colour print film for the type of photographs you will be taking is essential to achieve the best colourful results.

Basically the more intricate your needs in terms of capturing speed or low-light situations the higher speed film you require.

Kodak Gold II 100. Use in bright outdoor light or indoors with electronic flash. Fine grain, ideal for enlargements and close-ups. Ideal for beaches, snow scenes and posed shots.

Kodak Gold II 200. A multipurpose film for general lighting conditions and slow to moderate action. Recommended for automatic 35mm cameras. Ideal for walks, bike rides and parties.

Kodak Gold II 400. Provides the best colour accuracy as well as the richest, most saturated colours of any 400 speed film. Outstanding flash-taking capabilities for low-light and fast-action situations; excellent exposure latitude. Ideal for outdoor or well-lit indoor sports, stage shows or sunsets.

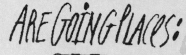

A
B
D
E
F
G
H
I
J
a
b
c
d
e
g
h
i
j
k
l